The New Physiognomy

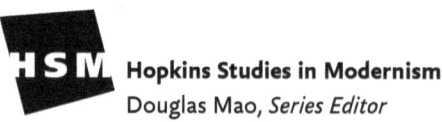

Hopkins Studies in Modernism
Douglas Mao, *Series Editor*

The New Physiognomy

Face, Form, and Modern Expression

Rochelle Rives

Johns Hopkins University Press
Baltimore

© 2024 Johns Hopkins University Press
All rights reserved. Published 2024
Printed in the United States of America on acid-free paper
9 8 7 6 5 4 3 2 1

Johns Hopkins University Press
2715 North Charles Street
Baltimore, Maryland 21218
www.press.jhu.edu

Library of Congress Cataloging-in-Publication Data is available.

A catalog record for this book is available from the British Library.

ISBN 978-1-4214-4837-4 (hardcover)
ISBN 978-1-4214-4838-1 (paperback)
ISBN 978-1-4214-4839-4 (ebook)

Special discounts are available for bulk purchases of this book. For more information, please contact Special Sales at specialsales@jh.edu.

But I, that am not shaped for sportive tricks,
Nor made to court an amorous looking glass;
I, that am rudely stamped and want love's majesty
To strut before a wanton ambling nymph;
I that am curtailed of this fair proportion,
Cheated of feature by dissembling nature,
Deformed, unfinished, sent before my time
Into this breathing world scarce half made up
And that so lamely and unfashionable
That dogs bark at me as I halt by them—
Why, I, in this weak piping time of peace,
Have no delight to pass away the time,
Unless to see my shadow in the sun
And descant on my own deformity.

—William Shakespeare, *Richard III*

Contents

Acknowledgments ix

Introduction. What's in a Face? 1

1 Facing Wilde; or, Emotion's Image 25

2 Realist Prosopagnosia; or, Face Blindness in Theodore Dreiser's *Sister Carrie* 54

3 Nothing "Conclusive": Optics as Ethics in Joseph Conrad's *The Secret Agent* 85

4 Modernist Prosopopoeia; or, Making Faces 116

5 Unreadable Persons: The "Face-Scape" of Old Age 150

Epilogue. "Getting Out" of the Face 181

Notes 193
Index 237

Acknowledgments

This book was largely completed before the start of a pandemic that brought front and center the question of what it means to look at other faces. I want to credit a number of people who facilitated the "face-work" I performed before we lost each other's in-person faces. At the British Association for Plastic, Reconstructive and Aesthetic Surgeons (BAPRAS), archivist Ruth Neave shared with me what she considered to be her career's greatest work, a painstaking reconstruction of Archibald Lane's dental scrapbooks. The scrapbooks contained photographs of his work on facially injured soldiers at Queen's Hospital in Sidcup, 1917-18. She knew each face and its history intimately, and our ongoing chats about the materials informed the visceral and emotional project of writing about injured faces. Along with access to their archives, the Hunterian Museum at the Royal of College of Surgeons of England granted me permission to view Henry Tonks's stunning collection of medical illustrations, which, due to renovations at the museum, were stored offsite. Bruce Simpson met me at an outlying train station, escorted me to the facility, and assisted my viewing of the portraits. At the William Andrews Clark Memorial Library, University of California, Los Angeles, Scott Jacobs patiently helped me navigate the library's "Wildeana" collection and has responded to my emails for the past ten years. A fellowship from the Clark Library and UCLA supported this research.

I would not have been able to complete this work without the support of a variety of grants and fellowships offered through my employment at the City University of New York. A Community College Research Grant from the CUNY Office of Research funded my research on Henry Tonks and Harold Gillies and also provided me with released time from teaching to work on the project. Various grants from our faculty union, the Professional Staff Congress, and two Chancellor's Research Fellowships for Distinguished Faculty offered more released time from teaching. Our faculty union also made possible two yearlong sabbatical leaves that framed the start and finish of this project. From the Borough of Manhattan Community College, I received two Faculty Publication Awards and Faculty Development Grants. Finally, the Mellon Foundation provided "mid-career" support and further released time from teaching through the auspices of the Interdisciplinary Committee for Science Studies seminar at the CUNY Graduate Center.

I owe much to my besties, Adele Kudish and David Bahr, with whom I was in daily contact during the three pandemic years we all lived on the other side of the ocean. Scott Herring has been the most generous friend. Joyce Zonana has been a wonderful mentor and an exemplar of resilience and strength. I must also mention my many inspirational colleagues at the Borough of Manhattan Community College: Mike Odom, Claire Pamplin, Leigh Claire La Berge, Tim Keane, Angela Florschuetz, Bob Lapides, Maria de Vasconcelos, Christa Baiada, Steffi Oppenheim, Jason Schneiderman, and my former department chairs, Phil Eggers and Joyce Harte. I thank a number of other allies, advocates, teachers, and generally helpful souls, all of whom have directly or indirectly shaped this book: Janet Lyon, Tim Dean, Nico Israel, Joseph Bristow, Andrew Radford, Jed Esty, Wayne Lesser, Mia Carter, Joe Malof, Jack Stillinger, Melissa Girard, Christina Walter, Kate Stanley, Julie Napolin, Sarah Blackwood, Loretta Clayton, Alix Beeston, Shane Vogel, Maria McGarrity, Rivky Mondal, Jim Berg, Charles Palermo, David Sterritt, and Megan Becker-Leckrone. The invaluable insights of the two readers of the manuscript assisted immeasurably with the final form of this book. Finally, I am extremely grateful for the generosity and support of Doug Mao, whose kindness, encouragement, and long-term attention to this project rescued me from many pandemic-related publishing and writing woes. I also thank Catherine Goldstead, Matt McAdam, and Adriahna Conway at Johns Hopkins University Press.

My thanks to Namwali Serpell for inviting me to share my work at the "About Faces" interdisciplinary conference she organized in 2014 at the University of California, Berkeley. Jesse Prinz and fellow seminarians at the Interdisciplinary Committee for Science Studies at the CUNY Graduate Center helped me work through revisions of two chapters of the manuscript. Graduate students at Pennsylvania State University offered valuable feedback on a different set of chapters, while a group of modernists affiliated with colleges across CUNY, Cliff Mak, Amy Robbins, and Melissa Dinsman, assisted me in evaluating my work's relation to "new directions" in modernist studies

Acknowledgments   xi

at the CUNY Graduate Center. Finally, I thank Anca Parvulescu and Tyne Sumner for organizing an illuminating three-day seminar, "The Face and/in World Literature," at the 2023 ACLA conference in Chicago.

An incredible network of hands made it possible for me to maintain my identity as a scholar, teach a community college course load, and raise two young children: my parents, Betty and Doug Rives; my mother-in-law, Phyllis Garral; my husband, Michael Garral; and a legion of teachers and caretakers, especially Millie Santos, Sandra Vargas, Jasmin Arias, Maria Tineo-Veras, Jennifer Mejia de La Cruz, and the comedor monitoras at CEIP, Gomez Moreno, in Granada, Spain, who served my children the most delicious food and braided my daughter's hair when I could not get it combed in the morning. Abrazos. This book is dedicated to you.

Permission to reprint selected illustrations of Henry Tonks has been granted by the Hunterian Museum at the Royal College of Surgeons of England, while the William Andrews Clark Memorial Library gave permission to publish images from its "Wildeana" collection. Other images appear courtesy of the Metropolitan Museum of Art and the Imperial War Museums. Photographs by Cindy Sherman appear as © Cindy Sherman, courtesy of the artist and Hauser & Wirth. The photograph of W. H. Auden by Jane Bown appears © Guardian News and Media Limited, 2023. Finally, the still from John Frankenheimer's *Seconds* appears as © Paramount Pictures and was provided courtesy of Paramount Pictures.

A small portion of chapter 1 appeared in *PMLA* 130, no. 5 (October 2015): 1363-80, as "Facing Wilde, or Emotion's Image," and earlier versions of sections of chapters 3 and 4 appeared, respectively, as "Face Values: Optics as Ethics in Joseph Conrad's *The Secret Agent*," *Criticism: A Quarterly for Literature and the Arts* 56, no. 1 (Winter 2014): 89-119, and "Modernist Prosopopoeia: Mina Loy, Gaudier-Brzeska, and the Making of Face," *Journal of Modern Literature* 34, no. 4 (Summer 2011): 137-59.

The New Physiognomy

Introduction
What's in a Face?

> Should we speak here of character? One of the leading portrait painters of our own day once remarked to me that he never knew what people meant when they talked about the painter revealing the character of the sitter. He could not paint a character, he could only paint a face. I have more respect for this astringent opinion of a real master than I have for the sentimental talk about artists painting souls, but when all is said and done a great portrait . . . does give us the illusion of seeing the face behind the mask.
>
> —E. H. Gombrich, "The Mask and the Face: The Perception of Physiognomic Likeness in Life and Art," 1970

> "But," said one fellow, "it's the face that you tell by." "Faces is it!" I screamed, "the face is for fools! If you fish by the face you fish out trouble, but there's always other fish when you deal with the sea. The face is what anglers catch in the daylight, but the sea is the night!"
>
> —Djuna Barnes, *Nightwood*, 1937

Sometime at the end of 2018, I joined Instagram just to see Cindy Sherman's strangely distorted examples of the by then seemingly trite genre of self-portraiture, the selfie. Hyperbolized satires of the catlike, fishlike "Instagram face," with its overly plumped cheeks and artificially ballooned lips, the photos use Instagram's own filters to exaggerate, stretch, and reproportion targeted facial features.[1] Sherman's portraits of her own face masked by the faces of other women aging ungracefully channel many of the questions I engage in this book, which, in its broadest sense, is about the modern face and its centrality to what reading and writing meant for a variety of twentieth-century writers and artists. In particular, what does it mean to have a face, to make a face, or to lose one, or to wear a face that is not one's own? Furthermore, how should we read other faces if our gaze is thought to deform or damage its object, and why is the face the form that, in many literary and visual texts, often allegorizes this type of violation? Finally, why *should* we look at other faces?

In considering these questions, I trace a basic correspondence between the aesthetic form of the face and the question of how we read literary and visual texts. I explore models of faciality that, often serialized, caricatured, wounded, or aged, emphasize the importance of the face as an aesthetic site of ambiguity linked to the distortion of modern vision. Beginning with nineteenth-century physiognomy and the subject of Oscar Wilde's face—as it was illustrated and caricatured in a variety of visual formats before and after his 1895 trials—the book ends by considering the facial paranoia of John Frankenheimer's 1966 Cold War film, *Seconds*, along with the specters of aging women performed by Cindy Sherman in her most recent photographic portraits. These points of entrance and departure create a significantly broader context for considering works by Theodore Dreiser, Edith Wharton, Jean Rhys, Joseph Conrad, Mina Loy, Henri Gaudier-Brzeska, Henry Tonks, and W. H. Auden, among others, illustrating their continued ethical relevance to the concerns of our present-day "facial society."[2]

My story begins with nineteenth-century physiognomy, itself a technology of reading, and its construction, through the meticulous plotting of facial expression, of a legible human subject. Adhering to this physiognomic tradition, Georg Simmel, writing in "The Aesthetic Significance of the Face" (1901), maintained that the face achieved its aesthetic effect by "mirroring the soul."[3] Distinct from the body, it acted as an "interpreter of mere appearance," synthesizing surface and depth so as to be clearly legible to the "trained eye."[4] I track this notion of legibility through a variety of discourses. It appears in treatises on art and aesthetics, pseudoscientific tomes on "personality" and endocrine glands, manuals for rejuvenating the face, extensively detailed studies of old age, and, given the horrors of facial injury during the First World War, records of surgical facial repair. Such examples, when considered alongside the literary fixation with faces that I bring to light here, suggest broader connections between the specific methods that inform our conclusions about art and literature and other scientific and political modes of apprehending human beings, challenging the work of contemporary "read-

Cindy Sherman, Instagram account, 2019. © Cindy Sherman. Courtesy of the artist and Hauser & Wirth.

ing" technologies—from "surface reading" to facial recognition technology—that privilege accuracy, mimesis, and automaticity.[5]

But faces ask that we read them; according to poet Allen Grossman, there is no poetry without faces because a "face demands a text."[6] In his account of the faces of Trojan priest Laocoön and the blind Homer, Grossman articulates an ethics that aligns the production of art, in this case poetry, with the alterity and strangeness that appears in the making and reading of faces. Essential to our reading of faces is what we cannot read or image, and this "scarcity" sustains the "moment of poetry," as well as "our capacity to value persons."[7] Sherman's photographs, for example, push the limits of what it means to put on a face, projecting, as I explain in chapter 5, an intractable strangeness, even vulnerability, that extends beyond their facing. Sherman "mobilize[s]," as art historian E. H. Gombrich would put it, a view that reflects not only her skill as an artist but also the face's very capacity for representing "ambiguity, ambivalence and conflict," what we typically think of as depth or dimension.[8] This is, for Gilles Deleuze, a primary "trai[t]" of faceicity [*visagéité*]"; characterized by its movement and "brilliance," the face possesses "content which . . . rebels against the outline."[9] For Gombrich, our own face-to-face interactions with "fellow human beings" guide our aesthetic responses to this "brilliance" and direct "projective activities" that "compensate for the limitations of the medium."[10] In other words, even when a concrete artistic medium arrests a face's particular movement or limits its representation to a surface, an artist's rendering of a face may still inspire a viewer's animating vision.

Georg Simmel would theorize a much less sentient model of expression in 1901, writing that the face's "inner unity" accounts for its "significance as a subject in art," as well as its ability to project legible expression by synthesizing the "diversity" of its shapes and surfaces.[11] At the same time, this unity also produces the face's vulnerability to "destruction" by "the disfigurement of only one of its elements," resulting in illegible and "aesthetically unbearable" expressions, "spiritual paralysis," and "loss of control."[12] Writing thirty years later, William Empson would reformulate this idea in *The Face of the Buddha* (1931), claiming that, in contrast to the illegible remoteness of the "whole face," such a "strain on unity" was necessary for making the Buddha's face "more human."[13] Confessing that he did not want to "appear crazy over" his "facial theory," Empson alleged that asymmetry allowed the Buddha face both to function as an "art-form" and to "portray character," and that it further accounted for the "work" of the face "on the spectator."[14] Like Gombrich, Empson theorizes a more expansive mode of modern viewing that accommodates "ambiguity, ambivalence, and conflict" into a model of animate expression.[15] These expressive qualities, which cohere contradictorily through disturbance, do not allow the viewer to see into the subject, but rather galvanize legible expression.

I outline these ideas about "faceicity"—and its accompanying tensions—to illustrate a shifting model of aesthetic expression. Both Gombrich and Empson theorize a more inclusive sense of modern vision that not only humanizes the potentially remote sphere of art and aesthetics but also emphasizes the viewer's ability to accommodate more—deformation, disturbance, even blind spots—into the field of vision. My account thus reflects Jonathan

Crary's characterization of a visual modernity marked by a "freeing up of vision, a falling away of the rigid structures that had shaped it and constituted its objects," as well as the simultaneous emergence of "a plurality of means to recode the activity of the eye."[16] In the case of various examples that appear within this study, such as the faces of Oscar Wilde, Dreiser's Carrie, and Ezra Pound, the ability to "recode" or recognize expression is linked both to our knowledge and experiences of individuals and to their presumed distinctiveness or depth, as well as to the expressive fields that produce the appearance of the individual "personality." This complexity, which also draws on the tension between individual and scientifically determined type, face and mask, not only characterizes the viewing of distinct art forms like caricature in the nineteenth century but also underlies many of our pandemic and post-pandemic facial realities, in which various obstructions, like surgical masks, occlude our view of what's in a face.

Mary Ann Doane has described this same kind of shift as the "displacement of face as a bodily phenomenon mirroring the soul—demanding legibility, marking the particularity of the individual—to a question of social status and intersubjectivity."[17] Doane references more specifically Erving Goffman's analysis of face-to-face interaction in his well-known essay "On Face-Work" (1955), arguing that his outline of the "terms of intersubjectivity" does not actually follow from the nineteenth-century physiognomic theories of Charles Darwin, Francis Galton, and French anatomist Guillaume-Benjamin Duchenne—which sought to excavate a universal human nature—but rather, as corroborated by his footnotes, originates from Chinese concepts of face that encode "the experience of colonialism" and otherness.[18] Goffman's well-known account of "face-work" advances the idea of "face" as an essentially "positive social value a person effectively claims for himself."[19] A "face" inscribes us in specific communities and social networks, but as Goffman also explains, having a face requires a "commitment" to participation in social life that may wear a person out because a person "cathects his face" and "his feelings become attached to it."[20] As I suggest of Dreiser's *Sister Carrie* or Wharton's *The House of Mirth*, this sort of "face-work" may age or "waste" the face.[21]

With all due credit to Doane's brilliantly researched tome, I offer here a minor adjustment to this story of the "face" in modernity. While Goffman's concept of "face," like Empson's idea of the Buddha face, does in fact reflect the "experience of colonialism" and otherness, it does not preclude the idea of "face" produced by physiognomy in the nineteenth century. As I demonstrate in chapter one, this idea of face as a master template for human nature was directly linked to the concept that would, in the twentieth century, emerge from it: "personality." In Goffman's account, "face" is not a literal face but a metaphor for social functioning that calls on the meaning of the face as an index of human personality. Like "face," personality functions in the twentieth century as a trait that may be more powerful or weak in sustaining the "positive social value a person effectively claims for himself," and, as Warren Susman has claimed, it could be constructed and managed to influence the perception of others.[22] This is not the labor of the body, but rather the work of the face, or "face-work."

In the contexts I examine, the face's failure at its work of synthesizing the interior and exterior dimensions of the human subject inspires new modes of reading it as an exterior manifestation of biologically determined traits and characteristics, or, in the case of visual arts or literature, scripted forms of transferrable expression, or "personality," as when a person "cathects his face."[23] In chapter one, for example, I argue that the production of scientific explanations for distinct personality and facial types had, in many cases, the effect of de-pathologizing them, routing them into the field of recognizable visual expression. Personality was not seen to reflect a moral interior or "soul" but understood as something to be seen, manifested on a visible, readable exterior. Whereas Simmel maintains that the face could simultaneously "signify . . . personality" and "reveal the soul," fusing "kind" or type and "differenc[e]," pseudoscientific studies such as Louis Berman's *The Glands Regulating Personality* (1922) presented human personality as a surface phenomenon related to distinct facial types—like Oscar Wilde's or Napoleon Bonaparte's—where the source of facial difference and personality traits was the distinct functioning of the endocrine glands. Similarly, modernist poet Mina Loy, writing in 1919, promoted alongside her claim that "the face is our most potent symbol of personality" a system of manual facial exercises designed to stimulate a harmonious correspondence between "facial contour" and the "youth of our souls."[24] In these cases, personality can be understood as a plastic social form that corroborates Goffman's concept of "face."

The relevance of plasticity to this idea of personality can also be briefly illustrated by the case of the mannequin face. In the nineteenth century, mannequins were essentially dressmaker's forms, torsos without heads or faces designed to fit clothing, not display it. As ready-to-wear fashion became available in the late nineteenth century, shop windows became more focused on humanizing wax figures with painstakingly executed faces and real hair, exhibiting a "face-first" realism that, by the 1920s, aimed to project emotion, facial distinction, and, as Sara K. Schneider argues, "personality," or a "sense of character that persisted through different poses, attitudes, and activities."[25] As it literalizes Gombrich's concept of "face-work," the mannequin's face offers insight into "what constitutes a believable reproduction of human presence," where the ability to convey personality and expression across a varied set of postures becomes the basis of its "display value."[26] I discuss this specific construction of modern personality more explicitly in chapters one and two, but for now, and following from this example, I define personality more broadly as an expressive or composite projection of a person based on a physiognomic ideal of a readable and relatable subject. As it is linked to an idea of kind or type, and as it emerges, in the early twentieth century, in the intersecting discourses of science, art, and commerce, personality also operates as a script that we understand from experience; it allows us to read others—even mannequins—as subjects as it simultaneously alters or exceeds the original image and pose of the body.

Personality is most often understood as a measurable category derived from specific assessments about modes or styles of individual judgment and perception, as in the Myers-Briggs test for personality types, which can be dated back to the 1920s and continues to be widely used today.[27] This connection notwithstanding, I approach personality as an aesthetic phenomenon that has its roots in the scientific and medical history of the face. I thus introduce new contexts for considering the well-known disdain that energized so many artists and writers in the period of aesthetic production we now term "modernism," generally dated from 1910 to 1939, building on, as in other recent studies, a more expansive notion of the period and its "long term aesthetic effects."[28] As is well known, the high modernist retreat from personality—as advocated by T. S. Eliot in his 1919 treatise on "impersonality," "Tradition and the Individual Talent"—was marked by a corresponding interest, in the case of Yeats or Pound, for example, in poetic masks, not faces, tools that, to borrow from art historian Hans Belting's description of ritual masking in cult ceremonies, "'disembod[y]' a face in order to 'embody' someone else."[29] In visual art, for instance, Man Ray obsessively incorporated masks into many photographs, most famously in his portrait "Kiki with African Mask" and in his commercial work for companies such as Elizabeth Arden. In his classic work, Robert F. Storey traced these same interests in masking—especially in pantomime—to the French poet Jules Laforgue, and further to the Parisian *commedia dell'arte* and the great mimes of the eighteenth and nineteenth century, as characters who could not be "unmasked," fusing "creator and role."[30] Whereas modernism has been said to turn away from such "figurative representation" of the face in its desire to "bypass" its "mediation" of an "interior world," texts such as Dreiser's *Sister Carrie* and Conrad's *The Secret Agent*, I argue, highlight the figurability of the face as it challenges the typological simplicity produced by viewers' efforts to "recode" it.[31]

As a way of thinking about the problem of facing in the context of modernist writing, I turn briefly to Djuna Barnes's novel *Nightwood* (1937) and its dystopic view of what faces do to seeing. In their rambling address to the lovelorn Robin Vote, illicit gynecologist and spasmodic talker Matthew O'Connor dissolves the fantasy that connects writing to the making of faces, waxing at length on what the night does to "identity."[32] A jack of all trades, O'Connor is an "anonymous" teller of stories, "a collector and a talker of Latin, and a sort of petropus of the twilight and a physiognomist that can't be flustered by the wrong feature on the right face" (*NW*, 98). Notwithstanding the dubious meaning of "petropus," the doctor aligns their loquacity as a storyteller and the pseudoscience of physiognomy.[33] While boasting of the accuracy of their readings, they simultaneously insist that our writing and reading of faces offers no conclusive narrative or story. One cannot ultimately "tell" what is in a face, yet it is the face that necessitates our telling. As writings produced in the day, faces do not speak accurately of the night, or the variety of life that populates the opaque and unfathomable sea (*NW*, 99).

What should we see, then, if not faces? The voluble physician, whose "talk," according to Vincent Sherry, unfolds in "immense stretches of uninterrupted text," advocates for a history rewritten from the standpoint of the night: "Was it at night that Sodom became Gomorrah? It was at night I swear! A city given over to the shades, and that's why it has never been countenanced or understood to this day" (*NW*, 92).[34] Here, O'Connor rallies against a physiognomic conception of history that concretizes an embodied, visual sense of the aesthetic. There are things—in this case, Sodom and Gomorrah—that resist facing, remaining "[un]countenanced," and likely untold (*NW*, 92). But how does writing get formed in the absence of faces? For O'Connor, a different kind of telling, a modernist narration, is unconnected to faces. It involves a third "eye that you fear," which sees from the "back of the head," as when "looking at the beloved in a dark place" (*NW*, 88).

The eye that we use to see darkness is not the eye we use to see faces. As a narrator, O'Connor is a person without a face, or, at least, their speaking voice, "torn into parts by a hundred voices," cannot be faced, or "countenanced" (*NW*, 92). This facelessness is indicated in the novel's first composite description of the doctor as "heavily rouged" with "lashes painted," but the passage connects these features to their personage more generally and to their "head," not to their face (*NW*, 85). This facelessness suggests that their own person is itself a kind of writing, deliberately unformed as a means, like other "careful writers," of "guard[ing] myself against the conclusions of my readers" (*NW*, 101). The doctor remains "[un]countenanced," maintaining his polyvocality against the formal, visually coded activities of reading and imaging, which typically seek closure and synthesis and, as a result, fragment the writer (*NW*, 92).

Uncountenanced: A Brief History of the Face

But writing that is "un-faced" remains unread. O'Connor's resistance to identification and countenancing describes a modernist problematic that is characterized through reference to physiognomy and the dilemma of facing. The face cannot accommodate or figure the novel's defamiliarized aesthetic view; connected to the materiality of writing and the "recod[ing]" of vision, it cannot image a history that cannot be written, or even begin to mediate an aesthetic view of it.[35] This problem of facing relates to a more general problem of expression that, according to Belting, originates in the European portrait. As it "exchanges a face for an image," the portrait removes its sitter from life by representing "the withdrawal of life from the face."[36] For Belting, the visual image of the face's death, its "stiffening into a mask" through the act of painting it, appears explicitly in Caravaggio's seventeenth-century paintings as a preoccupation that survives in Francis Bacon's attempts, in the twentieth century, to "tear" the mask "from the face that has become a portrait."[37]

This idea of expression that "devours the face" also informs Deleuze's idea that expression *is* the face, or "affect."[38] Deleuze traces this model of affect and expression back to René Descartes's and Charles Le Brun's understanding of the "passions" as reflected in the face's simultaneous coordination of "immobile unity" and "intensive micro-movements."[39] While Le Brun wrote to instruct painters, his elaborate taxonomy of facial expression claims a scientific basis for expression that reads in the physiological movements of the body the expressions of the soul. The idea of faces as *individually* expressive did not emerge until later, in the eighteenth century, when Johann Lavater claimed physiognomy as a science. As Lucy Hartley has argued, Lavater promoted physiognomy as a method of consolidating the physiological actions of the body, which were diverse and various, with a more universal "science of mind" connected to the "moral behavior" and intentions of individuals.[40]

The advent of photography in the nineteenth century made it possible to study this variety while freezing human expression in isolated settings of study. In "Little History of Photography" (1931) Walter Benjamin famously elaborated on the "new and strange" problem of portrait photography; whereas portraiture removes the sitter from life, arresting the moving image, the picture's "spark of contingency" supports the agency of a subject that "will never consent to be wholly absorbed in art."[41] This same challenge of intentionality informed the studies of Darwin, Jean Charcot, and Duchenne, all of which utilized photography as a tool for mastering the complex unruliness of the face's neurological movement. François Delaporte has argued that Duchenne's photographic study *Mécanisme de Physionomie Humaine*, or *The Mechanism of Human Facial Expression* (1862), centralized the face not as a reflection of character but in an "anatomy and physiology of affects."[42] Indeed, the expressions appearing in Duchenne's photographs were the result of electrical stimulation and consequently expose the fiction of the camera's claim to objectively record the discrete state of "natural" expressions.

This method of studying the face—much like the eugenicist programs of Cesare Lombroso, Alphonse Bertillon, and Galton, which I discuss in chapter three—anticipates modern facial typology and the physiognomic program of Paul Ekman, whose "expert" facial decoding systems were popularized after 2001 as a means of apprehending potential terrorists.[43] Among others, Ruth Leys has argued that the presumed universalism of Ekman's "physiognomic ideology," especially the distinction it maintains between the "genuine faces we have when no one is watching" and those that are primed or posed for the camera or observer, simplifies an "array of tremendously difficult questions about the nature of intentionality."[44] One might recall George Orwell's dystopian novel *1984* (1948) and the subject of *"facecrime,"* which means to "wear an improper expression on your face."[45] Here, "improper expression"—a "nervous tic, an unconscious look of anxiety . . . anything that carried with it the suggestion of abnormality, of having something to hide"—is natural expression, or an expression of one's actual thoughts, which must be distinguished from the feigned dissembling that is necessary to avoid being punished by the Party.[46]

The novel *1984* makes explicit the politics of having a face, as well as the often problematic possibility of its potential agency from the "face-work" that is the by-product of a biopolitical regime. Such power is more generally connected to the idea of physiognomy as a "hermeneutic system" specifically designed to "allay fear of the unknown," one that, as Doane argues, "predictably aligned" various "surface differences" in the human face with "racial differences."[47] This racialist connection is literalized at the outset of *1984*, where the "lean Jewish face" of Goldstein, a virulent detractor of the Party, appears on the ubiquitous telescreens.[48] It is used, along with "expressionless Asiatic faces," to intensify "Hate" and thereby inspire allegiance to the Party.[49] Difference is coded not overtly in terms of skin color but, as Ellen Samuels has pointed out of nineteenth-century "fantasies of identification," through the increasingly minute analysis of the physiological signs of racial difference, such as nose shape or hair, in the effort to ascertain a "verifiable, biological mark" of racial identity.[50] For Samuels, racist modes of surveillance used to taxonomize difference also underlay an emerging concept of disability in the nineteenth century that developed in response to the ambiguity and indeterminacy of disabled bodies. Similarly, Susan Schweik addresses more specifically how the "ugly laws" that populated the code books of American cities during the late nineteenth and early twentieth centuries cohered around the problem of determining exactly what was considered too "unsightly" to be seen.[51] And as Sander Gilman has illustrated, physiognomy responded to this very problem of appearance by forging identifications between the most visible facial features, most notably noses, and race.[52]

Accordingly, and in relation to the history of her own discipline, anthropologist Amade M'charek asks whether it is "possible to do the face in ways that do not necessarily enact race."[53] She argues that turn-of-the-century instructional prints of racialized faces offer an "invitation to learn types" that promote the "illusion of objectivity," as they invite the viewer to consider the "relation between one face and another."[54] These relationships, M'charek argues, create phenotypes that instruct vision and anticipate more recent visual technologies, in particular, forensic DNA technology, which uses biological markers to generate composite images of crime suspects to create a *"suspect population."*[55] While *The New Physiognomy* does not fully chart the fields of disability or critical race studies, it shares with the aforementioned projects a focus on the "visibility of human diversity" as it is "repressed," denied, deleted, or detected.[56] Culling insight from a variety of disciplines, discourses, and methodologies, ranging from traditional literary studies, to visual art theory, to science studies, to medical humanities, I address modern facial typology as it both attracts and directs seeing, a comparative enterprise enmeshed in the intersecting histories of race and disability.[57] Throughout this book, I draw on Georges Canguilhem's *The Normal and the Pathological* as a baseline for my consideration of how normative bodies "form" and direct legible expression.[58] In this sense, I focus similarly on the types of "recalcitrant and unruly faces" Namwali Serpell documents in her book *Stranger Faces*, which situates the "disjunction" of unreadable faces against an "Ideal" face that is "pleasing[ly] human."[59] However, in the case of racialized caricatures of Wilde, the blasted faces of young war veterans, Auden's aging face, or, conversely, Carrie Meeber's "very pretty" one, I examine how even seemingly unreadable and unclassifiable facial "types" may carry in them a deep structure of expression or form that in fact instructively informs the way we encounter the language, the images, and the faces of others. These at times illegible forms underline the possibility of alternate modes of vision that are consistent with Allen Grossman's account of the face as "witness to *a catastrophe of a particular sort*" or "represented destruction."[60]

Methodologically, Grossman's work is part of the larger theoretical arc that I construct and historicize in this book, represented by Eve Sedgwick, E. H. Gombrich, Emmanuel Levinas, Paul de Man, J. Hillis Miller, and Michael Taussig, among others—all of whom explicitly link faces to the joint project of reading texts and others, and who engage more particularly the face's capacity to both solicit and undo modes of visual perception and surveillance that would seek to abstract it into, to borrow from Sianne Ngai, "the face of no one in particular."[61] Essential to this project is Paul de Man's formulation of prosopopoeia, a technology of reading and writing based on the "fiction of an apostrophe to an absent, deceased, or voiceless entity," which "confers upon it the power of speech."[62] In chapter four in particular, I elaborate on prosopopoeia as a model for giving faces that, like a Levinasian mode of facing, dissolves totality and synthesis, but which also occurs as a more intrusive form of defacement that may model ethical relation. In Levinas's ethics, the face-to-face interaction is essential to the "consideration of the other, or justice," as it opposes the power and tyranny of "thematization and conceptualization," of mastery.[63] However different, both models describe a kind of "face-work" that defines expression, a labor that, on one hand, "cathects," or objectifies the individual.[64] On the other hand, however, efforts to instrumentalize the face and its expressions are in fact often responses to its potential dynamism, its "brilliance," or its ability to stymie even the most expert practices of reading it.[65]

This aspect of "faceicity" not only galvanized the nineteenth-century project of physiognomy but also has inspired the more recent development of automated systems such as facial recognition technology (FRT), which work by creating template faces that conform to actual images (e.g., driver's license photos) of a known face. As is the case with the Clearview AI app, these photos need not be perfect; the system, using an algorithm that "converts" facial images into "mathematical formulas, or vectors, based on facial geometry," works even with profile or partial shots of the face or when the face is partially obscured by a hat or sunglasses, as well as, more recently, surgical masks.[66] Organizations like the ACLU have been documenting the extreme expansion of the FBI's "massive facial recognition apparatus," as the consequences of such covertly applied technology for our autonomy and privacy are unparalleled.[67] Indeed, COVID-era masking has only accelerated the development of more enhanced facial analysis systems that can produce recognition with visual access to smaller parts of the face. Further efforts at creating real-time facial recognition—in which police, for example, would be able to wear devices enabling immediate identification—would potentially allow officers to search without probable cause in situations where privacy would have been required by law. In the most dystopic of scenarios, facial images are generated from DNA in blood drawn in apparently mandatory medical examinations, a method employed in China most recently to track ethnic and religious minorities.[68]

E. H. Gombrich and the Problem of Likeness: What Is a Reading?

FRT in particular diminishes the relevance of even the kind of expertise Leys problematizes in Paul Ekman's facial decoding techniques, replacing the work of reading a subject's intentions with automatic composite imaging, geometrical formulas, or vectors. As a technology that exchanges reading for recognition, the subject of FRT also underlines connections between our scholarly reading practices, which may be discrete and disciplinary, and the reading—scientific, technological, or social—of persons; it thus seems crucial in this climate to maintain an idea of facial form that accounts for its essential ambiguity, as well as the possibility of misrecognition or loss. Daniel M. Gross terms this ambiguousness "rhetoricity," noting Darwin's confused reaction to first seeing the famous photographic experiments of Duchenne, which impressed upon him *"how easily we may be misguided by our imagination."*[69] Following Darwin, we may see or read something—an ego, or personality—in a face, even though it may not be *there*.

What might it mean to read with the idea of such failure in mind—while simultaneously attempting to get the text "right"? I attempt to answer this question through a close reading of Gombrich's classic essay on the correspondence between our own observed experience of the world and the formal code of the artist, "The Mask and the Face: The Perception of Physiognomic Likeness in Life and in Art."[70] Given originally as a lecture at Johns Hopkins University in 1970, the essay, an extension of his earlier anti-fascist work on caricature from the 1930s, interrogates the sense of "likeness" that arises from our tendency to see faces in everything and, significantly for literary studies, explicitly connects the work of criticism to the way we encounter other faces.[71] Gombrich's work thus supplies an antidote to Theodor Adorno and Max Horkheimer's idea of a duplicative visual culture saturated with "synthetically manufactured physiognomies" and runs counter to some of the more dogmatic viewpoints of modernists such as Pound, who, in *ABC of Reading* (1934), expressed his belief that an astute critic or reader could simply look at something and "KNO[W]" what is in it.[72] Indeed, as Louis Rose has extensively documented, Gombrich's collaborative work on caricature with psychoanalyst Ernst Kris was an intellectual response to the emergence of an authoritarian aesthetic that privileged and even mandated uniform modes of vision. In contrast, the two highlighted the "fusions, distortions, exaggerations" of caricature, which indicated the "necessary ambiguousness of artistic messages and reactions."[73]

For Gombrich, reading emerges as a visually constitutive action linked to caricature and the resulting critical stance, as Rose explains, of "shifting distances."[74] In "The Mask and the Face," Gombrich addresses more specifically the question of portrait likeness and conjectures that what allows us to perceive or recognize our "fellow creatures" as separate from each other is something called a "physiognomic identity," or "constancy," which is, as Gombrich explains in "On Physiognomic Perception," based on a "global" or "immediate reaction" to an expression.[75] We see expression in a face, or something inanimate that we give a face, like a poem or even a piece of music, "without being aware of reading 'signs.'"[76] Consequently, our experience of what's the same in someone's face, "its underlying constancy," is so strong that we experience as a mask any impediment to this familiarity.[77] To put it differently, if we typically read the signs that familiar faces exhibit without self-consciousness, it's actually the mask that makes us uncomfortably aware of the activity of reading and its possible wrongness.

For Gombrich, masks indeed disrupt a physiognomic norm and are often what we see in the faces we notice, "the crude distinctions, the deviations from the norm which mark a person off from others."[78] Echoing Benjamin's account of photography, Gombrich argues that technological modernity has created impediments to an earlier form of physiognomic constancy exemplified by the legibility of the "arrested image."[79] For example, in the film shot, sheer speed at capturing images may leave an expression "uninterpretable" and therefore more like a mask, discouraging our projections or readings.[80] This idea may for some call to mind the cinematic close-up, as well as Roland Barthes's well-known description of "Garbo's face," with its eyes of "black . . . pulp" that are not "expressive."[81] As a "total mask," it "may imply less the theme of secrecy . . . than that of an archetype of the human face."[82] In this case, the mask does not obscure the more authentic face, but rather aestheticizes it into a remote and unrelatable distance.

Rather than the close-up, the idea of the portrait, with its lifelike proportions and projection of subjectivity, informs the examples I discuss in this book, including Henry Tonks's paintings, Mina Loy's treatise on facial construction, and caricatures of Oscar Wilde. For Gombrich, the great portraitist will "mobilize our projection" by "exploit[ing] the ambiguities of the arrested face" so that "the multiplicities of possible readings result in the semblance of life."[83] As viewers we in fact construct a face through a process of abstraction that, however automatic, is the performance of a reading "mobiliz[ed]" by the artist.[84] Ultimately, as Gombrich indicates, it is the work of "memory"—our experiences—that allows us to get the reading right, our envisioning of the portrait's subject, and their character, in the contexts with which we are familiar.[85] Just as Audrey Hepburn's face, as well as its place in time, is "individualized" by its association with her "person" and through its "specific thematics," Gombrich suggests that we do not possess a clear and unruptured view of an image that is not supplied by context or familiarity.[86] That view is always and automatically a reading.

Gombrich elaborates a mode of criticism that privileges both the automaticity of physiognomic response and the more deliberate intellectual action of reading. It is true, as Gombrich elaborates in "On Physiognomic Perception," that what we characterize as "expressive" evokes "physiognomic reactions" in which we attempt to "make sense" of something—a person, an artwork—by giving it a face.[87] But it is also true that such an automatic reading may "sometimes go wrong," especially when we misread and "assign" such a fixed meaning to the "variables" or details that present a challenge to likeness.[88] Ideally, "likeness has to be caught rather than constructed."[89] Otherwise, the "physiognomic approach," which identifies art with expression, "may lead to the suicide of criticism."[90] The critic's role, Gombrich writes at the end of the essay, is to "help the artist" do "justice" to the "mystery of ordered form."[91] The critic should, in other words, produce a reading—a "valid articulation" that is consistent with the organized "mystery" of artistic production.[92] Gombrich thus formulates a mode of critical reading that attends to the dynamism of modern pictorial representation—where likeness is "caught"—without dismissing the more constant expressive qualities that visibly embody a subject or a face.[93]

Reading Wrong, Reading Right

With this idea of criticism as doing "justice" to "form," I address how our consideration of what's in a face—as a figure for reading and relation that visibly engages both surface and depth, automaticity and deliberation, control and submission—might help us think beyond some of the recent polarization that has come to characterize the meaning of "criticism" in our profession. My point here is not to incite the "bad feelings" of the "method conversation" that, according to David Kurnick, more accurately reflect the "diminished standing of the humanities in general and of literary criticism in particular," but rather to look closely at some specific aspects of the logic that structure this "conversation."[94] Like Kurnick and quite a few others, I am interested in the particular example of Stephen Best and Sharon Marcus's well-known essay "Surface Reading" (2009), with its critical account of the "symptomatic" reader as one who chases after "latent or concealed" meanings derived from only "elements present in the text."[95] The case against symptomatic reading notwithstanding, I draw attention to the authors' political rationale for "surface reading," which rests on the example of Hurricane Katrina and the moment in which media coverage, they argue, made immediately visible the state's obvious "abandonment of its African-American citizens," as well as the government's lies.[96] This particular observation, which counts the public as a reader of a reality where "so much seems to be on the surface," is not actually an argument about the reading of texts, but rather is founded on a claim about images and their particular power of communicating so directly as to produce one way of looking and, by extension, one type of response, which cannot actually be a reading.[97]

The reduction of the written text to a media-generated image seems somewhat problematic for a methodological practice that values the historical accuracy ascribed to the empirical activity of description. With its claim that reading can take place at "first sight," the fantasy of description, as Ellen Rooney has argued, in direct response to Best and Marcus, assigns "immense value to the paraphrase," as it "disavows reading's own formal activities."[98] More specifically, I would suggest, description does not account for the problem of form, which, as a script that often deforms the subjects of our reading, works through a representational tension between the forms of inner life and their external appearance. Form does not merely synthesize but realizes an antagonism between surface and depth, between the materiality of words on a page, to follow Michael Fried, and our reading of those words.[99] When seen through the lens of classic narrative theory, form also abstracts the various temporal dimensions of a story; it is the package that negotiates the conflict between the story as it *occurs* and the story that later is *told* by a narrating subject. Form is also closely linked to style, as in the example of literary impressionism—a topic of chapter three, on Joseph Conrad's *The Secret Agent*—and its aim, as characterized by Conrad, of "render[ing] the highest kind of justice to the visible universe" in order to "make" the reader "see."[100]

With regard to this issue of reading's "formal activities," I have concluded that the recent panic over student use of AI apps to "enhance" and fabricate their college essays, at least in literature courses, may be misplaced, and that certain formal, even symptomatic, activities of close reading and explication may allow us to distinguish a "real" essay from a fake one.[101] At least at the present moment, such tools cannot perform a close reading and generally produce mere paraphrase, or synthetic documents that resemble computer-generated composite images. I offer such an anecdote in response to the perspective that readings that seem too formalist, close, psychoanalytic, or theoretical are the wrong kind of readings, or, as Sam Rose has observed, one must eschew aesthetics in order to avoid rearticulating the claims of "formalist modernism, elitist conceptions of beauty, and the like."[102] Anna Kornbluh has similarly indicted the "allergy to form in the humanities" as representing the "broad failure of humanists" to articulate a positive and relevant conception of what the actual study of literature or art might offer "beyond historic preservation."[103] The chapters that follow offer some solutions to these critical problems by following face-to-face interaction as it allegorizes modernism's own self-reflective inquiries into the discretely formal activities of reading and writing. In this light, faces are seen to represent "content" that may be undecipherable but solicit the formal activities of inference and explanation nonetheless.

Such a conception of formalism, I argue, animates the idea of an aesthetic surface and exposes the lack of thought behind the contention that explanatory reading is "paranoid" or bad reading.[104] The chapters that follow document various facial forms—caricatured, racialized, pretty, absent, wounded, aged, and otherwise—that complicate and even sabotage readerly attempts to assess, describe, or apprehend their surfaces. And while I do not always return to the aforementioned debates about reading as directly as their prominence in this introduction might indicate, I invoke them continuously through other kinds of frames—theoretical, philosophical, and historical—that problematize the nature of surface legibility by modeling forms of *"misguided"* or even failed reading.[105] Chapter one, "Facing Wilde; or, Emotion's Image," for example, brings together nineteenth-century caricatures of Wilde (which were highly racialized), the later depictions of Wilde that would emerge after his trials, pseudoscientific works on endocrinology, and classic accounts of visual modernity by Charles Baudelaire, Max Beerbohm, and Gombrich and Kris. When read closely together, I argue, these texts both anticipate and offer resolutions to some of the problems of intention and expression raised in contemporary theories of affect and emotion. Consequently, I do not see theory and history as opposed, but rather look to the archive, as it supports the historical relevance of models of explanation, like deconstruction, or affect theory, or even psychoanalysis, that have more recently been dismissed as ahistorical or universalist. Louis Berman's *The Glands Regulating Personality* (1922), for example, utilizes a physiognomic method of reading various "facial types" to articulate a physiological, surface model of reading human faces and personality as influenced by glandular activity; this model, I argue, anticipates the "corporeal account of emotions," or anti-intentionalist paradigm, to which Ruth Leys responds so strongly in her 2011 essay "The Turn to Affect: A Critique."[106] I similarly read a much earlier text, Baudelaire's "On the Essence of Laughter," as posing important resolutions to the problems of such anti-intentionalism, which separates, according to Leys, "meaning and signification" in a "non conscious . . . autonomic reaction system."[107] In Baudelaire's elaboration of comic expression, I argue, there is always a suspended moment between content and its expression, meaning and signification, that encourages our laughter "a moment late."[108] This response is bodily, and it is often out of sync with our perception of its source. Our "reading" of the comic, concretized especially in comic forms such as caricature, is by nature deforming and distorting.

Concepts like the comic, as well as one of its attendant visual forms, caricature, disturb the possibility of faithfulness to a text's surface by positing likeness or recognition in fleeting forms of expression that must be "caught," to return to Gombrich, at the moment of difference.[109] What's funny cannot always be immediately apprehended or articulated through objective description. Comic form demands subtle activities of reading, often marked by the reader's self-consciousness. More concretely, I also ask in chapter one how these explicitly racialized caricatures of Wilde that emerged from his trip to America in the 1880s could in fact code him as queer. Given this example, with its discordant masking of the queer body by the racialized one as the basis for the image's comic effect, we can see how the image may occupy what is, according to David Kurnick, a "symptomatic place of queerness" that strategies of surface reading do not make available.[110]

The next three chapters, which address realism and modernism from a period-specific lens, investigate how the face may block reading altogether and how it allegorizes the forms of dissociation that have now been deemed central to the modernist aesthetic. I formulate these chapters around a number of tensions that play out in the thematics of "facing," in particular, the ways in which the face's capacity for expression, its "brilliance," may actually occlude an accurate vision of its content, or what is "in a face."[111] Of importance here is the photograph, which produced a mobile or composite expression that problematized a discretely embodied sense of personality or form. Chapter two, "Realist Prosopagnosia; or, Face Blindness in Theodore Dreiser's *Sister Carrie*," returns again to Gombrich's idea of physiognomic perception, in which we make something readable by giving it a face. It argues that in Dreiser's novel *Sister Carrie* (1900) the text's preoccupation with Carrie's very pretty face narrates a form of modern vision that cannot produce the closure demanded by the realist project, situating the novel more closely with a modernist aesthetics that values dissociation and illegibility. Of particular importance to this chapter is Georg Lukács's well-known negative commentary on modernist aesthetics; his case for an idealized realist subject characterized by psychological totality points to the problem of persons *Sister Carrie* poses, where one can only be equal to one's face if one has a readable identity or self to express in the first place.[112]

This chapter also underlines the more general problem for women in naturalist fiction, which is, I argue, the problem of having a face. Drawing from Lois Tyson's classic account of Edith Wharton's *The House of Mirth* (1907), I suggest that, in texts ranging from *Sister Carrie* to *The House of Mirth* to Jean Rhys's late modernist *Voyage in the Dark* (1934), the "labor to escape existential inwardness through self-reification" and "self-aestheticizing" in fact wastes the face, literally ages it; face-work that dis-coordinates the subject supports neither intersubjectivity nor expression, instead signaling a lack of affective connection.[113] I also address texts like Stephen Crane's short 1894 sketch "When Man Falls, a Crowd Gathers," which connects this "waste" of the face to the problem of legibility and the urban environment, where the rapidity of visual impression renders the image unreadable. Similarly, George Bellows, the highly physiognomic American painter, either blots out the faces of his subjects or reimagines them as wolfish caricatures of exaggerated features. Such images, I argue, reflect the distanced stance of a modern, urban viewer, who, enclosed in a sphere of purely visual impression, either has given up or has lost a formal relation to their environment. The blank face, I argue, and the corresponding state of prosopagnosia, or face blindness, it entails reflect the absence of a scheme of readability through which attachments form. The chapter concludes by addressing the subjects that are so central to the novel, melodrama and theater, as historical contexts that help elucidate the prosopagnosia of an urban culture in which faces, and consequently selves, do not form.

This emphasis on the theatrical extends to chapter three, "Nothing 'Conclusive': Optics as Ethics in Joseph Conrad's *The Secret Agent*," which asks what happens to ethics in the absence of readable form, and which, like the previous chapter on Dreiser, looks to melodrama as a mode that dramatizes the problem of legibility and ethical irresolution. Conrad's 1907 novel is a specifically modernist commentary on the ethical reading of both texts and persons, addressing head-on the question of how we must read, even when the results of that reading may yield nothing "conclusive."[114] Set around the 1894 bombing of the Royal Observatory Greenwich in London, the novel explicitly links its commentary on surveillance to the development of new physiognomic systems, by Lombroso, Bertillon, and Galton, in particular. These systems, I argue, employed in the modernization of identification, were developed in response to the same problems of reading that *The Secret*

Agent examines—in particular the ethical ambiguity that attends the face's capacity for expression. Bertillon's anthropometric system and Galton's invention of fingerprinting responded to the ways in which faces could elude a viewer. Of more specific interest is Bertillon's science of identity, which involved practices designed to cultivate reasoned memories—through the study of photographs, for example—that would aid agents in the identification of criminals. The trained agent would not only be able to synthesize various views of a subject; they would also be able to absorb a whole range of perceptual data connected to an individual. Such a method offers a telling backdrop for reading Conrad's impressionism, which also recognized the inadequacy of the singular, surface impression and articulated methods for the management of numerous impressions. But Conrad's novels, as Jesse Matz has claimed, narrate the "undoing" of such a method, and I argue that *The Secret Agent*, like *Sister Carrie*, pursues this problem of representation by returning to the face of the actor and the subject of melodrama.[115] In illustrating the failure of impressionist synthesis and in exhausting the codes of melodrama, the novel ultimately dramatizes the *action* of reading as a practice that cannot offer an account of ethically unpardonable acts, but which it nevertheless characterizes as an ethical form of seeing.

The Secret Agent ends with Comrade Ossipon's attempt to "lay hold" of the memory of Winnie Verloc's blank and unreadable face, just after she has committed suicide.[116] This suicide occurs in response to the loss of another face, Winnie's brother Stevie's, whose body is blown to bits in the botched bombing of the observatory. Stevie's absent face is a haunting testament to the morally inconceivable nature of the bombing and, as such, is central to the ethical vision of the novel. In outlining this ethics, I make connections between melodrama as a highly gestural mode of expression that does not necessarily reinforce conclusion or meaning and Emmanuel Levinas's understanding of the "ethical relation" as it emerges in the "face to face" encounter.[117] Levinas's model of facial encounter offers insight into Conrad's own impressionistic use of the face as a site of signification that resists coercion into meaning and stands in particular contrast to the history of physiognomic ideology I have outlined—in which the meanings ascribed to particular faces inspire ever more intrusive modes of vision or "recod[ing]."[118]

Chapter four, "Modernist Prosopopoeia; or, Making Faces," draws on a quite different model of faciality, prosopopoeia, a model for reading and writing based on the resurrection and mastery of other faces. I take my formulation of the term primarily from de Man's reading of Percy Shelley's

"Autobiography as Defacement"; while we may all be aware of the dismissal of de Man's work on the basis of his questionable political activities, its cancellation was also a response to its perceived a-historicity and universalizing vision.[119] Nevertheless, I examine the relevance of this now-defamed model of analysis in three related historical contexts, all of which generated their own prosopopoeias and, like Bertillon's method, involved every possible visualization of the face: Mina Loy's pamphlet advertising rejuvenating facial exercises, *Auto-Facial-Construction* (1919); the critical context that formed around Henri Gaudier-Brzeska's sculpture *The Hieratic Head of Ezra Pound* (1914); and finally, World War I's devastating examples of facial injury and the corresponding "fantasy of repair" that accompanied them.[120]

When Ezra Pound contentedly observed that Gaudier-Brzeska's sculpture of him "does not look like me," he not only confirmed the loss of his real face to expression that "devours the face" but also foreshadowed the facial loss and injury sustained by soldiers in World War I, as well as the new innovations in plastic surgery it occasioned.[121] Alongside Harold Gillies's pioneering writing on the treatment of facial injuries during World War I, I look closely at some of Henry Tonks's pastel drawings of Gillies's patients, asking how prosopopoeia might operate as a mode of looking, a technology of vision, and a practice of reading through which we assign value to the wounded or injured face, the face in which we may not see an actual resemblance to its wearer, or, more generally, to ourselves. In doing so, I recast a critical binary that sees in surgical facial repair a state-sanctioned effort to rehabilitate normative masculinity against an authentically damaged, real face. I ask instead what Tonks's medical drawings teach us about doing "justice" to the wounded sitters of these portraits and inquire into the ways the images ascribe something like voice to their subjects. As de Man's description of prosopopoeia indicates, a speaking face solicits reading and, in doing so, actualizes its own defacement, or the destruction of that very form.

In the same way, any totalizing reading inevitably fragments, and prosopopoeia always encodes its own failure. Given this formulation, we may think more specifically about whether, in the case of Tonks's drawings, a damaged anatomy can elicit the "formal activities" required of reading, or whether it has a deep structure of expression or form.[122] To return to the logic of Grossman, who offers his own theory or prosopopoeia without naming it as such, these faces contain within them the "represented destruction" or "scarcity" that operates as a "final term of value" in "existence as such."[123] In claiming the face as a text and as a figure for reading that is essential to the *"justice* of acknowledgment," Grossman affirms the value of literary modes of analysis and production for the more general satisfaction of "human needs" and, by extension, ethics.[124] For Grossman, these needs involve "the building and just distribution of the descriptive terms that specify the value of the person," practices that affirm their "visibility" and "intelligibility."[125]

Chapter five, "Unreadable Persons: The 'Face-Scape' of Old Age," takes on the explicit question of how these "descriptive terms" specify both "visibility" and "intelligibility," given the apparent "damage" that attends old age as a "formed" category of scientific, aesthetic, and social inquiry. It begins by considering the deeply creviced visage of W. H. Auden, which, according to commentators such as Hannah Arendt, displayed the ravage of the poet's late-life misery, and examines how arguably modernist interventions in the aging process constructed a seemingly illegible body. Yeats, for example, quite famously pursued reinvigoration through elective vasectomy. Not only do I focus here on the literature surrounding Yeats's Steinach operation, but I also show how texts representing the nascent geriatric sciences of the period, following Charcot's work in the nineteenth century, defined the aging body as duplicitous, characterized by changes and transitions so imperceptible as to elicit a crisis in the mode of observation of the subject, a crisis in reading.

I also note Auden's own poetry, in particular "Old People's Home," which explicitly formulates the aesthetic category of "damage" and the corresponding process of defacement to theorize poetry as an act of writing that—in an action typical of prosopopoeia—"revisage[s]" older faces.[126] Through Auden's poetry, I connect "damage" to the concept of illegibility and perceived disfigurement, which has behind it an ideal of legibility that is symbolized by the unmarked, youthful face. The idea that aging bodies, and faces, disturb the idea that we can always know persons and thus connect with them on the basis of that legibility underlies the examples I discuss, such as tomes on rejuvenation and geriatrics; John Frankenheimer's 1966 film about age and masculinity, *Seconds*, in which an aging banker, played by John Randolph, undergoes a total body overhaul to become the "reborn" Rock Hudson; and Cindy Sherman's photographic portraits of herself in the personae of aging Hollywood women. Such examples, I argue, illustrate the tension that characterizes our viewing of other faces, between the violence of "revisag[ing]" and the "distribution of descriptive terms that specify the value of a person."[127] Michael Taussig characterizes this same type of dynamic as "defacement," a form of "criticism" that involves the viewer's desire to unmask a "worthy" but otherwise illegible face.[128] With this lens in mind, I conclude by emphasizing the importance of seemingly unreadable forms—aging bodies, bodies in transition, wounded faces, to name a few—that solicit our readings nonetheless.

In the epilogue to this book, I address various ideas about faciality that fell outside of its explicitly reparative frame, namely the biopolitical arguments of theorists such as Giorgio Agamben and Deleuze and Guattari, which advocate a "dismant[ling]" of the "face and facializations" as a means of resisting objectifying and dehumanizing biometric systems.[129] I also identify some contemporary issues that leave us concerned about the reckless misuse and processing of our faces, as in the example of FRT, and simultaneously wary of the obscurity that results when are faces are lost or unseen. I briefly examine the terror of losing one's face in relation to several contemporary contexts: two films, Jordan Peele's *Get Out* (2017) and Pedro Almodóvar's *The Skin I Live In* (*La Piel que Habito*; 2011); the complicated ethics of the face transplant, first performed in 2005; and finally, the experience of "facial loss" suffered by people with "facial problems," including more rare conditions such as Moebius syndrome.[130] I argue that the answer to the questions about facial loss generated in these contexts is not to "escape the face" but a return to the power of a visually constitutive form of reading that involves an imagining or witnessing of the faces of others.[131] Following de Man, Miller, and Grossman, I look to prosopopoeia and to the poetic "power of imaging," or the giving of faces, as it reflects the "capacity to value persons" at the same time that it makes room for consideration of what may not be apprehensible in them.[132] Rather than uncovering and explaining a void or chasm, this book ultimately attempts to think through the desire to read deeply into what we cannot read as productive and restorative in a world of surfaces.

1 Facing Wilde; or, Emotion's Image

> It is not the least important of the lessons of endocrine analysis that there is no soul, and no body, either.
>
> —Louis Berman, MD, *The Glands Regulating Personality*, 1922

> Perhaps it isn't given to man to express all his emotions on his face, especially when we consider the many different emotions that have been named and arbitrarily classified by the philosophers.
>
> —Guillaume-Benjamin-Amand Duchenne de Boulogne, *Mécanisme de Physionomie Humaine*, 1862.

In his 1862 study *Mécanisme de Physionomie Humaine* (*The Mechanism of Human Facial Expression*) Guillaume-Benjamin Duchenne argues that "emotions, sentiments, and passions" are only genuine when their "image" appears in "muscles" of the face.[1] If the emotion is not visibly evident in "isolated contraction[s]," it is unreadable, without an "image," having been arbitrarily classified by the philosophers.[2] Duchenne's charge here is to Plato, Aristotle, Cicero, Descartes, and Hobbes, but his complaint anticipates more recent inquiries into the relation among the face, expression, and our reading practices. Psychologist Silvan Tomkins, for example, has argued that our faces do not merely express our affects but define them, as "affect is primarily facial behavior."[3] If "facial behavior" can be thought of as the transmission of an "image," I am interested here in the fate of emotion's image and what a face—in fact, a particularly well-known face—can tell us about the meaning of expression, especially when that image is elusive, fleeting, or simply unknowable.

Whether one understands expression as physiological—as surface "facial behavior"—or psychological reveals a great deal about how we conceive of the individual as oriented around a depth, or interior, and its relation to an exterior. Evident in Arthur Symons's response to Henri de Toulouse-Lautrec's "appalling" watercolor of Oscar Wilde, painted on the eve of his final 1895 trial, a purely physiological form of expression can be quite shocking to a viewer.[4] Midway through the self-indulgent narrative of his own "morbid sense of aversion," Symons—in a scene of reading that is uncannily reminiscent of Wilde's *The Picture of Dorian Gray* (1890)—digresses into what is perhaps the most unflattering depiction of Wilde on paper.[5] This paragraph-long aside is a testament to the visibility of Wilde's physiological decline; in the early to mid-1890s, an assortment of print venues ferociously caricatured an engorged and fleshy Wilde. As Robert Sherard put it in his well-known biography, Wilde's was a "formidable physiological problem"; Frank Harris similarly "lay stress on" his feeling of "physical repulsion" toward the man, who, as early as 1884, appeared "fat and oily," as if "written all over" with "fleshly indulgence and laziness."[6] Toulouse-Lautrec's portrait offers no exception. Not only does Wilde appear "swollen, puffed out, bloated and sinister," but the painting also, Symons remarks, reveals his "womanish side."[7] One sentence, however, says it all: "The face is bestial."[8] This "hideous countenance," this "thing that is no more a thing," fashions Wilde into a "kind of Hermaphroditus," marked by a mouth that—as painted by Toulouse-Lautrec, and apparently by Wilde as well, with a cosmetic—"no man who is normal could ever have had."[9] Physiognomy, invested in establishing norms of expression, underwrites Symons's pathologizing discourse, which locates the meaning of Wilde's perversion in his face.

True, the mouth is most troublesome. Crimson red and tightly pursed, it appears as if painted onto a preexisting portrait, unlike the sagging flesh of the face, a more natural extension of Wilde's slackening body. "No such mouth," Symons writes, "ought ever to have existed," claiming it as the focal point of a pathologizing discourse that links Wilde's deteriorating body and "bestial" face to the "horror of his hideous countenance in a mirror": the expression of his "inversions," or, as Joseph Bristow has observed, his degeneration into a "racially regressive being."[10] In Toulouse-Lautrec's portrait of Wilde, the image transmitted by expression no longer reflects an inside, but rather arises from "personality." As the argument goes, the ideology of modern personality—in contrast to the nineteenth-century culture of character, which emphasized moral self-mastery and strength as indicators of

Henri de Toulouse-Lautrec, *Portrait of Oscar Wilde*, 1895. Lordprice Collection/Alamy Stock Photo.

one's internal state of being—posited the self as something that could be constructed and further managed to influence the perceptions of others.[11] I use this term similarly throughout this book, to refer to an external perception built around self-development and self-presentation, but I am more specifically interested in the ways physiology informs personality and vice versa. Toulouse-Lautrec's portrait illustrates how personality—linked in this case to physiological decline rather than creativity and attractiveness—is a projection based on a physiognomic ideal of a readable subject. At the same time, personality is a script that enables the reading of subjects, reframing or deforming the parameters of the image transmitted by the body. As it informs modern vision, personality thus complicates a purely physiological or mimetic account of expression. It also, as I argue more indirectly, upsets a purely mimetic account of reading that privileges exacting modes of description over criticism or analysis. My story of modern facial expression begins here, with investigations of three related contexts: the historical parameters established by a number of texts that converge around the subject of Wilde's face, more recent debates about affects and the emotions, and the theories of visual modernity advanced by Charles Baudelaire, Max Beerbohm, and Ernst Kris and E. H. Gombrich. These accounts of expression—which link an embodied, expressive subject to a modern, unsingular vision—see it as an essentially meaningful phenomenon that does not authenticate a human interior to be expressed, read, or analyzed.

Modern Physiognomy and *The Glands Regulating Personality*

Albeit in the service of a different ideological end—homophobia—American scientist and proponent of endocrinology Louis Berman, MD, corroborates a similar model of expression, which locates meaning in the absence of a psychologically expressive individual. In his 1922 study *The Glands Regulating Personality: A Study of the Glands of Internal Secretion in Relation to the Types of Human Nature*, Berman advances Oscar Wilde as a representative "facial type"; he examines photographs of Wilde's parents and claims that Wilde's homosexuality derives from both the "curiously animal" features of Wilde's father and the "masculinoid" characteristics of his mother.[12] Recalling characterizations of Wilde as tall and of *"great corpulence,"* Berman stresses the "thymocentric significance" of the "glabrosity"—the hairlessness—of Wilde's face.[13] Other traits of interest include Wilde's *"fleshy* and *plump"* hands, the volatile range of his voice, and his large breasts.[14] Finally, Berman notes "the exceptional size" of Wilde's head, which, he argues, "reinforced the love of the beautiful that is part of the feminine post-pituitary nature."[15] Given the artistic genius born of his homosexuality, Wilde is indeed one of the "abnormals" without whom there would "be a great gap, a yawning absence in the world's culture."[16]

Berman employs a physiognomic *method* of reading the face (not only Wilde's but also Florence Nightingale's, Charles Darwin's, and Friedrich

Nietzsche's, among others) as a "complex of brows, eyes, nose, lips and jaws" whose "modeling and tone" manifest what "each of the endocrine glands has . . . to say."[17] In his review of Berman's study, published that same year in the *Journal of Abnormal Psychology and Social Psychology*, Harvard psychology professor Gordon Allport, who rejected behaviorism for its too-shallow conception of the individual, worries that this rapidly accelerating interest in endocrinology, and physiology more generally, has become a reductive explanation for the larger "problem of personality," as well as the "emotional and affective life of the individual."[18] Berman, his reviewer concedes sarcastically, "brings physiognomy up to date and gives it a new lease on life."[19] That is, Berman's radical modification of physiognomy as a hermeneutic practice consists in reading individuals without reading *into* them. Put another way, he employs a physiognomic method organized around the presumed dimensionality of individuals only to render them dimensionless.

Physiognomy, claimed by Johann Lavater as a science in the late eighteenth century and further revitalized by Darwin in 1872 in *The Expression of the Emotions in Man and Animals*, predicated the expressive strength of the face on its ability to consolidate the interior and exterior dimensions of the human subject. For Berman, however, the face has become not the exteriorization of the soul's emotions but the exteriorization of various chemical secretions; physiology, not psychology, with its claims to understand the subject's inner recesses, becomes the basis for emotional expression and, further, personality. Berman's study corroborates François Delaporte's argument that expression did not exist before the mid-nineteenth century and the work of Duchenne, because the face itself did not exist. The body first had to be constituted as an object of study, as it was in the "anatomy and physiology of affects," or the corporeal account of the emotions that emerged from Duchenne's experiments, which employed a combination of photography and electrical stimulation to simulate and capture representative human facial expressions.[20] Duchenne believed that such expressions, which he claimed to have "induc[ed]" through electrophysiological stimulation, would assist psychology by producing a "language" for better understanding the emotions.[21] This "new grammar of signs," Delaporte argues, aided by the development of photography, made possible the modern face, along with a corresponding "image" of an inside.[22] In this case, meaning does not emerge directly from the inside, but is rather an image or projection derived from an analysis of the surface.

For this reason, Duchene did not have an ethical problem with the idea

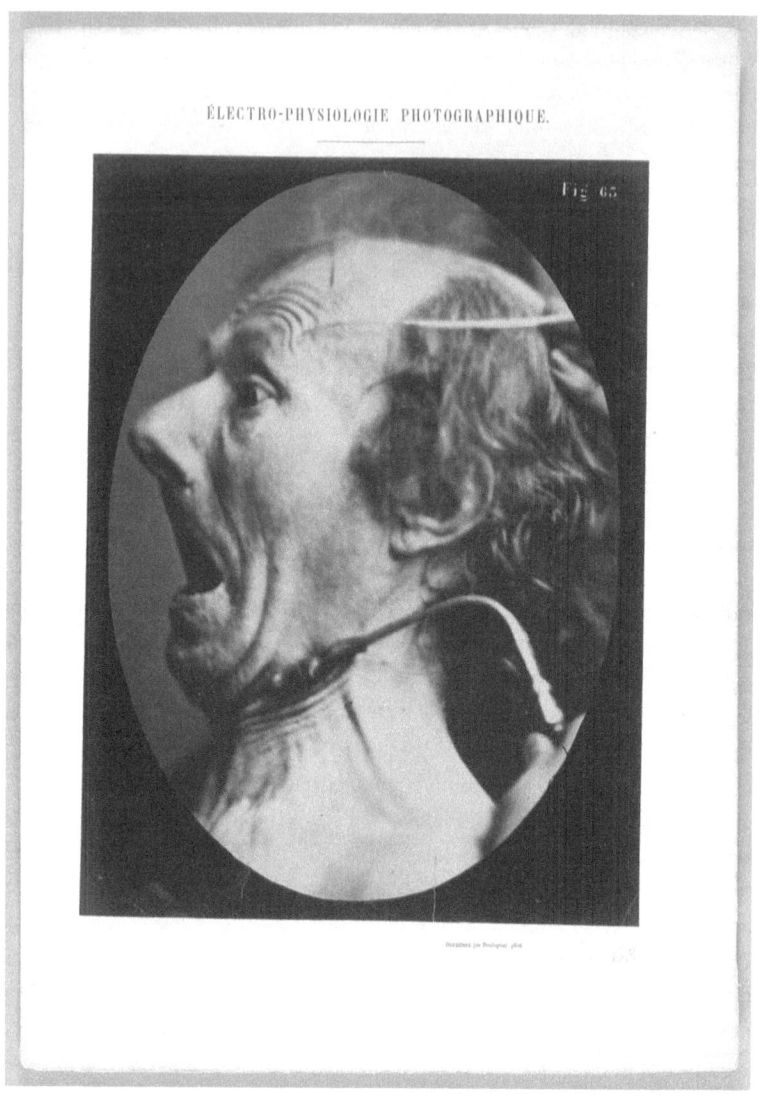

From Guillaume-Benjamin-Amand Duchenne de Boulogne, expression of terror, 1854–56, printed in *Mécanisme de Physionomie Humaine*, 1862. Photo © Metropolitan Museum of Art. Courtesy of Art Resource, NY.

of manipulating sensation to create correspondences between isolated muscle contractions and projected interior states. He indeed believed that a facial expression was more "complete when they [the facial muscles] contract in isolation," thus throwing any concern for the coherence of natural phenomena out the window.[23] With this disregard came a corresponding turn away from Lavater's obsession with common forms of appearance and order toward a focus on individual psychology. As Delaporte observes, Duchenne noted commonalities in human expression, but he understood them as signs derived from the body's organization, where shared forms of emotional expression were the product of a projection made possible in the first place by the body. Nonetheless, Duchenne, like Bell, retains an "*image of emotions, sentiments, and passions.*"[24] I am arguing here that such an image meets its fate in Berman's *Glands*, which lodges the meaning of individuality in the personality. For Berman, there is no psychological, or internal, basis for emotional expression, as personalities—"The Adrenal Personality," "The Endocrine Personality," and so on—are based on the dominance of glands that determine physical characteristics and direct individual behavior.[25] Other than a combination of glands, Berman does not offer a clear definition of what he thinks personality is, except that it "embraces much more than merely the psychic attributes."[26] Berman does call the personality a "soul-body, or body-soul," suggesting that it is the embodiment of characteristics, feelings, or traits generally connected to the projection or idea of a soul, or what one might call a psyche.[27] However, in Berman's account, these presumably interior dimensions of human experience are rerouted into the personality itself. In this formulation of personality, the interior, which is for Duchenne a projection born of an analysis of the outside, is no longer an image that is separate from the body's functioning.

As a physiological manifestation, personality also becomes the means by which the physiological tips into the pathological. Whereas Lavater's physiognomy sought to identify common forms and types, Berman's face reading seeks out the abnormal, the pathological, as the source of meaning. And what better subject for Berman's analysis than that very maligned and celebrated face, that notorious personality, which, after 1895, embodied a whole set of pathological associations—Oscar Wilde. With the previous sentence, I am suggesting that, in the twentieth century, Oscar Wilde *is* a face. In turning to him as such, as a representative "facial type," Berman's study becomes part of a lengthy preoccupation with Wilde's face, beginning with the explosion of visual images caricaturing the writer in the 1880s and moving through an assortment of accounts that emerged after the trials of 1895 and persisted throughout the twentieth century.[28] The argument that the 1895 trials "refashioned" an otherwise merely effeminate Wilde into a "pathological being"—a real queer, to say the least—is well known.[29] I will return to this argument later, but for now I reiterate the idea that the trials, as Ed Cohen has argued, were the stage for a "new 'type' of sexual actor: 'the homosexual,'" which "crystallized a new constellation of sexual meanings predicated upon 'personality' and not [sexual] practices."[30] This sense of personality can indeed be likened to the "pose" for which Wilde was interrogated in the first place. To replay the story, Wilde initially sued the Marquis of Queensberry, Lord Alfred Douglas's father, after receiving the former's calling card, on which was written the now-famous words "For Oscar Wilde Posing as a Somdomite [sic]."[31] As Cohen has noted, the trials played on the indeterminacy of the word "posing." The question was not whether Wilde *was* a sodomite but whether he was "the kind of person" who would have committed sodomy.[32] At issue was Wilde's self-presentation, his expression of an image or type, corroborated by his already-established notoriety as a public figure, the polish of his language, his flamboyant attire, and the general "effects of his 'persona.'"[33] As Cohen has illustrated, despite Wilde's obvious refinements, press reports and illustrations foregrounded Wilde's physical presence, as it embodied the "unarticulated meanings" of homosexuality—a "metonym for the 'crime'" of physical acts that could not be concretely represented.[34] In these grotesque stylizations, Wilde's fleshy lips and "monstrous" nose embodied the "physical degeneration that such nonnormative non-'manly' practices portend."[35] As corroborated by Berman's account, Wilde's physiognomy offered the public something to "read" only by way of his deviation from normative masculinity and, further, a normative face.

Expression and the "Turn to Affect"

It follows that if we would analyze our fellow man with regard to his personal capacities we have only to refer to certain characteristic features of the body to receive an unmistakable index of character.

Gordon Allport, 1922

The trials produced not only a new kind of personality, then, but also a new, and reductive, way of reading it, a practice that reaches its full culmination in Berman's *Glands*. In his sarcastic comment, Allport indeed refers to "character"—which seems to reference the complexity of human experience—in explicit contrast to Berman's physiological version of "personality."[36] I make note of Allport's response to demonstrate how a particular moment in the historical account of emotional expression I am constructing both anticipates and posits resolutions to some of the problems of intention and expression raised in more recent theories of expression and affect. In these exchanges, however, neuroscience has replaced endocrinology as an explanatory paradigm for the human personality and the affective life of the individual. I am referring to Ruth Leys's 2011 article "The Turn to Affect: A Critique" and the series of responses it received from William Connolly, Charles Altieri, Elizabeth Wilson, and Adam Frank, all of whom fault Leys for rhetorically packaging a diverse group—which includes Brian Massumi, Antonio DeMasio, Joseph LeDoux, Paul Ekman, Silvan Tomkins, and Eve Sedgwick—into a reductive anti-intentionalist paradigm.[37] For Leys, such "corporeal accounts of the emotions" support the idea that affective processes occur independently of the "cognition or knowledge of the objects that caused them"; in this scenario, affects have no cognitive content, no meaning or intention.[38]

Leys's thesis that the turn to neuroscience as an explanatory paradigm for the complexity of human affect and emotion is indifferent to how deeply we are embedded in culture and ideology—as well as her insistence that the phenomenon of aesthetic expression deserves actual inquiry—continues to be important and timely. More specifically, as I show here, the aforementioned debates not only establish a significant vocabulary for thinking about the meaning of aesthetic expression and experience but also connect questions about the expert reading of human beings to our reading of literary and visual texts. For example, though Leys grants him only a brief note, Daniel M. Gross's account of the seriously "impoverished" "social model" that characterizes the "brain science of emotion," as exemplified in the work of Antonio Damasio and Joseph LeDoux, is actually a tale of bad reading.[39] Reflecting on "early modern emotion," Gross faults Damasio in particular for reproducing a "reductive" Cartesian "psychophysiology of emotion" that strips certain social characteristics and phenomena of meaning by turning them into "localizable and theoretically measurable manifestation[s] of the body or brain."[40] Gross cites the conclusion of Damasio's well-known experiment, based on a CT scan of the impaired amygdalae of patient S, that a person with an abnormal brain—unable to distinguish a trustworthy face from one that intended harm—could not read a human face accurately. According to this logic, all persons with normal brains would share the same "adaptive human trait" that enabled them to read other faces correctly.[41] This assumption, Gross implies, overrides the sorts of social distinctions that make some people better readers of faces than others and elides "emotion's uneven expression over different sorts of people, its apparent dysfunction in the humiliated or depressed, or even its utter absence in the politically disaffected."[42]

Gross's critique of Damasio also presents the question of what it means for meaning to emerge from our "abnormal" brains, and for us to be bad readers of ourselves and others. This a question Leys overlooks when she faults Eve Sedgwick's work for flattening affective experience into a disorganized grab bag of bodily responses that affirm the "singularity of one's experiences," or Sedgwick's own political agenda of promoting "difference."[43] Sedgwick, following Tomkins, actually views emotions as "complex . . . assemblages" that cannot necessarily be linked to distinct cognitions or drives, but which may still find themselves "embedded in scripts that serve to negotiate our motivational realities."[44] For Sedgwick, again with reference to Tomkins, meaning (and "freedom") emerges from unintentional acts: the potential distance between affect and cognition, through the "possibilities . . . for being wrong about an object—and implicatively, about oneself."[45] Leys's mischaracterization of Sedgwick aligns with the former's "insistence on a radical opposition between affect and intention," further eliding the question of the meaning of expression in art, which, Leys herself laments, has been the subject of anti-intentionalist indifference.[46] The more significant issue, I would suggest, is what an expression can *mean*, especially if its object or source is absent, elusive, or simply unknowable.[47]

In terms of my own account of Wilde's face, I am concerned with how these expressions come to be embodied and are further recognized without being reduced to a flattened projection. As I suggest in what follows, the case of Oscar Wilde demonstrates how an expression itself may become so powerfully recognizable or enculturated that it can be seen in bodies that are physiologically not its source. In my analysis of visual images of Wilde, I show how the meaningfulness of a bodily expression can in fact exceed its relation to the individual body that produced it. In contrast to accounts that see expression either as intentional and meaningfully related to individual subjects or as automatic and without content, my reading of these images locates meaning in the visual scripts or fields that multiply the parameters of the individual body. Since expression can be separated from the individual body that is its initial source, the accuracy of our reading of expression must be related to our knowledge and experience of specific expressive fields that may resist our efforts to quantify or describe them.

This view is corroborated by Delaporte's historical argument that expressions only existed when the "muscular contractions" of the face could be "situated within a field of expressivity."[48] A "muscular spasm, a grimace," or other "insignificant movement" was otherwise inexpressive—unreadable—because it could not be "transformed" into a "sign" through "psychological thought."[49] An expression in this context is not fully without content but—to extrapolate from Tomkins, writing almost a century later—is situated within a "field" or script that informs the relation between the subject's intention and an observer. Expression or affect is produced in the body, but, contrary to Leys's assertion, this does not diminish its intentionality or meaningfulness, at least in terms of our possible awareness of or feeling about our affects. Much like Gombrich's idea of "physiognomic perception," which I discuss in the introduction, Tomkins's understanding of facial affectivity links affective expression to the viewer's memory and experiences, or the subject's rapid processing of prior responsive experiences related to the form of other faces.[50] In this account, the interplay between the image and its involuntary relation to memory best characterizes the script that informs modern expression. Viewing expression as produced in the scripts that create personalities and, further, identifiable facial forms—rather than in the singular individual—offers a potential resolution to the critical debates I have just surveyed, which situate bodies either as conscious and meaningful or as purely physiological, without individual intention and, consequently, meaning in the world. For Duchenne and Tomkins, the meaning of expression resides in the image as it is "generat[ed]" by the observer, or *what* the observer sees in a face.[51] In the logic I am outlining here, what an observer often "sees in a face" is personality. To return to Berman's *Glands*, personality is itself form, an image or expression of various hormonal combinations, transmitted through the medium of the face. This insight into the function and formation of the modern personality—via the rather unlikely genealogy of Duchenne, Berman, and Tomkins—provides what Leys's own critique of "the turn to affect" does not: an avenue for approaching the problem of what a physiological form of expression can mean, especially as it appears in the particular example of Wilde's face during any given point in its print circulation.

The Normal and the Pathological

In the accounts I discuss here, the meaning of Wilde's face underwrites larger questions of aesthetic and physiological form. For Berman, "normality means harmony," a definition that renders Wilde—whom Berman classifies among the "abnormals"—badly formed.[52] In Wilde's case, the perception that this foremost advocate of form was indeed irregularly formed lingered throughout his career and contributed to his popularity as the subject of caricature. As declared by one Oxford publication of 1893, a rival to Douglas's *Spirit Lamp*, "His [Wilde's] face is his misfortune."[53] There can be no doubt that Wilde's physiological irregularities—his overlong face, his stature, and, in the 1890s, his corpulence, along with the "uneven" display of his emotions—contributed to his popularity as a subject of caricature and established his connection to bad form.[54]

Modernist Wyndham Lewis was preoccupied with the possibility that Wilde's bad form—his excessive affect in conjunction with the group constituting power of his "personality"—might indeed become good form. In "The Physiological Norm and the 'Vicious'" (1926), Lewis inveighs against the "'Nancyism' of the joy-boy or the joy-man"—the "over-mannered personality," complete with a "grating or falsetto lisp" and a "queer insistence on 'delicate nurture.'"[55] He further credits Wilde with transforming these once pathological affectations into fashionable norms: "as he possessed to the full the proselytizing zeal that usually goes with sex inversion, . . . he prepared the ground with his martyrdom, ecstatic recantations, eloquent and tear-ful [sic] confessions, and the great prestige of his wit, for the complete reversal of the erotic machinery that has ensued or is ensuing."[56] In claiming so much for Wilde's excessive affect, his "well-advertised agony," Lewis is either speaking sarcastically or giving what he thinks is due credit to Wilde's effect on modern sexuality.[57] He is, in any case, wrong about Wilde's delivery on the stand, where his verbal polish and affective control actually frustrated his critics. Regardless, this charge to gay affection as a kind of bourgeois "material physiognomy" fuels Lewis's homophobia.[58] Indeed, "The Physiological Norm and the 'Vicious'" proceeds by way of an analogy in which Lewis compares the expression of inversion to the red of a drunkard's nose; inversion is thus the external, physiological expression of a vice. For Lewis, both inversion and its opposite, the "puritan conscience," are locked together in a "'vicious' circle": an essentially *"bourgeois"* dynamic that "gives sex inversion . . . its particular material physiognomy of *protest* and over-importance."[59]

Much of Lewis's rhetoric here builds on the relationship he sees between his idea of the *"physical"* or "material physiognomy" and the "person" as a physiological expression.[60] Speaking through another questionable analogy of a groom's reaction to finding that his bride has been previously deflowered, Lewis writes that "it is a person, a mind, that he has married; incarnated, and expressed, it is true, by a certain body."[61] The "person" is the expression—the form or the image—expressed by the body. Lewis excuses the *practice* of homosexuality but, echoing Symons, penalizes the "inverted fashion" primarily for its bad expression of a physiological vice.[62] And bad expression makes for bad persons. Indeed, the word "bad" here, which is my own, follows from Lewis's final and more interesting claim that the "moral indignation" and "loudly expressed disgust . . . of the Plain Man or Plain Woman" mirrors the "self-satisfaction and sense of outrageous discovery" that motivates the "other ('unnatural') side of the sexual pale."[63] Both sides, he suggests, are equally bourgeois in their theatricality, such that the "stimulus" against moralism actually reproduces it.[64] As Lewis puts it, excessive moralism, especially when "loudly expressed," is a "physiognomy," a face.[65] In highlighting Wilde's presumably intentional theatricality as the badge of bourgeois physiognomic display, Lewis's physiological account of form, problematic as it is, points to the ways in which physiological expression creates meaningful "persons." As with the example of Wilde, expression creates a person by way of its attachment to a meaningful history, not an authentic interiority, or even a singular individual. Only as a "person" can Wilde's embodied particularities, his apparently excessive expression of affect, be linked to the "inverted fashion," the script or expression, the image of his homosexuality.[66]

Writing in the 1920s, both Lewis and Berman drew on a particularly modern understanding of Wilde as "personality"—a threateningly fashionable aberration that, critics have argued, grew from the trials of 1895. It is in reference to these trials that Lewis makes his virulent jab associating Wilde's "inversion" with overblown physiological expression. Extrapolating from these aforementioned arguments linking the emergence of the modern, biologically defined homosexual to the development of a gay personality—as opposed to the merely effeminate dandy—it follows that the trials gave inversion a face, a physiognomy. Such a face, I have been arguing, consolidates a person and thus gives meaning to a physiological form of expression that is also pathological. As I have suggested, the distinct focus of pathology in Toulouse-Lautrec's portrait of Wilde, as well as Symons's analysis of it, is the playwright's mouth, which is seemingly isolated from the rest of the face and body. In the years following Wilde's trials, this mouth, which, according to Symons, "ought [n]ever to have existed," became the subject of a public conversation made possible by the trials.[67] In *The Life Sexual: A Study of the Philosophy, Physiology, Science, Art, and Hygiene of Love* (1905), for example, Edgar C. Beall, MD, looks to one of Napoleon Sarony's famous 1882 photographic portraits of Wilde as evidence of "Femininity in All the Features."[68] Of significance to Beall are the "rounded contours" of Wilde's body, his soft flesh and "narrow, drooping shoulders" along with his "large, full eyes," which testify to his "artistic talent" and "delicacy of taste."[69] Wilde's mouth, "exceptionally refined and beautifully feminine," is the ultimate proof of his sexual perversion.[70]

In contrast to Delaporte's claim that in the nineteenth century the pathological exceeds the "threshold" of "expressivity," the pathologizing discourses of Beall, along with those of Lewis and Berman, exaggerate the powers of Wilde's expression. Much in contrast to the physiognomic tradition inspired by Lavater, with its emphasis on common types, the focus here is on how the pathological characterizes a distinctly readable and expressive subject. Berman further opens ways for new "types" by arguing that the "individuality of the individual" emerges from the sheer variety of hormonal combinations that constitute the "normal body," through "numberless hereditary gradations and transitions, blendings, and mixtures."[71] For Berman, "pure types," those dominated by only one gland, are also the easiest to classify and thus come to represent the "norm" against the mixed types, in which the "lines of distinction are less clear."[72] Consequently, he writes, "it is possible to conceive of a million types of normals," championing the increasing sophistication of endocrine analysis as a means of extending the possibilities of "normal" to those mixed types who were not "measurable" before.[73]

In his important work *The Normal and the Pathological*, Georges Canguilhem argues that with the work of French physiologist Claude Bernard and the influence of his scientific method in the mid-nineteenth century, hereditary anomalies came to be understood as distinctly pathological alongside a corresponding category of normal that reflected phenomena with measurable, observable characteristics. Physiognomy concerns itself with this normal as a rule of averages used to categorize the individual according to various norms or types.[74] Such emphasis on measurement suggests an explicit, already-identifiable correspondence between an embodied human subject and a desired outcome—or an explicit sense of the very norm that one is measuring for in the first place. This logic in fact confirms Delaporte's historical account of facial pathology—which suggests that expression itself existed only insofar as it conformed to the field in which it could be recognized. That is, expression was understood as real, not only in relation to an embodied human subject but also in its connection to an identifiable "person."

Delaporte's account of expression—focused as it is on physiognomy as a practice of making visible the invisible—indirectly supports the view that inversion did not have an expression, or image, prior to the 1895 trials. As I suggest in the readings that follow, however, the phenomenon of expression itself—by virtue of its relation to the inaccessible, the indefinite, and the unknown—complicates the argument that the trials made homosexuality visible.[75] In his excellent reconstruction of the "cultural climate" of the trials, Michael Foldy has noted that the Victorian public was quite familiar with the "sex scandal," including the Cleveland Street Scandal of 1889, which featured a homosexual brothel and a member of the royal family.[76] The Wilde trials, Foldy contends, created a "single forum and a single frame of reference" for the "otherwise disparate concepts" of decadence, degeneration, criminality, male effeminacy, and, last but not least, homosexuality.[77]

Given this account, how does this range of "disparate" associations contribute to Wilde's physiological grounding in a world of signs before 1895? Decidedly nastier than their British counterparts, the caricatures from Wilde's 1882 trip to America have been addressed from a variety of perspectives: as the products of a culture of celebrity and self-advertisement that resulted from an easily accessible press; as the American press's vicious effort to transform the writer into both a "sexual predator" and a racialized subject, who threatened to seduce the young and impressionable with his message of "artistic and sensual dissolution"; and finally, as reflective of Wilde's racialized position as an Anglo-Irish subject, as well as scientific discourses related to non-Western peoples.[78] Indeed, the caricatures racialize Wilde's aestheticism, with its focus on art for art's sake and advocacy of leisure, which they register as a threat to American control over a potentially idle population. Here, racist constructions of affect and emotion are used to forge an ugly image, the bad form of the subject's (Wilde's) interior.

In the 1882 Currier and Ives print "The Aesthetic Craze," a "black-faced" Wilde appears as a slightly less enervated version of the "racially regressive being" of Toulouse-Lautrec's portrait, linked to a subjugated but potentially rebellious population of African American help.[79] The illustration does not

THE ÆSTHETIC CRAZE.
What's de matter wid de Nigga? Why Oscar you's gone wild!

Currier and Ives, *The Aesthetic Craze*, 1882. Courtesy of the William Andrews Clark Memorial Library, University of California, Los Angeles.

simply forecast the possibility that Wilde's effeminate costume might influence both male and female followers, resulting in the "feminization of American men";[80] rather, the subject's mouth—the frequently cited "sign" of Wilde's homosexuality in the twentieth century—is the primary visual and physiognomic link between him and his conspirators. Part of the *Darktown Comics* series issued from the late 1870s to the early 1890s, the print betrays a particular Reconstruction-era anxiety about race relations in America and Oscar Wilde as influencer. The illustrations were, as the company put it, "good natured hits at the populare [sic] amusements and excitements of the times," depicting African Americans as they attempted to enjoy the pastimes of "ordinary folks," meaning whites; they are hunting, riding horses, taking music lessons, getting married, and, in the image in question, dressing up as Oscar.[81] The caption—"What's de matter wid de Nigga? Why Oscar you's gone Wild!"—mystifies the target of the ridicule here, thus intensifying the disturbing effect of the picture. This sort of racialized image was, as Mary Blanchard has observed, the most "incisive indictment of the male aesthete," not merely for his effeminacy but for his threat to the forms of racial demarcation on which the social order was based.[82]

Such fears were clearly echoed in a comic biography published that same year, which lamented Wilde's influence on the wives and the help: "Our colored help stand speechless as he enters our hall and leave our work neglected."[83] The young subject of "The Aesthetic Craze" is not speechless but stands in the characteristic Wildean pose made famous in the Sarony portraits that were also taken in 1882, as if saying something. He is "crazed" or "wild," pathologized; something, not quite measurable, is "the matter" with him. Dressed in yellow knee britches with sunflower in hand, he speaks to an audience of two women. While one looks at Oscar with perplexed exasperation, the other, head tilted on clasped hands, has abandoned her work in admiration. Wilde's voice here is figured not as a projection of an interior but as a form of physiological expressivity that is the basis for the picture's comic effect. In this sense, this particular portrayal of Wilde, which connects his effeminacy to the exaggerated physiological expression, does not differ markedly from the depictions that emerged after the trials.

There is, however, one major exception: the face in this caricature does not look like Wilde's face. The major difference between this image and those that emerged after the trials is the set of associations and expressions—ostensibly moral in meaning—linked to what is not expressed in the picture, relegated explicitly to the realm of the pathological, the abnormal, the "wild."[84] In "The Aesthetic Craze," the visibility of the subject's racial "difference" from Wilde is the source of the illustration's humor and, to say the least, its racism. Consistent with the dynamics of blackface minstrelsy performances more generally, the joke behind the illustration relies on the viewer's participation in a racist visual field and the artist's racist constructions of the subject's affectations.[85] The nineteenth-century idea of racial "phenotype" is also relevant here, particularly as it emerged in efforts to classify and create racial types in fields like anthropology, which, as Amade M'charek has observed, were deeply "tainted" with "race science" and "colonial pedagogies of racial difference."[86] Much like the instructional prints of black faces M'charek examines, designed to teach viewers how to recognize racial differences, the black-faced caricatures of Wilde guide the gaze of the viewer through a "field of expressivity" that coheres around the connection the pictures establish between the exaggerated gestures of the black body and the effeminate male body, as well as the viewer's knowledge of the person, Oscar Wilde.[87] In asking "what's the matter," the picture makes it explicit that what is important in the expression cannot be identified. What gives expression meaning in this caricature is a racist set of visual assumptions about blackness, about pose and affect, and the outline or formalization of the person, Oscar Wilde. In this particular case, Wilde's characteristic pose and accoutrements give ideological meaning to the embodied subject of the illustration. The blackface in this picture is not a mask for Oscar Wilde, but rather a hyperbolic sign that indicates just how thoroughly racist constructions of expression can saturate the "anatomy and physiology of affects."[88]

Indeed, "The Aesthetic Craze" suggests how meaning and expression might cohere as a form outside of the phenotype, outside of actual physical resemblance, and, more importantly, even outside of a coherent "expressive field," or resolute image.[89] As with the twentieth-century depictions of Wilde, where Wilde effectively looks like himself, "personality"—and racist constructions of it—is just as powerful in creating an image of him as an expressive subject. In this case, however, caricature operates as a racist medium for devaluing the forms of expression with which Wilde's personality was associated. In other words, blackface comedy serves to channel Wilde's apparent homosexuality. This form or outline is recognized not simply in relation to Wilde's body but in regard to a range of affective displays for which this "bepuffed and advertised gentleman," this "irrepressible High-Priest of too too," attired in "knee breeches and sea green neckties," was famous.[90] In the caricature, Wilde's costumes of silk neckties, green velvets, and fur, along with his "exceedingly verbose" style of delivery and its "appearance of affectation," are now the subject of cheap and gaudy imitation.[91]

This picture thus exploits a racist field of vision to create unlikely connections that mock Oscar Wilde as an expression. Similarly, in a set of 1882 trade cards bearing the title "National Aesthetics," Wilde is parodied in the guise of a number of figures costumed in typically "aesthetic" garb: an Irish

E. B. Duval, from *National Aesthetics*, 1882. Courtesy of the William Andrews Clark Memorial Library, University of California, Los Angeles.

leprechaun, a Jewish Uncle Sam figure, an apparent "chinaman," a paunchy German, and an emasculated African American. Mocking the self-absorption of the aesthetic movement, the last card reads "Ise g'wine for to wushup dat Lily kase is sembles me." Much like other images from the era, the card parodies the male aesthete swooning over the ubiquitous lily that Wilde had reportedly carried down Piccadilly in London. As with "The Aesthetic Craze," the focal point of the face is the red lips, pursed as if to kiss the lily that "sembles me." The delicacy of the hands that hold the lily, along with the subject's billowy "dress" and tie, reinforces the irony of the character's refinement, his distance from the labor associated with his skin color. In this series more generally, the use of dialect becomes a way of devaluing the forms of "refined" expression with which Wilde was associated in 1882 and after. Long after this date, in 1926, Wyndham Lewis would underline this same "refaynement," which, he argued, "goes with male inversion (the *obligation* of culture, of a 'refayned' speech, and the unreality of millionaire luxury as a necessary background)."[92] Consistent with remarks made much earlier about Wilde's self-presentation, Lewis's assessment underlines the coherence characterizing the reception of Wilde as an image both before and after the trials.

Charles Baudelaire's Deforming Vision

In deforming or inverting its subject, caricature draws on the meaning of expression as a form or outline by demonstrating the likeness in two images that are essentially different. While personality makes expression recognizable in its relation to a person, caricature can deform this expression until it is almost unrecognizable—thus problematizing any singular account of a visual surface. The moralism of the images, however, compromises the modernity of their expression. That is, at least, how Max Beerbohm, Wilde's own caricaturist and contemporary, would likely have responded to such drawings. Since the scope of this chapter prevents me from addressing Beerbohm's actual caricatures of Wilde, I turn briefly to his 1901 article "The Spirit of Caricature," which theorizes caricature as a modern "art of exaggerating, without fear or favor, the peculiarities of the human body, for the mere sake of exaggeration."[93] By "proportionately diminish[ing]" the subject's "subordinate" qualities and "magnify[ing]" the "salient" ones, caricature creates a "new" man, "wholly transformed" but still the same, so much that by "the uninitiated he will not be recognized."[94]

According to such logic, the "National Aesthetics" trade cards are indeed caricatures, as they do not resemble their subject, Oscar Wilde, but rather draw on the viewer's familiarity with various nineteenth-century racial phenotypes. Nonetheless, the power of Wilde's "personality" allows us to read the expression as Oscar Wilde's. The caricature itself is this reading—albeit a racist one—which is, as Beerbohm observes, "the epitome of the subject's surface, the presentment . . . of the most characteristic pose, gesture, expression."[95] If we view caricature as "expression," as the "epitome of surface," then we are still left with the question of content, or what the expression is expressing. While Beerbohm criticizes the "moral impulse" that he attributes to certain caricaturists, he does not say that caricature should be without meaning, what might otherwise be understood or read as the form's content.[96] Beerbohm's account of caricature aligns with Wilde's historical situation, but it no doubt extends from the positions advanced by Charles Baudelaire in his 1855 essay "On the Essence of Laughter," which describes caricature, particularly French caricature, as a *"plastic* expression of the comic."[97] I turn to this idea of *"plastic* expression" since it resolves some of the issues I raise in earlier portions of this chapter, as well as later, about the caricatures of Wilde—concerning the relationship between expression as perceived by a viewer and the content or meaningfulness of that expression. Baudelaire advances an understanding of what aesthetic expression—and the viewing of it—can mean when it is neither a simple read out of a work's content nor a projection produced by the spectator.

The difficulty of "On the Essence of Laughter" lies in Baudelaire's rhetorical tendency to question or even invalidate the viewpoints that he initially takes on and, further, encourages in his reader. The first of these—which he attributes to the "orthodox," or Christian, mind—connects man's "fall, of a debasement both physical and moral," to the appearance of human laughter ("OEL," 150). For Baudelaire, neither laughter nor "tears" exist as expressions in the "paradise of delights" because man is not yet afflicted by "trouble": his "countenance was simple and smooth, and the laughter which now shakes the nations never distorted his face" ("OEL," 150). That is, without "trouble," there is no physiognomic model for laughter as expression, a "nervous convulsion, an involuntary spasm" that "disfigure[s]" the human subject ("OEL," 152). Formless and incomprehensible, laughter is, put plainly, part of man's "ugliness," a pathological deformity that emerges from the "unknown" ("OEL," 151). Baudelaire explains this phenomenon through the perspective of *Paul et Virginie*'s Virginie, a figure of "absolute purity and naiveté" ("OEL," 151).[98] By imagining that Virginie "shudders" in "fear" and "suffering" when brought "face to face with caricature," having "sensed that there is offence in it," the author revises his original position that the "good" prevents laughter ("OEL," 151). "Gazing at the unknown," the girl "hardly understands either what it means or what is it for" ("OEL," 151). Nonetheless, the caricature has meaning as a "double thing . . . both drawing and idea—the drawing violent, the idea caustic and veiled" ("OEL," 151). What then is this ugly "idea," which Virginie can sense but fails to know or understand?

Given this problem of what we sense but cannot see, know, or understand, the essay elaborates rather circuitously on the question of how the "comic" in art becomes comprehensible as expression. In claiming that comic expression begins with man's fall, Baudelaire suggests that the "moral impulse" Beerbohm denounces indeed motivates comic expression and caricature.[99] And while Baudelaire later claims that comic expression and human laughter are "satanic," he does not give up the idea that their roots are moral. Virginie, the "immaculate angel," "shudder[s]" at the "offence in" the caricature she witnesses ("OEL," 151). The suggestion here is that moralism contributes to the perception of expression, the "offence," in the first place. For Baudelaire, laughter, "essentially human . . . essentially contradictory," is born of man's feeling of superiority over others and his anxiety that he will in turn be the subject of laughter ("OEL," 153-54). "What more striking token of debility," Baudelaire writes, "could you demand than a nervous convulsion, an involuntary spasm comparable to a sneeze and prompted by the site of someone else's misfortune?" ("OEL," 152). This dilemma, however, is essential to laughter, because from it emerges the capacity for analysis that allows for laughter in the first place ("OEL," 152). For Baudelaire, the "absolute comic," exemplified most specifically by the grotesque, is a *"unity,"* in that the laughter is immediate, as the image affects the "intuition" of the viewer ("OEL," 155). But the comic is rarely absolute, it seems. In the "significative" comedy of Voltaire, there is always a pause, where "it is quite permissible to laugh a moment late" ("OEL," 157).

But is it? To laugh "a moment late" may mean that we are slow to get the joke or did not get it at all. It may be that we are only mimicking the laughter of others, or that laughter may be inappropriate, not "permissible" at all, considering that, for Baudelaire, the most "exaggerate[d]" form of the "significative" comic is the *"savage* variety" ("OEL," 159).[100] In this case, laughter may follow a cringe, as if we are uncomfortable with the very "idea of superiority" that allows us to respond to such an expression in the first place ("OEL," 159). Laughter is in fact a "comic emanation" or "explosion" in which there must be "two beings face to face with one another," where the comic is a gestural, bodily expression itself and an affective response to an expression that requires the accompanying laughter of the spectator ("OEL," 165). If a third party is introduced and the person laughing becomes the subject of laughter, the comic becomes a mimetic chain, however removed from the original content of comic expression. Incomprehensibility then becomes the rule, not the exception.

The takeaway here is that an expression does not mean in and of itself; rather, the spectator gives expression its meaning. This meaning, however, is compromised, according to Baudelaire, by the "permanent dualism in the human being," the insecure uncertainty of being two places at once, and the condition of not knowing ("OEL," 165). Baudelaire's essay on the comic thus does not diminish the contradictory, ambiguous phenomenon of expression by resolving the question whether there is meaning behind it. For Baudelaire, the laughter of a madman or a child, a little "budding Satan," may not have an object, but it does have an "ambition" ("OEL," 156). Through these examples, Baudelaire affirms our knowledge that what we don't know is in fact magical, absorbing, corrupting, and alluring. Ultimately, this understanding of expression—in which meaning *is* our insecure not knowing—anticipates, and even resolves, the debates I reviewed earlier. More particularly, Baudelaire's treatise on laughter annuls the distinction Leys draws between the anti-intentionalist view of affect as corporeal surface and the idea that our affects mean something by virtue of their identifiable relations to particular objects. With this model of comic expression, we can also see the caricatures of Wilde as staging cringeworthy and anxious scenes of reading, where racist visual scripts deform the subject into something almost unknowable or unidentifiable, something more or less than "what [one] thinks it is," while simultaneously affirming the superiority of the viewer's powers of analysis and perception.[101]

In this account of analytical reflection and viewing, the dynamic that emerges from the formal encounter of these "two beings face to face with one another" is multidimensional, textural, and temporal. In this sense, Baudelaire confirms something like the "anti-intentionalist" paradigm Leys critiques, which, she argues, separates "meaning and signification" in a "nonconscious . . . autonomic reaction system."[102] Similarly, for Baudelaire, the suspended moment between content and its expression, between meaning and signification, may cause us to laugh "a moment late," in a bodily response—a "spasm" and "convulsion"—that is out of sync with our mental perception of its source ("OEL," 152). If the virtual is, according to Brian Massumi, "reality in the reality of change" or a fleeting "sign of the passing of process," a "deformational field," then we need not look to Deleuze and Guattari, or even resort to this lingo to understand how expression (or image) unfolds in time or, further, how our readings of aesthetic expression may be complicated by this formal suspension.[103] My point here is not to equate Baudelaire's understanding of the comic, or these ugly pictures of

Wilde, with Massumi's notion of a virtual experience of the image mediated by various screens and interfaces, a fully "imageless" form of "interrelating";[104] rather, I am suggesting that "deformation" is a condition of expression itself and of modern forms of perception that are hardly nonconscious or anti-intentional but rather riddled with self-consciousness of the superiority that allows us to perceive, or read, comic expression in the first place.

To think of expression as the product of perception as a form of deformation and delay might help us understand what these "ugly" pictures of Oscar Wilde really mean—and, ultimately, how we are to interpret the degenerating image of Wilde's face in Toulouse-Lautrec's 1895 watercolor. For art historian E. H. Gombrich and psychoanalyst Ernst Kris, writing at the onset of World War II, caricature is not simply an art but a psychology of deformation—a "psychological mechanism" that developed at the end of the sixteenth century alongside the notion that art was a "*projection* of an inner image."[105] Prior to this time, pictures were considered not representative but real embodiments of a person, such that "distort[ing] a man's face" was tantamount to injuring him.[106] For Kris and Gombrich, distortion is a defining element of modern vision that influences the forms of "*projection*" through which the subject is visualized, so that the "inner image" itself is in fact always a "readjustment."[107] This process, the pair argues, resembles Freud's notion of "primary process," a dreamlike, nonconscious state, in which a particular mental image diminishes the frustration of not having an object.[108]

In connecting caricature to Freud's primary process, Kris and Gombrich, however indirectly, qualify the position they articulate earlier, where they define caricature as a physiognomic genre. Like the physiognomist, the caricaturist penetrates, or reads, the outer surface of the subject but, in contrast to the tenets of nineteenth-century physiognomy, does not attempt to synthesize its interior and exterior dimensions: "The caricaturist . . . does not seek the perfect form but the perfect deformity, thus penetrating through the mere outward appearance to the inner being in all its littleness or ugliness."[109] Modern caricature produces a different, deformed surface, to be read and further "readjust[ed]" by the spectator. In its link to personality as a script that enables reading, modern caricature is itself a reading, an art of deformation based on misrecognition. To return to Baudelaire, the moment of not seeing our own faces in the mirror is also the point where we may laugh "a moment late." This suspension of perception in time, for Kris and Gombrich, is tantamount to the way "a joke is thought out." While the aim of the joke may be intentional, or "thought out," its dynamics are not.

That particular aim, "ridicule," offends its viewer through its concretization of a momentary, even unglimpsable expression that is only a projection itself.

As it captures these projections, caricature can ultimately be understood as a recording of the spectator's encounter with a surface. To return to Baudelaire, caricature is a picture of a scene of reading, of "two beings face to face with one another" ("OEL," 165). This scene, as it comes to stand in for the larger phenomenon of modern aesthetic expression, is characterized by the temporal suspense of laughter "a moment late." Laughter is a form of reading that, unlike Symons's insidious analysis of Toulouse-Lautrec's portrait of Wilde, is unsure of itself. As an expression that deforms an expression, caricature underlines the value of the unreadable, of the possible suspension or gap between our affects and our conscious understanding of them.

The Picture of Dorian Gray: On Not "Feeling Like" Oneself

Since I have not addressed how Wilde himself would have responded to these questions about vision and the meaning of expression, and in particular the deformation of his own image, of "not seeing his own face in a glass," I want to do so briefly as a means of concluding this chapter.[110] For Wilde, the question of likeness, the coherency of the image, trumps any consideration of its content, "as those who find ugly meanings in beautiful things are corrupt without being charming" (*PDG*, 21). In these epigrams from *The Picture of Dorian Gray* (1891), Wilde is elaborating a practice of modern reading that involves not looking into things too deeply. But the novel also underlines the often fatal costs of these reading practices, which privilege distant and bored subjects who, to return to Silvan Tomkins, do not generally "feel like" themselves.[111] *The Picture of Dorian Gray* details the pitfalls of a personality that remains uncountenanced, or unfaced—unlinked to an image of an actual person. My brief reading of the novel thus looks closely at what happens when there is no meaning or intention behind a face and connects the chapter's foregoing discussion—about affect, expression, and their meaningful relation to an individual—more explicitly to the act of reading. Regardless of Wilde's overt injunctions against deep reading, the novel's reflections on the subject suggest that reading in the "face" of too much distance is both erroneous and deadly.

The infamous painting at the center of Wilde's explicitly physiognomic novel is, like caricature, a record of a scene of reading that fuels its subject's

(Dorian Gray) conscious interest in the potential fissures between his affects, to return to Leys, and his intentional understanding of them. Indeed, one can read the text as a commentary on the art of caricature and the act of reading it. It is not so much that the painting registers the distortion of Dorian's "soul"; rather, the affective distortion that characterizes his own projections of it—his own feeling of "shame"—shapes his vision as a modern reader (*PDG*, 102). To echo Gombrich and Kris, the caricaturist manipulates a physiologically based form of expression to expose the inner "ugliness" of the caricature's subject. For Dorian, the portrait becomes a way to "follow his own mind into its secret places," but he may perform this reading only through his prior knowledge of his deeds and his consequent visual projections about what his mind is doing (*PDG*, 103). Dorian does not have a Cartesian problem with other minds as much as he does with his own. At least, this is what much of the drama in the novel seems to revolve around—Dorian's deficiency in the reading skills that, to return to Tomkins, allow us to know what our expressions "feel like."

Like one of Damasio's brain-damaged patients, Dorian is a bad reader of both himself and others. My analogy here is not arbitrary, as Wilde took a noted interest in brain science that can be dated back to 1874 and his years at Oxford. Elisha Cohn has closely documented the development of Wilde's interest in the brain cell; understood as a "molecular object" with only "surface qualities," he connected it to the impossibility of fully knowing the self, as well as to the idea that mental life may be "biologically determined" and consequently inaccessible.[112] *The Picture of Dorian Gray* literalizes this notion of a remote self through Dorian's consuming obsession with his own portrait and his lack of a felt relation to his own expressions as manifested in it. The painting is, in fact, Dorian's self, hypermaterialized in a surface, but it lacks its subject's—his own—intention. He indeed muses that the material change may be scientific: "Might there not be some curious scientific reason for it all?" (*PDG*, 103). The question points to the paradox at the heart of Dorian's life; despite all of his efforts at self-invention, there is no essential access to or identification with a self that would allow him the freedom he desires. He must watch the painting as a literalized "expression" that exceeds his own physiology, especially as his image—with its "misshapen body and failing limbs"—becomes more deformed with each passing sin (*PDG*, 124).

While Dorian may alter or cultivate his "personality," the portrait's expression, linked to his body, is beyond his control. Dorian notes earlier in the novel, however, that his most charming physical attributes remain unchanged: his "gold hair, blue eyes, and rose-red lips—they were all there. It was simply the expression that had altered" (*PDG*, 119). In line with nineteenth-century physiognomy, we may be tempted to read this "expression" as a sign of Dorian's corrupt interior state. However, Dorian views the painting as an external phenomenon that is unrelated to his internal state, for which there is actually no image. The painting is merely the external screen on which Dorian's emotional states are projected and further deformed until they are, by the end of the novel, not identifiable as his own. When he wonders whether there might be "some curious scientific reason" for the change in the painting's expression or whether things "external to ourselves vibrate in unison with our moods and passions," he offers an account of the individual in which one, to return to the critical discourse I have surveyed in this chapter, is totally free from one's cognitions and inner drives (*PDG*, 103).

Unlike the pre-1895 characterizations of Wilde, which see expression as a manifestation of the subject's corrupt moral interior, Dorian anticipates Ruth Ley's characterization of the anti-intentionalist paradigm at its most fatal extreme; with our affects ever distant from our intentions, we are not just "wrong about ourselves" but cannot even begin to know or "feel like" ourselves.[113] Dorian suffocates himself in what Sedgwick would call "texture"— layers of tactile things, clear from his obsession with Catholic ritual: embroidered tapestries, ecclesiastical vestments, perfumes and scents.[114] All seem to be focused more specifically on nonvisual acts of feeling, touching, and, in the case of perfume, smelling. Such items evoke sensation and thus align themselves with what he believes are his "unpictured sins," the content of which remains a "mystery" (*PDG*, 118). Dorian's deeds are sins, and therefore pathological in their resistance to visualization or imaging by a spectator. If there is no spectator, there is, to echo Delaporte, no expression—and ultimately, no reading of it.

As much as Dorian's interest in his own picture signals his desire for a readerly understanding of his self, he protects his opacity when it comes to the reading eyes of others. He therefore murders the one reader of his portrait, its creator, Basil Hallward. When Dorian tells Basil that he may in fact see the portrait, he introduces it as a narrative record of his life, as an object that solicits reading: "I keep a diary of my life from day to day, and it never leaves the room in which it is written. I shall show it to you if you come with me" (*PDG*, 147). Basil begrudgingly assents, asking that he not be required "to read anything tonight," as "all I want is a plain answer to my question"

(*PDG*, 147). Dorian, alluding to Basil's imminent death, replies, "You will not have to read long" (*PDG*, 147). In its disconnection from Dorian's actual body, the expression offers nothing to read and is in fact a surface projection of what the spectator, Basil, already knows.

If Dorian's "unpictured sins" are indeed visualized in the expression on the painting's surface (they aren't), they are recognizable to the experienced reader not as manifestations of internal wretchedness but as part of a visual expressive script that Basil has already encountered through his prior knowledge of Dorian's deeds (*PDG*, 118). Dorian is mistaken, however, in his fantasy that the painting can be completely occluded, that his past, in other words, won't catch up with him, and that he will forever be free from whatever roots him in relation to his own affects and drives. He thus believes that with the same knife he can murder Basil and his work, the portrait, and also "kill the past" (*PDG*, 213). This is, in effect, an effort to disable the expressive scripts to which he is linked and that account for the contorted expression of the painting. But Dorian is unable to be truly free from his expression, his "feeling" about his own face. Ultimately, his becoming his own expression is an instantaneous death, which highlights again the impossibility of knowing, at least consciously or intentionally, what our expressions "feel like."

Dorian's death occasions a final scene of reading in which the servants who find his body deem him unrecognizable. Removed from the world of artistic representation and deformed to the point of unrecognizability, except for the rings on his fingers, Dorian is no longer even a caricature of himself. In light of recent debates about whether our affects are intentional and thereby meaningful, and whether we can, in fact, identify with them, I have shown in this chapter how caricature both performs and solicits a reading, where likeness emerges from the presumed difference between the content or intention of a work of art and its actual expression. "Personality," I have argued, is itself an expression that forges this sense of likeness or identification, linking the person to a coherent and recognizable image incapable of being fully corrupted by the deforming vision of the modern spectator. But in *The Picture of Dorian Gray*, Dorian's mercurial and "unpictured" nature—his impersonality—does not link to a script for interpreting him (*PDG*, 118). In contrast to Dorian Gray's, Wilde's actual face, as I have suggested of posttrial depictions in particular, is recognizable by virtue of its connection to a personality that links his expression to his person as a readable organization. This modern construction of a face—which I continue to theorize in the following chapters—does not offer an avenue into character, but rather, as is evident in Symons's account of Wilde's degenerating visage, informs the construction of a seemingly readable subject based on the physiological expression of the "person" or "personality." As I have demonstrated, however, through close readings of texts such as Baudelaire's "On the Essence of Laughter" and Wilde's *The Picture of Dorian Gray*, immediate and accurate readability is often a fiction, as the most overt intentions of a work and its content are always subject to the deformation of the modern viewer.

2 Realist Prosopagnosia; or, Face Blindness in Theodore Dreiser's *Sister Carrie*

> Of what value *is* a portrait . . . which, although it represents exactly every line and tint of a face, does not produce on the beholder the effect which the face itself produces?
>
> —Richard Grant White, "A Morning at Sarony's," 1870

Circa 1895, Theodore Dreiser's aspiring actress, Carrie, enlists a photographer for some headshots. This nonfictional figure is Napoleon Sarony—who, in 1882, produced the famous set of photographs with which we now associate the face of Oscar Wilde. The relationship between Sarony and his subjects was mutually advantageous, as photographers would often either pay their subjects to sit for them or waive their fees while retaining full rights to sell the resulting photographs. The sitters would then benefit from the potential celebrity promised by the rapid circulation of their image. How Carrie, fresh from her stint as a scantily costumed chorus girl in an Orientalist musical comedy, scores such a session with the most famous portrait photographer of the time is not explicitly disclosed in Dreiser's 1900 novel, *Sister Carrie*. Dreiser's narrator, however, suggests that the draw is her face. Carrie is "sweet-faced" and "very pretty," but in a "demure," diminutive way that does not get her a speaking part, only the role of the "silent little Quakeress," with which she achieves her fame.[1]

The idea of the photograph is important as a metonymic representation of the novel's own narrative strategy, its deforming of realist aspirations that privilege vision and legibility. As Jonathan Crary has argued, following the work of Foucault and Benjamin, "modernity subverts even the possibility of a contemplative beholder."[2] With every image in circulation, "vision is always multiple," and there is "never a pure access to a single object."[3] While the camera appears to ground the singularity of its subject, its actual function is to disturb that ground. As I have noted in relation to the physiognomic experiments of Duchenne and others, the camera was essential in introducing the face as the focal point of human expressiveness and, further, made it possible to study the face in motion.[4] At the same time, Duchenne's experiments aimed to present a legible subject based on the artificial suspension of natural movement, temporarily restricting the subject to a fixed and stable position.

However unlike Duchenne's expressions of joy, pain, and benevolence are to Carrie's "very pretty" face, the camera in both cases operates as an instrument of form that, as it supports the fiction of a situated observer and subject, reinforces the itinerancy of modern vision (SC, 325). Consider Richard Grant White's description of "A Morning at Sarony's," penned for the March 1870 issue of *Galaxy* magazine, where Sarony is touted as both an artist and an "operator" in his Union Square studio filled with "glare, bareness, screens, iron instruments of torture, and a smell as of a drug and chemical."[5] As for the "instruments of torture," they are posing braces and stands that force the subject to remain motionless during long exposure times. In the various sittings White observes, Sarony, often in prolonged conflict with his subjects, installs himself as manipulator and extractor of expression: "He has succeeded in selecting, and then in fixing by a process almost instantaneous, the position and expression that will transmit . . . [the] moment to posterity."[6] In one particularly fraught scenario, the camera "degrades, vulgarizes, and grossens" the "lovely face" of a "radiant beauty" who thwarts the photographer's instructions, centered as she is on the particularities of her "fashionable head-dress" and "artifices of toilet."[7] She "submits" to the photographer in his "mingled office of high priest and executioner," and hopefully an image is formed, a likeness that, without degrading the subject, may not in reality mirror her exact features.[8]

As White observes, Sarony's photographs do not produce a realistically "embodied" subject, but instead a "spirit" or form that problematizes a mimetic reading of that form.[9] Rather than present an accurate rendering of a subject's features, Sarony's photographic technique reveals a basic understanding of the face as aesthetic and essentially mobile, unsituated form. In this case, and as I argue in the preceding chapter on Wilde, form is itself a deforming of the actual features of the subject. This turn in my story of modern expression shares with my earlier analysis of Wilde an emphasis on technique, but in this case the jarring ugliness that is insistent in caricature—where readability or likeness, however "caught," is still an aesthetic and political aim—gives way to a much different aesthetic interest in the harmonious surface legibility of Carrie's "very pretty" face (*SC*, 325).[10] Unlike the caricatured face of Oscar Wilde, Carrie's face at least seems to be "like" her, as what she desires, I will argue, is to be equal to her face. The novel, however, underlines the increasing impossibility of such closure. Through this problem of facing, I argue, *Sister Carrie* illustrates the deforming of realist technique, with its focus on comprehensive environmental description and psychological closure, into a more typically "modernist" forming of dissociation and illegibility.

Stuart Burrows has more recently argued that the "photographic fiction" of American realism suggests a more "sympathetic," if not continuous, relationship between realist and modernist fiction, where realism's fixation on the visible—and corresponding engagement with the camera as narrative lens—signals "a loss of faith in fiction's ability to represent the world."[11] The idea of "photographic fiction," Burrows contends, changes the topic of the conversation from fiction's ability to objectively represent the world to the question of how it does so.[12] This change is made explicit through the role of the photograph in *Sister Carrie*. Its form deforms modern vision, acting as an agent of erasure that produces missing persons and lost faces. For example, when the homeless Hurstwood stumbles upon the place where he has just seen Carrie's poster, he is shocked to find that she is "gone," covered now by "the new signs" (*SC*, 323). Hurstwood's is essentially an encounter in which the form-giving powers of Carrie's increasingly mobile poster-face literally paper over the features of her actual face. In this case, Carrie might be seen as an example of the "serialized woman" whose "conspicuous appearance and disappearances" define, as Alix Beeston has argued, a mode of modernist narration.[13] The poster *is* Carrie, now covered by "new signs" and, we can imagine, new faces. The camera makes Carrie into such an image, the rapid proliferation of which, critics have suggested, removes her from the standards of comparison that characterize everyday life.

This evaporation from life is accomplished by the "insipid prettiness" of her face, and I argue in this chapter that Carrie's silencing by the form of her face points to a formulation of the person that runs counter to the novel's ostensibly realist aspirations (*SC*, 2). As Carrie herself seems to intuit in an odd moment of interior musing, the circulation of her face, and the money that comes with it, "brought her nothing, no warm, sympathetic friendship back of the easy merriment with which many approached her" (*SC*, 311). For Carrie, what is typically the main arbiter of affective connections with others, the face, produces only distance and isolation. Robbed of voice, its affects and emotions are not expressed, but rather cordoned off to some other dimension located outside of the subject of realist fiction. I follow here, albeit briefly, this dynamic of facing through a number of other examples: novels by Edith Wharton and Jean Rhys, stories by Edgar Allan Poe and Stephen Crane, and paintings by John Sloan and George Bellows, all of which, I argue, explore the crisis of representing or picturing the urban environment through the blank and featureless face. If expression conventionally refers to the presumed correspondence between the inner dimensions of a subject and external signs, then *Sister Carrie*, as do the supporting texts I examine here, reframes the realist project of fusing the subject's interior and exterior through the exactness of its social description and analysis.

I am certainly not the first to suggest that in *Sister Carrie* Dreiser appropriates conventions that are seemingly antithetical to a documentary realism invested in material descriptions of urban life at the turn of the century. Douglas Mao, for example, offers an alternative picture of Dreiser whose "environmental obsessions" were informed by an uneasy relation to the aesthetic, reflecting the tension between beauty and "meaning in human existence."[14] In her now-classic account, Amy Kaplan addresses the problem of Dreiser's sentimentalism, arguing that *Sister Carrie* in fact generates an opposition between its depictions of the sentimental excesses of "consumption and desire" and the realism of "work and deprivation."[15] Accordingly, sentimentality, "divested of its traditional familial ties and reinvested in market-engendered values and consumer goods," becomes a key feature in the novel's examination of its own narrative strategies.[16] If realism, at least for the purposes of my argument, can be understood more broadly as a mode that seeks to present the social world as the product of an act of seeing, then Dreiser's appropriation of sentimental codes might be seen to illustrate the struggles of that project, the various ways in which one's vision gets clogged, or at least distracted.

As I suggest here, *Sister Carrie* appears to reflect Dreiser's consciousness of the potential failure of realism as a narrative strategy of optical mimesis— and, further, of mimetic reading practices. Describing the novel "as a picture of conditions done as simply and effectively as the English language will permit," he goes on to characterize it as adhering to a particular dramatic form, where the "tragedy of man's life is being displayed."[17] In noting the goal that narrative objectively "displa[y]" or "picture" the tragic conditions of "man's life," Dreiser underscores the problem of his own form-giving power by imagining *how* he might "displa[y]" such "conditions" as reality.[18] I refer here to Dreiser's realism with this problem in mind. Given this contradiction, the photograph, formed and manipulated as it is, comes to stand for the realist project of directly representing "life." Rather than a stable or coherent narrative mode, realism in Dreiser's work emerges as an unstable narrative aspiration, informed by the abstractions that influence modern social relations and modes of vision.

Lionel Trilling, in the second part of his tirade against the American Left titled "Reality in America" (1946), helped shape the idea of a modernism that broke radically from realism, the style he connected to an "American metaphysic" invested in "material reality, hard, resistant, unformed, impenetrable and unpleasant."[19] Trilling's quarrel in the essay is with a political vision advanced by the likes of historian V. L. Parrington; insufficiently concerned with beauty, it values "reality" over "mind," lauding badly written work.[20] Such "mind," as represented in Henry James's "extraordinary moral perceptiveness," enables the individual, not the social field, to shape reality through "a complex and rapid imagination and with a kind of authoritative immediacy."[21] To be Dreiser is to be unnecessarily political, vulgarly ideological, a "cultural risk" for the cannon easily sabotaged by insufficient "power of mind."[22] Trilling thus dwells on Dreiser's aesthetic deficiencies, criticizing his prose for its "roughness" and "ungainliness"—basically, its lack of form.[23]

These distinguishing assessments of realism and modernism offer an illuminating backdrop for considering Georg Lukács's similar attempts to classify literary practice, albeit in the service of a politically different end. In this particular discussion, I align Trilling's version of "realism" with Lukács's references to "naturalism" to indicate, as Christophe Den Tandt has noted, a period of "literary decline . . . in which the very possibility of writing organically structured fiction" is linked to the development of a monopoly capitalism that undermined the potential for aesthetic works to synthesize abstract aspects of human existence with the concreteness of the social world.[24] Naturalism is thus the "decadent avatar" of the early nineteenth-century realism of Balzac, which Lukács idealizes as a healthy antidote not only for the chaotic and "lifeless symbolism" of naturalism but also, as we shall see, for the distorting effects of modernism.[25] As Lukács inveighs in "Narrate or Describe?" (1936), naturalism both warps and "contemporizes everything."[26] Whereas epic art properly hierarchizes and orders its content in a way that highlights the "significant and vital aspects of social practice," naturalism's relentlessly descriptive cataloguing "levels" the social world, producing a flattened literary terrain in which "objects determine the organization of the novel."[27] Since one thing does not receive more attention than the other, characters do not take shape, plots do not develop, and details make action superfluous. Given this major deficiency, naturalist writing thus lacks "ideology," so that whatever disillusion it can express with the capitalist annihilation of spirituality is in fact "feeble and purely subjective."[28]

Consequently, writes Lukács, "naturalism is not the innate style of the novel."[29] Rote empiricism cannot approximate the real structure of society, nor does it encourage the development of complex literary forms—like novels—as reflective of social ideas. Furthermore, Lukács sees this breakdown in artistic order as contributing to the potential diminishment of the reader, who will less likely engage with the "complexity of patterns of life," given the absent "proportions" of the naturalist work.[30] As Cannon Schmitt has observed, Lukács's "virulently anti-descriptive stance" welds narration with action; whereas description encourages readerly passivity, proper narration, according to Lukács, "involve[s]" the reader in a "rich web of variegated motivations," of which the omniscient narrator has both special knowledge and power to divulge at will.[31] With no "tension" or "suspense," description does not "awake[n]" the expectations or curiosity of the reader or create a feeling of oneness and confidence with the "fictional world."[32] This relationship between reader and text is both close and distant; guided by changes in narrative "perspective," or the "necessary distance in narration," the reader will pay close attention to some things and not others.[33]

While Lukács faults naturalism for maintaining a diminished perspective that elevates description over actual composition, or what we might also term "expression," he ascribes just the opposite shortcoming to modernism: its privileging of "technique" over "historicity" in a way that reifies subjectivity as reality.[34] Dreiser does not feature anywhere in this account of modernism's social disinvestment and its neurotic "*angst*-ridden vision of the world," but he very well could.[35] At least, the terms set by Lukács's schematic partitioning of modernist psychopathology from healthy realist totality offer a useful model for considering Dreiser's own critical attention to an ideal that offers the promise of realist closure and legibility, the "personality." My interest here in personality reflects the claims of the previous chapter on Wilde—where I argued that, in twentieth-century depictions of Wilde, an embodied "personality" replaces an image of a readable interior as the agent of expression. As another way of articulating this formulation of expression, I emphasize here the centrality of "personality" to Lukács's negative characterization of modernism and his sense of it as an organizing social and aesthetic principle. In modernist ideology, Lukács claims, referencing T. S. Eliot's "The Hollow Men," personality disintegrates at the cost of the external world, leaving no "outer reality . . . only human consciousness," producing a "schizophrenic dichotomy" in which "there [is] in man's personality no coherent pattern of motivation or behavior."[36] Without a "consistent view of human nature," Faulkner's *The Sound and the Fury* and Beckett's *Molloy* display no "unity of thought and action" or calculable sense of human motivation.[37] "Personality" thus supplies the foundation for a coherently coordinated, legible character whose internal motivations are in balance with their actions in the outside world. When the subject is "reduced to a sequence of unrelated experiential fragments," Lukács writes of Eliot's *The Cocktail Party*, "he is inexplicable to others as to himself."[38]

Lukács thus articulates major questions about "impersonality" that concerned many modernists, which is how to think about expression—and the reading of it—outside of the organizing function of the legible personality.[39] This critique of modernism is significant to the context I am elaborating because it articulates a vision of the person that motivates *Sister Carrie*'s particular realism. According to Lukács's view, a coherently unified person has expressive qualities that depend on the possession of a psychology—an inner self-consciousness—capable of being explained "to others as well as to himself."[40] The realist subject, as in Greek drama, must be legible. Form as well is only form insofar as it inspires reading practices that result from the conditions of expressive legibility that support realist totality, or the cohesion of inner experience and outer world. In *Sister Carrie*, I argue, the consistent link between the face and aesthetic expression gestures at the possibility of such realist closure and legibility.

As a realist novel, *Sister Carrie* employs a physiognomic mode of narration that both undermines and affirms the work that a face does. It can't quite do away with faces, which seem essential to its forming as a novel. To the extent that this is a periodizing claim, we might situate it in relation to the idea, most recently articulated by Sarah Blackwood in her analysis of Henry James's portrait novels, that "defacement" is an essentially modernist strategy of "bypass[ing] the face's representation of an individual world."[41] To some extent, Blackwood affirms Lukács's characterization of modernism, arguing that the modernist turn inward was reflected in a retreat from "figurative representation" toward a "stream of consciousness" style that privileged an "aesthetic view of inner life."[42] Regardless of their explicit periodization, the texts I examine here all, in one way or another, test the limits of figurative representation as it occurs through "physiognomic perception," which is, according to Gombrich, a mode of aesthetic experience in which the "'expressive' qualities" of "shapes and forms" are seen through their connection to the human face.[43] Though less polemical and more "descriptive" than Lukács's, Gombrich's body of work is concerned similarly with the assumptions underlying Freudian and Marxist thought, the problem of form and content, the historicity of art forms, and the more general nature of expression. For Gombrich, the "application of physiognomic categories," such as "smiling" or "menacing," becomes our most basic way of giving meaning or, in Lukács's terms, "totality" to things; even things without faces, such as "sounds, colours, and shapes," are capable of producing "physiognomic reactions."[44] Through this process of formalization, images are built, and consequently falter, as other impressions—a frown, a waiver of the voice—alter one's initial projections.

As in Lukács's critique of modernism, what is at stake in Gombrich's analysis is the meaning of "personality," or our "basic physiognomic hypothesis of a unified character behind all the manifestations we register," which, as a script that informs both the reading and giving of faces, is at odds with the "mystery of ordered form."[45] In *Sister Carrie*, this tension between personality and mystery is integral to a realist strategy in which the narrative perpetually questions its own claims, based as they are on "the vagueness of that first physiognomic guess."[46] As an example, Dreiser endows the city—in the first case, Chicago—with the expressive qualities of a face, adopting such a physiognomic perspective in the novel's first paragraphs: "There are large forces which allure with all the soulfulness of expression possible in the most cultured human. The gleam of a thousand lights is often as effective as the persuasive light in a wooing and fascinating eye" (*SC*, 1). The description is ironic, as "expression" does not emanate from a soul, but is rather the product of persuasive artifice and manipulation, more specifically acting. The lines thus set the stage for the importance of acting as a thematic commentary on the novel's realism. In *Sister Carrie*, acting is a practice of self-preservation that highlights the face as form, a metonymic marker of the problems attending realist modes of narration. Consequently, the face's capacity for "expression" undermines the realist project of representing modern society from the standpoint of an observer. Gombrich's analysis is most useful in this regard, especially as it allows us to locate the contradictions that attend physiognomic perception in *Sister Carrie*. That is, the novel both employs and narrates modes of physiognomic perception that, as a process of formalization, undoes its realist investments in the actual shape and form of things. While form itself, as much as it can be seen to reflect a unity, results from the mystifying tendencies of our "initial projections," it also thrives on a kind of "mystery" that develops against objective detail.⁴⁷ For Dreiser, form reflects the very dissociation of the person made literal by the face of the actor.

This dissociation might also be said to reflect the novel's "pseudo-totalizing" strategies, which, as Den Tandt observes, following Lukács, aim to "piece together a unified representation of an object" that in fact "exceeds a totalizing gaze."⁴⁸ In *Sister Carrie*, Dreiser invites the reader to view the "pseudo-totality" of Chicago, by cataloging it not in extensive visual detail but, as Den Tandt argues, in "distant, abstract terms."⁴⁹ As a potentially failed totality, the city is also a face. As such, the city—like a face—stands in for a text that inspires the success and failure of reading it. Put another way, this "pseudo-totalizing" form of perception is also, to return to Gombrich, physiognomic perception, and the novel offers its characters, and by extension its readers, no avenue for escaping it. One can either become a more acute reader of the total fantasy of a city or a face or, alternatively, wallow in the mire of vague physiognomic guesswork.

And so Dreiser's novel illustrates the ways in which readers can become better or worse. At the outset, Carrie is "possessed of a mind rudimentary in its powers of observation and analysis" (*SC*, 2). Her poor reading skills are matched by her directness. Having looked upon Drouet "in full," the narrator pronounces her unclever for looking "a man in the eyes so steadily" (*SC*, 5). In any case, the mutual looking here yields only the most superficial results—as in the rather well-known description of the drummer's wool suit and ringed fingers—since "neither was wise enough to be sure of the working of the mind of the other" (*SC*, 6). Carrie's analytical skills, however, develop very quickly, just as she begins to understand herself more acutely as the object of others' gazes, specifically those of the neatly dressed, "handsome" shop girls, in whose eyes she might "recognize . . . a keen analysis of her own position" (*SC*, 17). Having graduated from description to critical reading, she begins to understand that looking "more closely"—as she reminds herself to do in the case of a "fine stepper" Drouet notices while the two walk down the street—need not mean looking more directly (*SC*, 17).

Walter Benn Michaels has argued that this scene privileges the woman's "closer look" over the "aestheticizing 'distance' of the man's [Drouet's] gaze."⁵⁰

Where Drouet's passion is purely for observation, Carrie's imitative desire, according to Michaels, resembles capitalism in its "ability to imagine ways out of what appear to be biologically immutable limits."[51] Female desire, as well as capitalism, becomes a way of being not oneself but rather what one sees. According to the parameters elaborated by Lukács and Trilling, such desires make a subject less readable and, consequently, more modernist. Carrie's face can thus be understood as the "mark" that, for Michaels, writing about Charlotte Perkins Gilman's "The Yellow Wallpaper," *"exemplifies"* the culture of consumption within the naturalist writing project.[52] To leave a mark means to inscribe oneself as a producer into the consumer culture. At the same time, marking involves consuming oneself, putting something out of oneself, putting oneself out there. To move this logic toward the terms of my own argument, to have a mark, a face—or, for that matter, an image or form—is itself a "using up" of that face, a defacement.

"Face-Work" in Edith Wharton's *The House of Mirth*

I will generalize a bit more here to say that for other women in naturalist fiction, the "problem of persons"—which is also the problem, as Michaels argues, of female desire and capitalism—is the problem of having a face, or "face-work."[53] This is nowhere more pronounced than in Edith Wharton's bleak tale of a young woman's decline, *The House of Mirth* (1905). I turn just briefly to the novel's first pages and their introduction of Lily Bart, which occurs by way of a taxonomizing male gaze, Lawrence Selden's, a socially inappropriate suitor for a penniless woman with elite social status. He "feel[s] how highly specialized she was"—a bright contrast to the "dinginess, the crudity of this average section of womanhood" on the streets of "sallow-faced girls in preposterous hats."[54] While Lily excels at producing such contrasts, she is also an expert reader of others. At Bellomont, her friend Judy Trenor's opulent country house, Lily arranges herself into a "graceful abstraction" for the viewing benefit of a potential suitor, the wealthy Percy Gryce (*HM*, 83). She knows how to "throw her charms into relief," exuding polish alongside the "volubility" of Mrs. Carry Fisher, whose "energy of eye and gesture" renders her only a voice (*HM*, 83). At the same moment, she deftly considers the "expressions on [the] faces" of her cousin, Jack Stepney, and his love interest, Ms. Gwen Van Osburgh (*HM*, 83). Gwen's face, which Lily likens to an "empty plate held up to be filled," reveals only a "lack of modelling," as if "painted on a toy balloon" (*HM*, 83) As a "deeper attribute" held by "most of Lily's set," Lily muses that this blank receptivity is a "force of negation" that "eliminated everything beyond their own range of perception" (*HM*, 83, 84).

Lily actually values such a "force," which she explicitly contrasts with her own interior life of "intuitions, sensations and perceptions" (*HM*, 84). As Lois Tyson has argued, Lily's predicament lies in not simply her financial dependence on others but her actual "labor to escape existential inwardness through self-reification" and "self-aestheticizing."[55] Lily's inwardness makes her an astute reader of her social scene, but this kind of reading, an affective and intellectual skill that may be more developed in one person and not another, involves a further self-abstraction that ironically amplifies the "intuitions, sensations, and perceptions" she seeks to escape. This inward sensibility both motivates and sustains her desire for "transcendence"—the project of being, as Tyson contends, an "*objet d'art*."[56] Lily thus wants to be seen, not touched. "Physical intimacy," Tyson writes, "endangers the transcendental project" of fashioning oneself into a priceless or "rare" treasure.[57]

Both Dreiser and Wharton explore the dynamics of this labor by attending meticulously to the work a face does, its maintaining of itself *against* a vision that simultaneously seeks to classify and aestheticize it, form and deform it. As I've noted, this vision first appears in Lawrence Selden's masculine scrutinizing of an "average section of womanhood." For Wharton, the problem of the realist novel is thus a distinctly gendered one, where the potential "waste" of a woman's face is linked to the formal collapse of transcendent narrative vision—one that is, in fact, represented by Lily's more comprehensive perception of her social and aesthetic environments—into Lawrence Selden's masculine one.[58] Just as women are seen to be more proficient in forming themselves and others, they are more vulnerable to waste or decline. There is, of course, the fabulous upper-crust party held by the Wellington Brys, where Lily, part of the night's course of entertainment, appears in a *tableau vivant*—posing provocatively as the center of Joshua Reynold's 1775 portrait *Mrs. Lloyd*. As Blackwood remarks of the scene, Lily's filmy white garment has the opposite of its intended effect, encouraging its audience's inquiries into the nature of her "'real self.'"[59] In other words, Lily's "performed portrait" invites too much scrutiny, sabotaging the "transcendental project" that occupies her from the novel's outset.[60]

It makes sense that Lily's fall involves the performance of a portrait. Self-aestheticization has its limits, and Wharton explores this through the construction and demise of Lily's face. Isolated in her own room after her first big loss at Bellomont's gambling tables, Lily is caught by her reflection:

"her face looked hollow and pale, and she was frightened by two little lines near her mouth, faint flaws in the smooth curve of the cheek. 'Oh, I must stop worrying!' she exclaimed. 'Unless it's the electric light—' she reflected. . . . She turned out the wall-lights and peered at herself between the candle-flames. The white oval of her face swam out waveringly from a background of shadows, the uncertain light blurring it like a haze; but the two lines around the mouth remained" (*HM*, 62). Alone and without an external observer, not even the soft filter of candlelight can mute the jarring result of the face's initial illumination. Inexpressively "pale," her face seems less like the image of her own face and more like the "sallow-faced girls in preposterous hats." Given the harsh backdrop of modern electric light, the form of the face falters, and the two fatal lines permanently disrupt its harmony.

With this idea of expression as the product of labor that is often specific to women in naturalist fiction—and as exceeding visual efforts to contain or control it—leaving lines or marks, I return to *Sister Carrie* and the subject of acting. Early on, and in keeping with a realist style of narration, Carrie's expression ostensibly coordinates with her inward plight; her "plaintive face" distinguishes her in her search for work, leading onlookers to feel sympathy for her (*SC*, 15). Later in the novel, her face revives its connection to work as expression becomes production for Carrie. Upon moving in with Drouet, Carrie understands that expression need not be a fixed determinate of one's character or type. In her naive trysts with the mirror, newly acquired habits of self-expression turn her into a "girl of considerable taste" (*SC*, 75). Indeed, Carrie's first theatrical rehearsal, where the director commands the ostensibly blank-faced Carrie to "put expression in [her] face" and implores that she "look shocked," is an exaggeration of Lily Bart's "graceful abstraction" (*SC*, 117-18; *HM*, 83). The director later commands his actors to "run right through" their lines, "putting in as much expression" as possible (*SC*, 119). As she performs in Augustine Daly's 1867 sensational melodrama about young women who have been switched at birth, *Under the Gaslight*, Carrie begins to express more and, consequently, to "feel the part" (*SC*, 120).[61]

The exteriorized script of expression is represented by the form of the face in the novel, which is central to a theatrical process that represents a mode of feeling. As Carrie's uneven performance in the pathos-laden melodrama suggests, feeling must come faster. In other instances, as when Hurstwood abducts Carrie, feeling comes too fast. In the rather heavy-handed dialogue that follows, Hurstwood implores the sobbing Carrie not to "act this way," announcing that he had no intention of hurting her "feelings" (*SC*,

190). Nonetheless, "sobs of fright cut off her desire for expression" (*SC*, 190). At this point, Carrie is unable to act, to effectively coordinate feeling and expression in a way that preserves the self rather than consumes it. In this way, as Philip Fisher has argued of the novel by way of Trilling and Rousseau, acting means "representing what one is not."[62] Fisher more importantly claims that Dreiser does not set up opposition between "the representation of what one is not" and "authentic self-representation."[63] Acting is rather understood as a "practice" of self concomitant with modern society. In extending Fisher's observations, I return to the face as the primary agent of this "practice" through which the self as a coordination is realized. In contrast to Lily Bart's inescapable "intuitions, sensations, and perceptions," this self, as Dreiser sees it, is not supported by inwardness or, for that matter, feeling (*HM*, 84). Fisher notes Carrie's blankness, "her lack of attachment or even mood, her easy forgetting of her family, her sister, Drouet . . . her passivity . . . even her absence of desires as proved by her realization once she has a great deal of money that there is nothing that she wants to buy."[64] What Carrie has to offer is that "force of negation" with which Lily credits her friends (*HM*, 84). This "force" is represented by a blank face, a receptive surface that does not exteriorize but rather receives the imprint of personality.

Whereas Carrie proves rather dull, Hurstwood, in a way that typifies successful masculinity, is initially marked by his "personality," his ability to reflect "the ambitions of those who greeted him" (*SC*, 125). Even though he looked "blandly on," he is "acknowledged, fawned upon, in a way lionized" (*SC*, 125). I bring up once more Warren Susman's definition of "personality" as the twentieth-century phenomenon that grounded "human behavior" and "destiny" within the individual, all the while displacing the ego and self from its center.[65] For Susman, an increasing interest in the "mastery and development of the self" meant that "personality" was also just as susceptible to decline.[66] Hurstwood embodies this vulnerability, and the narrator registers his decline in these terms, noting that "he had not the same impressive personality which he had when he first came to New York" (*SC*, 135). His personality having diminished, his face is no longer captivating. Carrie finds the "gloom" in his face "sinister" and "disagreeable" (*SC*, 139). As Hurstwood's "expression of manhood" becomes "rapidly . . . stultified," the "faint stirrings of shame" begin to more predominantly mark Hurstwood's expression, so much so that he responds to the world "shamefacedly" (*SC*, 295). In being "shamefaced," one becomes shame, turns into shame. This facial condition thus accompanies his physiological decline, along with the expiration of his personality, much in the same way Carrie's "sweet-faced[ness]" attends her physiological blossoming and budding personality (*SC*, 325).

Nothing about Carrie, however, is "sweet," an obvious contention that begs the question of what is in a face. While personality preserves a fiction of readability, it—and Carrie's face—is reflective, but the reflection itself distorts the subject. A good reader of personality is thus neither a "surface reader" nor a deep, "symptomatic" reader, but rather recognizes the various formal scripts that codify a subject's expressive performances, whether in the theater or, more literally, on the street.[67] In *Sister Carrie* the performance of this reading is also a performance of sociability. Indeed, once Carrie achieves success in the part of the Quakeress, she is met by those who may have formerly snubbed her with the "smile of sociability, as much as to say; 'How friendly we have always been'" (*SC*, 315). Janet Lyon in particular has addressed the idea of sociability as it informed the bohemian modernist salons held by the likes of Mabel Dodge and Lady Ottoline Morrel, grounding her analysis in the work of German sociologist Georg Simmel and his essay "The Sociology of Sociability" (1911). According to Lyon's account of the essay, sociability occurs by way of the "formal, impersonal intimacy among three or more people which effaces both the superficial conditions of social standing and the deep currents of personal psychology."[68] I would extend this analysis to suggest that sociability, as conceived by Simmel, affirms personality as a contradictory construction based on both the centralization and evacuation of an unreadable self. Carrie receives the "smile of sociability" when she appears in a costume of plain Quaker garb, in the "simple habit" that removes her from her real life, characterized by her obsession with attire as an advertisement of one's personal taste and social status (*SC*, 315).

Since sociability, as proposed by Simmel, is related to form, its potential function as an ameliorative balm for the alienation of modern existence counters the idea of reading both as an analytical practice of the eye that reinforces distance and as a strategy of mimetic description. Hurstwood is a case in point. As his personality weakens, so does his physiological form. The decline of the formerly "hale, lusty manager" into a "weakly looking object" accompanies Hurstwood's reversion into compulsive reading (*SC*, 326). Fisher observes that the newspaper in Dreiser is "the essential symbol of decline because it involves a preference for all experience as retrospective rather than lived."[69] Taking this perspective into account, reading is a practice of a-sociability that removes one from real life. In this function, Hurstwood's newspaper reading parallels realist narrative practice. Journalistic fiction is so readable that it requires no reading—literalizing the fantasy of surface reading, or what may be called an "immediate reading."[70] This is particularly true if we accept Lukács's view that reading involves the sorts of negotiations required of narrative forms, as opposed to compressed, flat descriptions. Nonetheless, just as Hurstwood devolves into a benchwarming newspaper junkie, his destitution sharpens his physiognomic skill in "sizing people up," having recognized "that there was a science of faces, and that a man could pick the liberal countenance if he tried" (SC, 327).

Hurstwood's interest in physiognomic analysis links his own very particular reading practices to the writing of naturalist fiction and to our roles as readers. Michael Fried has most famously underscored the link between the question of legibility and the authorial obsession with the materiality of writing, particularly in the work of Joseph Conrad and Stephen Crane. While Conrad, as I will discuss in the following chapter, centers his anxiety on the blank page, Fried argues that Crane thematizes writing as a "violent disfigurement" in "unconscious responsiveness to the production and physiognomy of his own handwriting."[71] To extend this logic, and to return to Michaels's analysis of *Sister Carrie*, if writing has a physiognomy, a face, then it can be thought of as an exteriorization of self that is ultimately consumed by a reader. In the same way, realist writing, based as it is on the reading of faces that is literalized in Hurstwood's "sizing people up," is a using up of some self or the other (SC, 327). Faces, however, are not so easily "sized-up," as Fried indicates, focusing on the ways in which the face's disfigurement in Crane calls into question "a mode of literary representation that involves a major emphasis on acts of *seeing*, both literal and metaphorical, on the part of author, characters, and reader."[72] As it stands in for a text, the idea of the disfigured face challenges the idea of criticism that lauds descriptive synthesis and the immediate apprehension of representative texts—without attending to what gets lost in such strategies. More specifically, while Fried links Crane's work to the "impressionist" principles famously articulated by Joseph Conrad in the preface to *The Nigger of the "Narcissus,"* the former's attention to faces most notably resembles Dreiser's own.[73] As I shall suggest of Crane, disfigurement operates as an authorial strategy for blocking both the intrusions of the reader and the forging of sentimentality around the affectively coordinated face.

What coordinates a face? Carrie's friend Ames offers an answer. Playing the part of physiognomist, he suggests that there is "something about [her] eyes and mouth" that "fits" her for "good, strong, comedy-drama" (*SC*, 341). Ames credits himself with noticing her "natural look": "expression in your face is one that comes out in different things. You get the same thing in a pathetic song, or any picture which moves you deeply. It's a thing the world likes to see, because it's a natural expression of its longing" (*SC*, 340). As Michaels has noted of this scene, Carrie is titillated by Ames's description of her because she wants to be equal to his reading and thus to her own face value (*SC*, 340). Put another way, what Carrie desires, oddly enough, is the transparent totality that characterizes Hurstwood's shamefacedness. Nonetheless, the very fact of her desire makes such equality impossible, for desire circulates around what one's body is not.

We thus return to the "problem of persons" in the novel, as Ames's own understanding of expression contradictorily suggests that the value of the face can never be equal to its physical features.[74] Carrie's commonly pretty face means nothing; it's rather her expression that gives other things a face, a physiognomy. The physiological features available for narrative description (by Ames and, more specifically, the narrator) take form only through the deforming desires of the world. While Ames's attention to Carrie's "large, sympathetic eyes and pain-touched mouth" suggests that there is a "natural" correspondence between Carrie's interior and her exterior, his analysis actually foregrounds expression, as well as the further reading of that expression, as it reflects the deforming vision of the viewer (*SC*, 340).

Georg Simmel and the Glance

In taking on the question of sociability, *Sister Carrie* also addresses the inverse question of how other people are "known"—or read—and how we know ourselves as these acts are compounded by the urban environment. In his short essay "Sociology of the Senses: Visual Interaction" (1907), which later appeared in Robert E. Park's and Ernest W. Burgess's uber-text *Introduction to the Science of Sociology*, the foundational book for the Chicago School of urban sociology, Georg Simmel explained that our reliance on the senses, most specifically vision, frustrates a reciprocal knowledge of other selves.[75] The embodied characteristics or "features of a person" produce "affective responses" that "do not enable us to understand or to define the other person"; we in effect become acquainted with others largely through certain objectivizing tendencies that confirm their formal characteristics, by way of the "eye" and its "uniquely sociological function."[76] Simmel calls this sizing up the "glance," which, he suggests, is not reciprocal but "expressive."[77] What Simmel means is that glancing always occasions a return to the sorts of immediate "affective responses" produced by a person's "features" or even "tone of voice."[78] These responses appear to prevent us from knowing others; the "expressive" qualities of the glance actually dissolve intimacy between persons, where expression, according to Simmel, is formalization, a "crystallization" of the person into an "objective structure."[79]

Consistent with his theory of sociability, Simmel does not advance a readerly model of knowing other minds, based on analysis or appraisal, but instead focuses on the glance as a model of direct perception that attends the formalization of the person. That is, our first glance at an individual, specifically at their face, "transmits to us" something that "cannot be analyzed or appraised."[80] This intimacy, he suggests, is made possible by the expressive capabilities of the face, which effectively blocks "analysis into individual traits."[81] This function of the face is especially crucial for the city dweller, who must depend purely on the visible for knowledge of others. Such dependence amplifies the "problems of the emotions of modern life," including loneliness and lack of "collective orientation," from which Carrie and Hurstwood both suffer.[82] If anything makes Carrie into a self, and in particular a gendered self, it is the consciousness of being "gazed upon," "stared at," or riddled with "sidelong glances" (SC, 18). Of course, Carrie eventually learns to return such glances, but here vision works to defend the self, rather than act as a disclosure of it, as in Simmel's assessment. In the famous "walk down Broadway" Carrie takes with Mrs. Vance, mutual glancing and staring does not yield a formalized view of the other. Rather, pure physical visibility replaces personality—a sort of urban looking that, much like Lawrence Selden's taxonomizing vision, reduces its participants to components: "a dark-blue walking dress," a "nobby hat," "affected smiles," and sets of gloved arms (SC, 217, 218). The marchers do not exceed their face value; they also do not equal it. In this "parade," where "to stare seemed the proper and natural thing," the face does not have a value (SC, 217).

Baudelaire and "Artificial" Form

In the street scene, the conditions of modern viewing render the face meaningless as a countenancing agent, in consolidating persons or personalities. In Dreiser's urban physiognomy, embodied particularities create a form of blindness that works against the objective "crystallization," or form, of the person.[83] The odd paradox here is that the particularities Carrie notices, all connected to "vice"—the "rouged and powdered cheeks and lips," the "large, misty and languorous eye"—are artifices designed to enhance the form of the person by masking their embodied reality (SC, 218). But these enhancements do not perform their form-giving function, pointing to the much larger issue of the narrator's or author's own form-giving powers. In the previous chapter, I argued that, at the turn of the twentieth century, the idea of "personality" no longer reflects an interior or even an image of one; rather, as in the case of Oscar Wilde, character traits that were traditionally connected to the inner dimensions of a subject are oriented around a physiological form in which affects are no longer expressed but instead appear on the body. Both Hurstwood and Carrie are testaments to the strength and vulnerability of this construction of personality. Hurstwood's demise follows, in effect, the collapse of the form-giving powers of his wardrobe. His personality diminishes as his body begins to speak for his condition, to become equal to itself. In a modernist vein, *Sister Carrie*'s Broadway parade suggests just how far this deterioration might go, to the extent that there is no longer an actual body or face around which personality can lodge. Consequently, the project of the realist writer is one motivated by lack, the project of how to imagine realist form in the absence of readable personality.

What is lacking in Dreiser's street scene is the "profound harmony" that, to return to the urban catalog of Baudelaire, fashion supplies to history. For Baudelaire, writing in 1863 in "The Painter of Modern Life," "the idea of beauty," or fashion, "which man creates for himself imprints itself on his whole attire, crumples or stiffens his dress, rounds off or squares his gesture, and in the long run even ends by subtly penetrating the very features of his face. Man ends by looking like his ideal self."[84] Put another way, the aim of one's face is to be equal not to one's face but to one's ideal, which is a mask. For Dreiser, in contrast, the flux of fashionable self-presentation distorts vision to the point that the viewer is no longer able to recognize other selves, but merely extensions of them in the form of "hats, shoes and gloves," or, in earlier parts of the novel, "lace-covered heads" and "white teeth showing through parted lips" (SC, 217, 57). This is, in *Sister Carrie*, most notably an affective dilemma. To return to Simmel's logic, if in glancing there is no expression, no formalization of the person, there is also no self-disclosure, no loss, and no intimacy. Carrie's experience of the street thus leaves her feeling particularly pained, "exceedingly receptive" to the "pathos" in the comedy she sees later that day with Mrs. Vance and company (SC, 219). Remembering her triumph in Chicago, Carrie dreams about acting again, but not for the prospects of fame and celebrity. Rather, her desire is to be part of the scenes she witnesses in order "to give expression to the feelings which she, in the place of the character represented, would feel" (*SC*, 219). In other words, through acting, Carrie wants to give feelings that are not her own expression, or form.

Like Lily Bart, she doesn't want to be touched, but rather wants to acquire the form Baudelaire identifies in urban pageantry. Incognito, Baudelaire's ideal spectator, the *"flâneur,"* or *"man of the world,"* possesses "a soul," a signature that marks his expression as his own.[85] As an artist figure "gifted with" both "the capacity of seeing" and "the power of expression," he uses experience to synthesize his extraordinary sensitivity to detail into vision.[86] Significantly, Baudelaire's ideal of "expression" is linked to the "childlike perceptive-ness" he most values in the artist.[87] Carrie is childlike in her perceptiveness of the motley pageant of the streets, but by Baudelairean accounts, she is no artist. In the work of the artist, the vision of the child, exceedingly keen to the gradations of the body and the movement of the muscles, is "reborn upon his paper, natural and more than natural, beautiful and more than beautiful."[88] There is no such coherence in Dreiser's street, characterized as it is by the sheer chaos of consumption and the clouded vision of the modern spectator.

Imaging the City: Edgar Allan Poe, Stephen Crane, and the Ashcan School

Dreiser's street scene draws attention to the problem of a realism that cannot formalize itself and further highlights the affective dilemma of the modern viewer who, unable to "face" others, can no longer read. As Ben Highmore has argued, this illegible environment—characterized by new and diverse social groups and "unregulated social and sexual identities," or what Carrie terms "vice"—produced an anxious experience of viewing, especially for those interested in standardizing and planning urban culture (*SC*, 217).[89] While Highmore's argument is more historical than literary, one such urban planner might be the realist narrator or author, pressed with the task of representing or forming these unreadable subjects. This dilemma does figure into one of the central literary texts in Highmore's account, Edgar Allan Poe's short story "The Man of the Crowd" (1840), which, Highmore argues, "foregrounds the theme of illegibility at the heart of urban culture."[90] Highmore's own reading of Poe's account of mid-nineteenth-century London focuses on its fissuring of the "very premise of *studying* the urban," situating the narrator in an epistemological "field" that is unknowable.⁹¹ And so the narrator's attempt to construct a "taxonomy of an urban crowd," however "absurdist and ideological" its "foundations," is thwarted by the sight of the old man who fuels his ramble through the urban underbelly.⁹²

Highmore adroitly links his reading of Poe's story to a historical account of London's physical modernization in the early nineteenth century, particularly as recorded by Friedrich Engels in *The Condition of the Working Class in England* (1845). My own reading of the story extends this focus on legibility to the literary, in particular the ways in which the narrator's attempt to make epistemological sense of the city's mystery overlaps with the problems that attend both reading and writing. In the story, these problems are manifest not simply in the aged *man* as the subject that the narrator cannot read or interpret but also in his *face*, the foundation, however absurd or imagined, for his readability as a subject. Furthermore, despite the powers of perception the convalescing narrator grants to himself, this is the story of an observer who initially cannot "face" his subject and who later, upon seeing the old man, attempts to give him a face that is, the narrator admits, unreadable. As with Dreiser's New York, the struggle here exists between the form-giving attempts of the narrator and the chaotic jumble of the labyrinthine city streets.

The narrator of the story at least initially grants himself the power of "abstract and generalizing" observation, such that he regards the trampers in "masses" and in "aggregate relations."⁹³ He further divides this pedestrian mob into numerous social and racial types—the upper classes, various orders of clerks, pickpockets, gamblers, "Jew Pedlars," and then the even more lowly "street beggars" and "invalids," and finally, at the bottom of it all, women and the contagiously ill and dying. "Enchained to an examination of individual faces," he professes his ability to "read, even in that brief interval of a glance, the history of long years" ("MC," 217, 218). The narrator's actual descriptions suggest otherwise, that his generalizations are indeed shallow, mired in pure physiological detail. He admits to as much at the beginning of the story, claiming that his vision "descended to details"; knitted brows, rolling eyes, gesticulating extremities, "solid-looking shoes," "slightly bald heads," protruding ears, "gold chains," and "thick sensual lips" are a few characteristics that fall in his arsenal of urban types ("MC," 217). In *Sister Carrie*, Carrie does not pretend to understand the urban streets, but is rather unsettled by what she witnesses. This narrator, unable to accept the anxiety that accompanies his ability to see only parts of people (i.e., their features), resorts to ridiculous modes of classifying them. And then, quite suddenly, he is able to see the forms of "individual faces," along with their history ("MC," 217).

The narrator's turn to physiognomic perception is indeed a mechanism for diminishing the anxiety occasioned by the numerous unclassifiable types that populate the city streets. These are, in actuality, subjects without personalities, men and women without faces, who rarely stop to look at each other, except in "search of some chance consolation" ("MC," 216). Ironically, he employs this mode of apprehending knowledge on the subject most immune to this sort of analysis, the "decrepit old man," lurching as he does erratically through the streets. Indeed, the old man's "countenance" and "the absolute idiosyncrasy of its expression" motivate the narrator's entire pursuit ("MC," 218). I noted in the previous chapter the argument that, in the nineteenth century, whatever exceeded the "threshold" of "expressivity" was not considered expressive, or subject to formalization, but rather pathological.[94] As the narrator puts it, "anything remotely resembling that expression I had never seen before" ("MC," 218). The narrator envisions the man as a text: "How wild a history," he says to himself, "is written within that bosom!" ("MC," 218). As a writing, the old man is particularly illegible; he "shudders" and "plung[es]" incomprehensibly, all movements related not to "expression" but to its unreadable or pathological underside ("MC," 220).

This recourse to the pathological as a specific kind of unreadable writing is linked to the narrator's, and arguably the author's, obsession with the materiality of writing, with the irreducibility of narrative matter to narrative itself. The narrator is indeed suffering from the terrifying consequences of his inability to "face" a man whose glance has the power to give him his own face. Insofar as the old man is a projection of the narrator's psyche, or even his double or alter ego, his "idiosyncratic expression," which the narrator never fully describes, symbolizes the narrator's own facelessness, his erasure from the "as of yet unwritten page."[95] In this crisis of facing, writing that does not have a physiognomy, or a face, remains unread. The writing self is not used up, consumed by a reader in its exteriorization, but rather saved. Thus, the narrator is convalescing, preserving his strength, such that illness becomes an indication of his writerly condition and, more generally, his status as a person. The narrator is flummoxed by the new physiognomy that emerges from the urban landscape, in which the human "countenance" preserves no recognizable image of a "person," decomposed by the various effects of costume.

Such questions about the changing form of the person appear within a host of turn-of-the-century texts that feature urban life. Michael Fried has argued, for example, that Stephen Crane's short sketch "When Man Falls, a Crowd Gathers" (1894) "has as its central focus a disfigured upturned face" and "thematizes that face as an object of an almost insane collective will-to-see."[96] This "will-to-see," Fried contends, also parallels the narrator's claim to see what the crowd cannot, even though he is, in effect, of the crowd. As with Poe's "The Man of the Crowd," the question of the narrator's vision and ability is centered on the perceived meaning of the face. Fried's focus is just this, the "difficulty of point of view" of the narrator and writer and its relation to the "encounter with a disfigured, upturned face."[97] Crane's story further explores the problem Simmel identifies in "The Sociology of the Senses," the making of "persons" and "personalities," which are arguably essential to narrative fiction, from a landscape created largely by lightning-quick impression. Indeed, the subject of the story is not a person but a crowd, which forms on the street around the body of a man of foreign extraction, who has had what seems to be an epileptic fit while walking with a boy on the East Side of Manhattan: "Two streams of people coming from different directions met at this point to form a crowd. . . . Down under their feet, almost lost under this throng, lay the man, hidden in the shadows caused by their forms which in fact barely allowed a particle of light between them. Those in the foremost rank bended down, shouldering each other, eager, anxious to see everything."[98] The defining feature of the crowd is that it is itself a faceless, disjointed body composed of feet and shoulders. Its inscrutability mirrors that of the fallen man, who does not have a face, but rather "pallid half-closed lids" revealing only "the steel-colored gleam of his eyes" ("WMF," 601). The man looks at his spectators, but only "as a corpse might glare at those live ones who seemed about to trample it under foot" ("WMF," 601). There is no mutuality to this look; indeed, the onlookers are "chained" to their very inability to get a reading of this primarily surface or visual experience. Crane uses the word "glare" more than once, evoking a prolonged experience of looking that counters the suddenness of the physiological event, the fit that lands the man on the ground, as well as the abrupt movements of the crowd, the "dodging, pushing, peering group about the man" ("WMF," 601, 600). This prolonged looking, however, produces only more impressionability, "the madness of their desire to see the thing" ("WMF," 602). They are thwarted, as stated in the story's last sentence, by an "impenetrable fabric" ("WMF," 604). For both the crowd and the narrator, this fabric represents a struggle with vision in a landscape that redefines persons and, consequently, the project of writing itself.

Or, to put it more broadly, the man's fall exposes the problem of the image in a world that depends exclusively on signs. As Rebecca Zurier has noted in her magnificently researched tome *Picturing the City: Urban Vision and the Ashcan School*, reading signs was essential for negotiating the "unstable atmosphere" of an urban life, in which people lacked shared traditions and a common language.[99] Interestingly, at the beginning of "When Man Falls, a Crowd Gathers," the boy and man are conversing in Italian. "Quick gestures" replace any comprehensible dialogue ("WMF," 600). In brief, Crane's description outlines the realist dilemma in which the sheer rapidity of the isolated visual image, centered on hands, feet, or other extremities, sabotages the very will to find meaning in an image. This same crisis of the image underpins turn-of-the-century visual culture more generally, including, for example, many paintings by members of the Ashcan School. According to Zurier, Ashcan artists focused on the question of how to convey the "diversity and difference" of the urban population, directly addressing "the meaning of pictures in an age of multiplying images."[100] Dreiser's own pictorial realism was influenced by Ashcan artists he knew in New York, including John Sloan and Everett Shinn, who became models for the artist-hero of his controversial novel *The "Genius"* (1915).[101] Like Dreiser, many of these artists began their careers in journalism, specifically as sketch reporters. Besides their urban subject matter, Zurier also notes the common "lack of finish" in the work of Ashcan artists, in which brushstrokes serve more as "notational (jot it down) device[s] . . . than representational ones," reflecting the immediacy of the encounter between painter and subject.[102]

This technique characterizes paintings such as John Sloan's *Chinese Restaurant* (1909), in which men sitting at an adjacent table observe a woman eating with another man in a place of questionable respectability, a Chinese restaurant. As Zurier points out in her analysis of the painting, the heavy rouge on the woman's cheek mirrors the red plume of her hat. The vividness of the red in juxtaposition to the black attire of all four figures is suggestive of the "vice" Carrie witnesses on the street in New York City (*SC*, 218). The woman's face itself does not speak of her trade as much as do the smears of red paint that artificially extend her skin's surface. This urban physiognomy exceeds the physiological to place meaning in the artificial. In paintings by other Ashcan artists, the effect is grotesque. I have in mind paintings by George Bellows in particular; their realism revels in techniques

John French Sloan, *Chinese Restaurant*, 1909. Courtesy of xennex, WikiArt.

of caricature and distortion that flatten out faces while exaggerating various facial features. This is especially apparent in Bellows's boxing paintings, such as *Club Night* (1907) and *Stag at Sharkey's* (1907). In both paintings, the faces of the spectators farther from the fighting ring are outlined but blotted out, while the wolfish facial features of those closer to the ring appear in sharper focus. In contrast, Bellows's famous streetscape *New York* (1911) obliterates the faces of the perambulating mass of New Yorkers. This wintery portrait of Madison Square—an admirable "surface reading" of the city—is marked by Bellows's distance from it, his attempt to capture the biggest slice of New York he possibly can. Faceless, with nothing more than occasional smudges or slits for eyes, his New Yorkers have no mark, other than the occasionally vivid street wear in emerald green, blue, and red; the repetition of these isolated colors organizes the picture. Worn by women, the garments connect the transitory nature of fashion to other images evoking mobility, a bus, and an undecipherable advertisement. To return to Simmel, such images reflect the distanced stance of a modern, urban viewer, locked in the world

George Bellows, *New York*, 1911. Courtesy of the National Gallery of Art, Washington, DC, collection of Mr. and Mrs. Paul Mellon.

of purely visual impression, in which one need not be equal to a face they do not have.

Bellows's former experience as a cartoonist suggests that he was indeed adept at techniques of caricature and exaggeration, but *New York* departs somewhat from the model of urban physiognomy I have been elaborating, in which the artificial embellishment of various facial features signifies specific character traits—to embrace what I am calling a modern prosopagnosia. More fully elaborated in the work of physician Oliver Sachs, the term "prosopagnosia," like its cousin, "prosopopoeia," derives from the Greek *prosopon*, or "face."[103] Whereas prosopopoeia generally refers to the making of faces, prosopagnosia, interpreted broadly, refers to the inability to make faces. It is literally a face blindness, a disorder of visual processing in which the viewer is unable to recognize other faces. My interest here is less in the actual disorder than in what this sort of blindness, this inability to make a face, might mean in terms of the realist aesthetics I am describing. *New York* seems to self-consciously explore the dilemma of a modern viewer who, in their zeal to represent all, cannot "face" their environment. The blank face is thus a compensation for the act of formalization necessary for face making, so much so that it appears as its own hollow form. This same unreadable face is the specter that complicates Dreiser's realism, fueled by the question of how to imagine realist form in the absence of a readable personality.

Defacement in Jean Rhys's *Voyage in the Dark*

The context I have been describing is not conventionally attributed to Dreiser and realism, but rather to Poe, Zola, and Baudelaire, one in which features and their artificial appendages eclipse faces. This prosopagnosia in many ways positions *Sister Carrie* closer to a modernism that is, if not dismissive, highly skeptical of "figurative representation."[104] With the idea of prosopagnosia as a gauge, we might also distinguish between *Sister Carrie*'s interest in the kinds of dissociation that attend urban vision and *The House of Mirth*'s nostalgic idealizing of Lily Bart's more comprehensive view. In concluding this chapter, it also seems useful here to test these presumptions about realism and modernism by turning briefly to a text where no one is smiling, Jean Rhys's *Voyage in the Dark* (1934). With its link to the world of the stage, the novel's grim portrait of affective dissociation and urban prosopagnosia offers an interesting juxtaposition from which to consider Carrie's face-work.

Rhys's appropriation of naturalist discourse and style into her fiction is evident in the novel's opening scene, which features Anna "lying on the sofa," reading "a book about a tart," Zola's *Nana*.[105] Anna is a struggling chorus girl who, quite like a mute marionette, cannot arrange or voice her feelings. After her migration from the West Indies, she is unable to coordinate her affective life with a cold and grainy London. Her contemporaries do not understand her, and no one likes the look on her face. A flatmate says that she looks "potty" and describes her *"eyes staring out of her head looking quite silly"* (*VD*, 127; italics in the original). Her first lover in the novel subjects her to a physiognomic racial classifying scheme. Another boyfriend wonders whether she takes "ether," because "her eyes look like" she "took something" (*VD*, 153-54). Unlike Lily Bart or Carrie Meeber, Anna is a poor facial manager. Her feelings are not coordinated with her expression, and the novel relates this facial maladaptation to London as a specific aesthetic environment where faces either do not form or, when they do, block communication altogether. Unreadable and opaque, facial features are neither conduits for intersubjectivity nor reflective screens of the desires of others. They signal not only affective disengagement but also a void of communal solidarity and empathy. Anna thus observes flatly of her landlady that "she always made her expression blank when she spoke to me" (*VD*, 76). In a restaurant, Anna and her friend meet the disapproving stare of a woman with a "face like a hen's" (*VD*, 119). It's "the way they look at you," Anna thinks, with "glassy eyes that don't admit anything so definite as hate" (*VD*, 120).

The paranoid mood of the novel reflects this ambiguous sense of expression, where actual feeling is motivated but not sustained, and thus does not take form on a face. Unable to classify others, Anna similarly cannot claim a relationship to her own face or feelings. Like Dorian Gray, she does not understand what her emotions "feel like."[106] In one representative instance, she rebuffs an American suitor to find that, inexplicably, "something came out from my heart into my throat and then into my eyes" (*VD*, 127). Feelings—which cannot be identified but have some origin in a bodily source—resist figuration in a face. This move away from "figurative representation" does not offer a more expansive view of a subject's "inner life," but rather marks their distance from one.[107] Anna's prosopagnosia—regarding her own face and others—is the result of the multiple ways her environment abstracts her into particles and pieces.

Facing Carrie

In *Voyage in the Dark*, the face does not serve a woman's "transcendental project," having already been marked or used up.[108] A good fur is a better investment. For Lily Bart, the form of face still holds value, and the labor of transcendence is connected to a sense of the face as a shield *against* inner life. With these distinctions in mind, we return to Carrie's commonly pretty face, made unreadable by the frown for which Carrie achieves notoriety on the stage. As the "silent little Quakeress," Carrie does not speak, but rather stands by the side of the stage and scowls (*SC*, 325). While the audience does not notice her at first, she soon attracts its attention and desire, and she becomes the "chief feature of the play" (*SC*, 313). Carrie's frown evokes unbridled, almost inexplicable laughter. Why is the frown funny, and why does it make Carrie's face desirable? The obvious answer is that the "portly gentleman" on the front row would love to "force [it] away with kisses" (*SC*, 313). Most evidently, a frown or grimace is an asymmetrical expression that disrupts the ideal form of the face. Like aging, it introduces gravity to the face, and unlike a smile, which typically discloses a desire to please and be liked, a frown is generally a sign of a-sociability. Whereas one often pretends to smile, a dissimulation often expected of women, frowns might seem more authentic, or, at least, more accurately indicative of one's present mood or emotional state. The frown pulls in its audience with the promise of something real—a face, a personality—within a controlled, fabricated environment that counters the world of the street. As Rae Beth Gordon has observed of similar gestures, an audience would likely laugh because it sees in the expression a mirror of itself. In forms of comedy such as cabaret, she argues, "spectators become the doubles of figures whose involuntary gestures belie nervous pathologies."[109] In *Sister Carrie*, as in *Voyage in the Dark*, hysteria characterizes the capitalist economy and the theater of the streets, where faces, eclipsed by their features, are difficult to make and recognize. But in contrast to the prosopagnosia of the latter novel, Carrie's frown offers an artificial, reassuring salve for the spasmodic unpredictability of an urban mode of viewing that abstracts persons, diminishing face value.

The theater, with its figurative emphasis on faces, provides the ideal setting for Dreiser's exploration of modern forms of affective expression—in particular, through the subject of melodrama. As Peter Brooks has argued, the idea that emotion could be fully "externaliz[ed] in legible, integral postures" was essential to melodrama as a mute and "expressionistic form," where gesture receives even more meaning than it can "literally support."[110] The exaggerated facial grimace was thus part of a lineup of stock gestures and hyperbolic expressions, which the actor often used to communicate directly with the audience, in a sort of false face-to-face dialogue. Whereas the gestures and grimaces of traditional melodrama are seen to exteriorize an internal reality, Carrie's frown is not a projection of her own interior. As stated explicitly in the text, her expression does not reflect her own desires, nor does it reflect the interior longings of others. To assume that the audience projects something of themselves onto her face is to assume that they have something to lose or disclose. They are rather titillated by the apparent legibility of an otherwise blank face that acquires form through the props of melodrama.

Quite literally, the surface that is Carrie's face does not speak. In her silent role as Quakeress, Carrie leads a purely visual existence. Voiceless, she is a hollow form, and in keeping with the novel's melodramatic investments, she fulfills many of the same functions as the professional mime. Carrie's particular role nods to pantomime and its formational influence on melodrama, especially as the form gained notoriety in the eighteenth century outside of major theatrical establishments such as the Théâtre Française, which exercised a monopoly on plays in dialogue.[111] Secondary theaters were restricted to wordlessness, and consequently, roles were conceived with the dramatic interplay of posture and gesture in mind.[112] As Brooks has argued, this intensely "visual representation of meaning" came to define melodrama in its recourse to "silent gesturality," especially as such a style was advocated by prominent critics such as Diderot.[113] Judith Wechsler has made similar arguments about the importance of mime as an art form that took the "modern" as its explicit theme.[114] Not only did mime, according to Wechsler, reflect the physiognomic classification of human types and bodily expression made popular by daily mass printing, but it also addressed many of the concerns of modern society while blurring the lines between high and low art. In the Théâtre des Funambules, for example, which opened in 1816, silence became a subversive vehicle for crossing such boundaries. A rather sordid and seedy affair, the Funambules resembled a sort of variety show featuring acrobats, trained dogs, and fire-eaters. But the retinue included, as Wechsler observes, a professional *grimacier* or *physiomane*, also known as Leclerq.[115] In "Some French Caricaturists," Baudelaire characterizes him as a "puller of expressive faces," who "sitting between two candles . . . used to illuminate his features with all the passions in turn."[116] Baudelaire describes the performances of this *"physiognomanic* clown" as "grotesque," given his "aptitude for make-up" and his powers of imitation, so *"objective"* as to block audience projection.[117]

Carrie's own facial displays in fact inspire masculine projection, but one can see in her stage performance the semblance of this tradition. For the professional *grimacier* or *physiomane*, the focus of performance is the face, as it is in the tradition of Pierrot. As Robert F. Storey has pointed out, the Pierrot figure, as immortalized in the performances of Baptiste and Charles Debarau, as well as other famous mimes such as Paul Legrande and Mime Séverin, is a "duplicative" type, characterized both by an "essential slackness of personality" and the "elasticity of his passions."[118] This "impersonality" certainly contributed to the attractiveness of Pierrots as subjects in Romantic, Symbolist, and Decadent literature and as figures for the artist in the modernist poetry of Jules Laforgue, T. S. Eliot, and Wallace Stevens. In the visual arts, a range of artists as diverse as Aubrey Beardsley, Pablo Picasso, Paul Klee, Juan Gris, and (in film) Charlie Chaplin drew on the Pierrot figure to explore the very duplicative functions of modern identity and expression. Regardless of its capacity for expression, the face of Pierrot in Gris's *Pierrot with Book* (1924), or Picasso's *Seated Harlequin* (1901) or *Pierrot* (1918), or Klee's *Captive Pierrot* (1923) does not have its own features. Such images essentially sever the relationship between the face's expressiveness and self-identity—the authenticity of the speaking self—figuring the strength of Pierrot's emotion, his sadness, as materially figurable. For *Sister Carrie*, positioned as the novel is on the border of modernist aesthetics, the clown figure is linked to the affective dilemma of modern existence.

Carrie's performance, as well as the rapid circulation of her face, hinges on a form of "duplicative" expression that reaffirms the problem Lukács elaborates in "The Ideology of Modernism."[119] If the personality is understood to be an ordering principle for expression, how does expression come to mean anything in its absence? Furthermore, insofar as individual personalities are connected to individual faces, such a "duplicative" mode of expression can only facilitate a prosopagnosia marked by an extreme sociability in which faces do not form. Such an exaggerated prosopagnosia, I have suggested, appears in Rhys's late modernist *Voyage in the Dark*, where the face does not cohere as a form. In other words, the mode of visual perception it conveys is not "physiognomic"; expression is neither seen nor figured in a face, nor linked to a unified character behind it.[120] Thus, in returning to the subject of Carrie's face, we might think of the novel as gesturing toward a vision of expression that rests somewhere in between a realist authentication and figuration of the human subject, on one hand, and a meaningless, consumerist prosopagnosia, on the other, a defacement or using up of oneself in an attempt to be the self that one produces or manages on the streets, as it were.

Perfectly formed as form, Carrie's face is the hallucinatory antidote both for a realist project motivated by lack and for an urban culture in which faces do not form. As Ames observes, Carrie's face is "a natural expression of [the world's] longing" (*SC*, 341). Her face is an expression of what her world lacks, as Michaels claims, but what does the world lack? Ultimately, it lacks other faces. I have attempted to probe the meaning of the term "expression" here in keeping with its use throughout *Sister Carrie*, and in realist aesthetics more generally, which consistently turns on the separation between the subject's interior, psychological recesses and the physiological manifestation of "feelings" that are presumably connected to such depths. Carrie's desire, as Michaels's analysis suggests, stems from the fact that she is not equal to a "feeling written upon her countenance" (*SC*, 341). In the language of Dreiser, Carrie's face is a text that can be written upon and further read. Expression is by nature not only physiological, surface matter in this context; it is also readable. But as I have suggested, a reader cannot always apprehend what is written on a surface. "Written" on, Carrie's perfectly pretty face is marked by the disfigurement of a viewer who reads it—both the audience and the realist narrator. As a narrative strategy that anticipates the explicitly modernist concerns I explore in the next chapters, Dreiser's realism is a mode of writing that disfigures other faces.

3 Nothing "Conclusive"
Optics as Ethics in Joseph Conrad's *The Secret Agent*

In a sense the face is equipped to lie the most and leak the most, and thus can be a very confusing source of information during deception.

—Paul Ekman and Wallace Friesen, "Nonverbal Leakage and Clues to Deception," 1969

He that has eyes to see and ears to hear may convince himself that no mortal can keep a secret. If his lips are silent, he chatters with his finger-tips; betrayal oozes out of him at every pore. And thus the task of making conscious the most hidden recesses of the mind is one which it is quite possible to accomplish.

—Sigmund Freud, *Dora: An Analysis of a Case of Hysteria*, 1905

"What are you making that face for? You see, you can't even bear the mention of something conclusive?" "I am not making a face."

—Joseph Conrad, *The Secret Agent*, 1907

For Freud, secrets are destined to leak out, if not from mismanaged bodily conduct, then from inevitable slips of the tongue. Prior to this conception of unintentional self-disclosure, Darwin, writing in *The Expression of the Emotions in Man and Animals* (1872), identified the face as the primary vehicle of self-expression, both intentional and otherwise, arguing that our faces, while responsive to our control, inevitably betray our wills. Paul Ekman and Wallace Friesen, drawing from this physiognomic tradition, termed such unguarded disclosures "micro leakage[s]," clues that thwart the liar's attempt to "perpetuate deception through his face."[1] Admittedly, Ekman and Friesen are writing here about telling lies, and Freud is writing about keeping secrets, two acts that carry ostensibly different moral valences, since lying is almost always unethical, whereas secret keeping is more ambiguous. Despite this difference, both theories of "leakage" posit an observer who reads these bodily and facial surfaces as a means of "making conscious" the subject's interior.[2]

This confidence in the ability to determine the meaning or intent behind presumably unintentional acts of disclosure stands in contrast to the third epigraph, taken from Joseph Conrad's *The Secret Agent* (1907), which is, like *Sister Carrie*, an urban novel about the making of faces. So far in this book I have addressed faces that do form, as in the case of Oscar Wilde's, and faces that do not, challenging the formalizing vision of the realist observer. As we move forward to texts more firmly identified with modernist aesthetic practices, faces often defy or evade conclusion altogether. In a scene from *The Secret Agent* that foregrounds this epistemological uncertainty, Comrade Ossipon, a member of a secret anarchist cell, meets with the explosive-wielding anarchist known only as the "Professor." The former hopes to "know the inside of this confounded affair," a bombing in Greenwich Park, in which a man has died.[3] The Professor chastises Ossipon for believing that any such knowledge could be a "matter of inquiry" to others, and this profound skepticism regarding the ability to "know" continues into the conversation when he accuses Ossipon of "making a face" (*SA*, 53, 58). Ossipon misunderstands the charge, contradictorily insinuating that he can intentionally control his face because his face is not something he is intentionally making. Suggesting that there is something to "know" about his face, he subscribes to physiognomic logic, defensively declaring that he has nothing to hide.

Ironically, the very notion of concealment runs counter to the Professor's entire philosophy; the distinction on which concealment turns—between intention and action, the interior and its expression—is, according to the Professor, characteristic of "conventional morality," which "governs your thought, and your action too, and thus neither your thought or action can ever be conclusive" (*SA*, 59). According to this same logic, a face does not offer its reader an inside to be known. It thus cannot function (as "conventional morality" and physiognomic logic would have it) as a potential arbiter of trust, transparency, and mutual accountability, or, alternatively, as a mask or tool of concealment. Having a face does not give one an interior, a psychology or depth, capable of being explained, read, discussed, analyzed, or even hidden. Rather than corroborating the Professor's moral nihilism, this failure of the face to *mean* in the novel, as I suggest here, is the source of its ethical potential. In refusing to locate being behind (or in) a face, *The Secret Agent* examines the possibilities for ethics in the absence of competent readers and, further, readable subjects.

As numerous critics have observed, *The Secret Agent* is a novel about various texts and how people read them. As a cover for his secret agency, Verloc, the secret agent charged with the bombing in question, runs a pornography shop, and critics have connected this "shady" commerce both to the novel's undermining of "homogenous reading publics" and to its "masculinist" reorganization of the nineteenth-century espionage novel.[4] While such conventions do inform the novel's operations, I suggest here that *The Secret Agent*, like *Sister Carrie*, negotiates a melodramatic understanding of personhood that locates the being of a subject in a speaking face. In doing so, the novel challenges the status of the face as the basis for both ethics and narrative construction, engaging the question of how we might conceive of ethics beyond conventional modes of reading. Whereas melodramatic narratives often employ the face as a fully expressive symbol that supports a fantasy of unified, ethical resolution, *The Secret Agent* engages these same codes of expression to allegorize the dissociation typically associated with the modernist aesthetic.

Given its interest in the illegibility of persons and faces, the text investigates the ethical possibilities of the face-to-face encounter as a context of mutual defenselessness and resistance that preserves the enigma of the other's face. While the novel only gestures at this Levinasian ideal by illustrating corrupted versions of it, as I will illustrate later, it challenges the physiognomic understanding that a subject's true intention will inevitably "out" itself in facial expression. This zeal for full disclosure was essential to the nineteenth-century melodrama, the form that, in Peter Brooks's well-known account, idealizes complete expression as a means of replacing a lost ethical consciousness. As I shall demonstrate, *The Secret Agent* stages this substitution as an anxiety that appears in the physiognomic guesswork of the narrator and characters. In engaging melodramatic conventions and codes, the novel tests the belief that the body or face will somehow give up its secrets to the expert reader. Melodrama is thus connected to text's related negotiation of a "vigorous" late Victorian interest in "hermeneutic method" and "the value of close reading," which, according to Stephen Arata, "links together practitioners from a variety of disciplines: medicine, psychiatry, criminology, sociology, and literary criticism, among others."[5] For Arata, the Victorian fin de siècle saw the emergence of a more general cultural faith in interpretive abilities of the "professional reader," who could derive "meaningful patterns out of unruly experience."[6] As it examines this culture of reading, *The Secret Agent* underlines the problem of "face values," which, to return to Ekman, leave no room for ethical ambiguity (*SA*, 144).

While Ekman is not writing about modernist literature, his extensive physiognomic program—which idealizes the expert observer in his ability to account for the actions and motivations of others—offers some insight into *The Secret Agent* as a particularly modernist commentary on a logic of reading that presumes a humanist subject built around the correspondence between one's "hidden recesses" and their manifestation on a visible surface.[7] In her compelling critique of Ekman's work, Ruth Leys connects the question of surveillance—more specifically the reading of faces—to the cultural need for ethical certainty, along with a new "science of fear" that believes it can "reliably distinguish authentic facial expressions from false ones, genuine from feigned."[8] That is, in the presence of others, we are all automatically liars, yet the trained observer has the expert capacity to decipher the real, unintentional content behind the surface of the lie. As Leys asserts, to say that the emotional states people experience when they understand themselves to be alone or unobserved are more "real" or nonintentional constructs the expressions of these states as universal and thereby readable or detectable. The consequence of the logic, she argues, is the sense that "the body cannot lie."[9] As I note in the introduction, reading technologies like facial recognition technology, with their aim of producing completely legible, dimensionless bodies, do away with the expert reader and, ultimately, the idea of reading altogether. This scenario, I suggest, is the logical extension of Ekman's program, which seeks to create a master template for explaining emotions and human psychology as codified bodily states.

Such templates are the basis of a physiognomic ideology that, as I'm arguing here, emphasizes a humanist notion of individual responsibility that idealizes the ethical comfort of making lies and deceptions public, where the ethical individual must account for his words and actions in the presence of others. In *The Secret Agent*, however, characters are often either misguided or plain wrong, and thus far from expert in their reading of faces. As illustrated by Winnie Verloc, who prefers to "put her trust in face values," the attraction to the face as a site for reading is matched by the effort to avoid reading altogether, as well as the compulsive evasion of its horrifying suppositions (SA, 144). The conclusions born of reading in the novel, as the Professor appears to recognize, are almost always misreadings. Conrad himself emphasized the ethical and "criminal futility" of an act that could not be read, the 1894 attempt to blow up the Royal Observatory Greenwich in London. In the novel, the repercussions of this act are the death of a boy whom Conrad's conversant in the preface describes casually as "half an idiot" and the consequent suicide of his sister.[10] In the novel, the blundering Adolf Verloc has done a less-than-exemplary job as a secret agent of an unnamed embassy (most likely Russian), and to save face (literally), he is charged with the task of destroying the observatory. Daunted by this mission, Verloc enlists his emotionally susceptible young brother-in-law to participate in the bombing, which does not go as expected; the resulting narrative follows the domestic melodrama that develops around Stevie's death and Winnie Verloc's slow but fatal recognition of her husband's deception.

Winnie's reluctance to do much "looking into" her husband's occupation is an uncanny complement to the observatory as a device through which one reads the seas and heavens (SA, 149). As it symbolizes both the limits and powers of visual perception and surveillance, Conrad could not have, as Stephen Kern has observed, "picked a more appropriate anarchist objective."[11] Given the observatory's role in the standardization of world time, Kern counts *The Secret Agent* as one of a number of modernist works centered on the conflict between the "heterogeneity of private time" and the uniformity of public time.[12] Indeed, the International Meridian Conference of 1884 established Greenwich as the "precise beginning of the universal day" and the point from which twenty-four time zones extended to define the earth.[13] Significantly, the events of the novel take place just two years later; the role of the observatory in establishing the new universal time would have been fresh on the public's mind, ensuring the anarchists that the bombing would attract global attention as an assault on such authority.

My point here is not to align the "modernist" with the anarchist in the common refutation of homogenous time. The modernist preference for heterogeneity over totalizing systems should be old news by now; rather, I want to draw attention to Conrad's irony in offering the observatory—a "graphic symbol of centralized political authority," or arbiter of truth or meaning—as a setting for a philosophically "unpardonable" act that "could not be laid hold of mentally in any way."[14] It is not the "unreason" of the act that troubles Conrad, for even "perverse unreason has its own logic," but the difficulty of reducing such violence to a reading or narrative, a story that can be told.[15] As Randall Stevenson has observed, Conrad does not align modernism with anarchism, but rather sees the observatory as a symbol of British surveillance and superiority that represents the "stresses imposed on the 'total human personality' by the great and perfect new systems Greenwich had imposed on modern life."[16]

The narrative difficulties of *The Secret Agent*—based on, as I am arguing, the disintegration of personality rather than the construction of it—are indeed a response to such stress. The bombing, which occurs outside of the novel's central narrative, produces the further narrative challenge of identifying Stevie's fragmented body, which has actually lost its face, the form through which personalities are generally recognized and read. But, in the account I am constructing, personality is not simply generated by the form of the face. It also forms a legible face, fusing, as in the case of Oscar Wilde, unlike representations to create likeness that may be momentarily "caught" by an observer.[17] Realist texts, I have argued, fret more anxiously over the loss of legible facial form. The decline of personality, as well as the face's inability to match its own claims, compromises the observer's ability to form the face and, consequently, their ability to read and write fictions. In the modernist scenario I will describe, anxiety about facial loss becomes critique; Stevie's absent face, illegible in the extreme, confronts the codes through which we read and generate stories.

Alphonse Bertillon and the "Sciences" of Identification

What is "conclusive" about a face? In an 1890 article from *The Monist*, titled "The Physiognomy of the Anarchists," criminal anthropologist Cesare Lombroso—whose name appears in *The Secret Agent*—argues that the face of the "political criminal" does look like something definite, although "among the anarchists there are no true criminals"; they merely "possess the degenerative characteristics common to criminals."[18] In examining one hundred imprisoned Turin anarchists, Lombroso remarks that only about 40 percent were actually endowed with the sort of "facial asymmetry"—characterized by "protruding ears," "enormous jaws," and an enlarged "frontal sinus"—that defines the "criminal physiognomy," regardless of their "true moral insensibility."[19] This logic of criminality as imperceptible or confusing to all but the trained eye necessitates the work of the professionally trained observer, anticipating Ekman's program by positing an expert reader who not only is able to perceive the objective signs of criminality but also can detect the absence of criminality behind an ostensibly criminal exterior. According to Carlo Ginzburg, such a semiotic enterprise developed alongside "more secure and practical methods for determining identity" that involved "the analysis of specific cases which could be reconstructed only through traces, symptoms and clues."[20] In Ginzburg's account, the late nineteenth century saw the development of a new "bourgeois concept of property" that created the conditions for more crimes, more prisons, and, consequently, more criminals, who could easily escape identification given new possibilities for mobility within urban settings.[21] In France in particular, where recidivism was a problem, it was necessary to prove that the perpetrator of the crime had been previously condemned and that the perpetrator of both crimes was the same person. Thus, new physiognomic systems accompanied the expansion of an "enormous criminal photographic archive" designed to create personal criminal records.[22]

In this "modern drama of detection," as Tom Gunning has illustrated, Lombrosian physiognomy—which attempted to read criminality through a set of consistent physical features—began to give way to an idea of the "unique body imprinted with its particular, inherited physiology."[23] Under these modern conditions, the study of facial characteristics seemed far less useful in determining identity than the potential observation of "unconscious habits and adaptations" as the "product and residue of a life history."[24] Photography informed this enterprise. However, slow shutter speeds made it possible for criminals to resist the photographic process by manipulating their facial expressions to effectively disfigure themselves, making recognition impossible. For Alphonse Bertillon, the question of how "to isolate distinct features in the continuum of an image" posed problems for distinguishing one criminal from another. Consequently, new systems of recording, such as Bertillon's anthropometric method, attempted to match "minute" bodily measurements with personalized records of criminal activity.[25] This method of quantifying criminality was integrated with something called the "spoken portrait," a primarily verbal description that sought to "restor[e] the image of the individual."[26]

Bertillon's anthropometric method and his system of verbal portraiture were flawed because they excluded individuals who did not "match" that visual and verbal data. Only with Francis Galton's contributions to fingerprint analysis in the late 1880s could individuals at last be identified and controlled. As Ginzburg points out, through fingerprinting, formerly unidentified subjects, by means of the state, "became at one stroke individuals, each one distinguished by a specific biological mark."²⁷ Ellen Samuels has called this development "biocertification," arguing more particularly that race and disability were "mutually constitutive and imbricated" in the development of fingerprinting as an effort to "control racial and disability identities."²⁸ She contends that while Galton's "racialist agenda" is well-known, "disability was as crucial to his interests"; indeed, Galton collected prints from the "lowest" and "worst" "idiots" in London to serve as constants in his attempt to discern racial and mental distinctions in contrasting fingerprints.²⁹ Even though Galton reportedly found no distinguishing marks in the prints, he still continued to insist on a "characteristic" quality of the "Negro print."³⁰

To claim that there were "discernible patterns" in the prints of various subjects where there actually were none was, according to Samuels, part of the "eugenic frenzy of the early twentieth-century."³¹ *The Secret Agent*, set only a few years after fingerprinting was introduced in England, engages many of these discourses and developments, including fantasies about "idiot" and racial typology. While fingerprinting is not directly mentioned in the novel, the text directly probes the fantasy on which such technology rests—the presumption of an immediately readable bodily surface or mark, asking to what degree the body is able to lie, to go against the suppositions of its appearance. As Lombroso's analysis of the physiognomy of anarchists suggests, the body of the anarchist *does* lie. In fact, its primary characteristic is its lying, in the failure of personality, character, or intention to match the criminal characteristics it displays. And perhaps this is why the subject of fingerprinting evades Conrad's, as well as his narrator's, interest. Like Ekman's system of facial decoding, fingerprinting leaves no room for ethical ambiguity. It cannot account, as other types of images do, for the "unavoidably elusive nature of the individual."³²

Nor can the fingerprint account for the question of what motivates unpardonable acts, even though Galton unsuccessfully attempted to link various degenerate racial types to peculiarities in the fingertips. Consequently, the face (not the fingers) is the narrative means by which *The Secret Agent* explores these questions of identity, primarily because of the potential for complication, mystery, and ambiguity that attends its capacity for expression—its form. If the novel possesses a coherent political content or ethical imperative, then it is set against this movement toward this concretization of identity or "fantasy of identification."³³ The ethics and politics elaborated by the novel are instead connected to the impression of the absent face,

Stevie's, which, in its ontological and epistemological uncertainty, deconstructs the idea of the individual as containing any particular content, or "something conclusive" (*SA*, 58).

This is especially true of the text's investigation into the nature of terrorism. The novel explores the question of what makes a secret agent or terrorist from a variety of perspectives, but I turn now to a particularly illuminative, albeit darkly humorous, scene, the introduction to Verloc, which occurs through a series of observer perspectives: first through the narrator, who describes Verloc as "undemonstrative and burly in a fat-pig style," and then through the perspectives of Wurmt and Vladimir, both employees of the unnamed embassy for whom Verloc is a spy (*SA*, 16). To the disappointment of his inquisitors, Verloc does not look like a secret agent. Wurmt attests that Verloc is "very corpulent," and Vladimir agrees: "You're right . . . He's fat—the animal" (*SA*, 16). Vladimir further admonishes Verloc for getting "out of condition" (*SA*, 16). Lacking the "physique" of his "profession," Verloc "wouldn't deceive an idiot" (*SA*, 18). While it is true that Verloc's body renders him unable to enter the ranks of the "starving proletariat," Vladimir's assessment here is ironic, since it is the "idiot" boy Stevie—convinced that Verloc is "*good*"—whom Verloc deceives (*SA*, 18, 146; italics in the original). Nonetheless, Verloc is inefficient as a terrorist because of his grotesque physical unfitness, which contributes to the shameful accident in which the boy is blown to bits. Verloc's body and its inadequacies, not his face, are linked to his ability (or inability) to carry out acts of deception. Indeed, terrorism and secret agency are essentially faceless occupations, and Wurmt and Vladimir seemingly agree that there is no content—no hidden, secret recess—to secret agency.[34] Quite problematically, Verloc's "gross bulk" disguises his occupation, such that his corpulence gives him a face, making him recognizable and therefore unrecognizable as a terrorist (*SA*, 21).

While Lombroso receives explicit mention in *The Secret Agent*, Bertillon does not, but Vladimir's and Wurmt's comments in this scene appear as rather comic and flawed applications of Bertillon's anthropometric system, in which physiological measurements provide clues to a subject's identity. Bertillon described his own duties at the Paris Prefecture of Police as requiring that he "fix the human personality, give to each human being an identity, a certain individuality, durable, invariable, always recognizable and easily demonstrable."[35] As Josh Ellenbogen has observed in his intriguing study, Bertillon's photographs and corresponding "science of identity" reflected the discrepancy he saw between the "body of a criminal as it readily presents

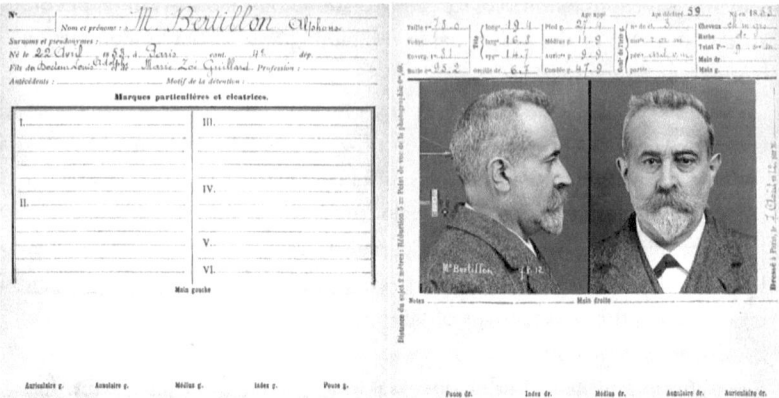

From Alphonse Bertillon, *Identification Anthropométrique*, 1893. Courtesy of Jebulon, Wikimedia Commons.

itself to vision" and his own attempt to register criminal bodies as "particular forms of data."[36] His ultimately quite complex system concerned itself not only with the problems photography posed for identifying criminal bodies but also with the issue of memory and its relation to the perception of images. One could not simply put trust in "face values," as it were, because they were too marred by the problems surrounding human perception. Concerned with how one uses the material we take from memories to identify individual characteristics, Bertillon aimed for a memory practice with the point of creating trained agents capable of studying photographs, committing them to memory, and then extracting data "that go unperceived by those without ocular education."[37] A "reasoned" memory could only develop in relation to an archive of specific auditory, visual, and tactile data regarding an individual.[38]

The idea that perception can be translated into forms of data that make a terrorist or criminal recognizable should be quite familiar to twenty-first century readers of *The Secret Agent*, given the rapid proliferation of profiling and surveillance methods and the climate of radical insecurity after 9/11. According to the physiognomic logic I have been examining, the face (and body) can be read by experts as an expression of a totality—a verifiable human identity or "personality." In *The Secret Agent*, Verloc's girth in particular breaks this fantasy of representative totality that makes a terrorist a terrorist. To his own detriment, Verloc himself ironically corroborates the logic of Vladimir and Wurmt by emphasizing another form of bodily content or data utilized in Bertillon's method (and a recurring trope in Conrad's novels): his voice, "famous for years at open-air meetings and at workmen's assemblies in large halls" (*SA*, 20). Vladimir has "no use" for his voice and, shouting "right into Verloc's face," demands "facts—startling facts—damn you!" (*SA*, 21). Unlike voice, facts are not read or interpreted; they do not express anything, but rather are certainties that annul the pressure of interpreting the true foreignness behind the face. Instead of exposing a secret, facts threaten the reality of secrecy in the first place.

Conrad's narrator, not Verloc, responds to this demand, limiting his eye, and his physiognomic inquiry, to surfaces while observing characters observe. Jason Coats has similarly drawn attention to Conrad's "physiognomic description of characters," arguing that the author's frequent allusions to criminal anthropology, scientific racism, and physiognomic ideology assume an "authorial audience" that would have "discredited" Lombroso and other proponents of degeneracy such as Max Nordau, instead recognizing "the narrator's slavish devotion to scientific racism as an outmoded relic of the 1890s."[39] Coats argues that Conrad as author aligns himself against the narrator's "discursive role"—which favors "typological simplicity" over "individual complexity."[40] Certainly, type fragments into complexity quite readily in the novel, as the narrative layering of perspectives and viewpoints exposes the inanity of the narrator's tendency to approach each character as a "specimen to be read for 'strong representation' of degenerate pathology."[41] To return to the scene in question, through the narrator's perspective, the reader sees Vladimir studying the "gross bulk" of Verloc's reflection in a mirror as he simultaneously examines the "advantage" of his own face, "clean shaved and round, rosy about the gills, and with thin sensitive lips formed exactly for the utterance of those delicate witticisms which had made him such a favourite in the very highest society" (*SA*, 21). This face, later likened to a "dog-fish"—a "noxious looking, altogether detestable beast"—is a "witty" speaking face (*SA*, 179); mediated by the mirror, however, and in a radical dissociation of form and content, it does not have a voice. That is, there is no correlation between the sensitivity of thin lips "formed for utterance" and an actual utterance (*SA*, 21). The "advantage" Vladimir views in the mirror is made even more ridiculous by the narrator's perspective, which superimposes Vladimir's head on Verloc's body. Here, the narrator's observations of a Vladimir (himself a foreigner) embodied by a foreign other, Adolf Verloc, underline the irony of Vladimir's own physiognomic self-inspection while highlighting his transient position in the "highest society." To return to Bertillon, the narratorial perspective is quite comically unable to fix or demonstrate the totality of personality or further transpose the image of the body into manageable data. Indeed, the reader's image of Vladimir's awkwardly embodied self affirms the very separation between interior and exterior, between content and form, that he indeed desires to close by seeking a synthesis in his own face.

The resulting Vladimir/Verloc body is an exaggerated reflection of the same body that was concretized in the photographic charts of the Bertillon method, with their assemblage of ears and other body parts expertly arranged for observation, analysis, and juxtaposition. Beyond its ostensible processing, this "body of modernity," as well as the potential success of its identification, offers a narrative promise.[42] As Bertillon's system of verbal portraiture illustrates, the process of identifying a particular body is also the process of telling a story about it—of constructing a life history. Certainly, Bertillon's system demonstrates how the expertise of the "professional reader" is tied to larger questions about the production of narrative more generally, and this is where I draw connections between the novel's focus on face—as a politics of apprehending, identifying, and processing persons—and its aesthetic aims, namely its related engagements with literary impressionism and melodrama.[43] Vladimir's viewing of himself through the narrator's perspective narrates the compulsion and failure to give oneself and others a face and thus create an essentially narrative understanding of the person as a readable organization, or personality. The synthesis Vladimir narcissistically seeks to realize in viewing his own face amounts to just such a fantasy, put into perspective by Inspector Heat's later conclusion that "a man must identify himself with something more tangible than his own personality" (*SA*, 97). The face itself is often presumed to project personality, but in *The Secret Agent* the face's illegibility weakens the personality's ostensible project of fusing individual uniqueness with the social self. In doing so, and insofar as Conrad can be categorized as an "impressionist" writer, the face functions as an impressionist problematic connected to the novel's ethical and narrative irresolution, apparently undermining the impressionist aim of merging a specific set of sense data into a utopian notion of consciousness as totality—of revealing "something conclusive" (*SA*, 58).[44]

Impressionism, then, can be thought of as the writer's mode of resistance to the narrator's tendency toward "typological simplicity."[45] As an aesthetic aim or philosophy, it can also be understood as a historical antidote to Galton's racialist science, Lombroso's reductive physiognomy, Bertillon's criminal archive of data, and Max Nordau's assortment of degenerate types. In its apprehension over the perception and retention of images, Bertillon's method of collecting and archiving data anticipates many of the concerns that would later inform literary impressionism. For Bertillon, memories must be trained so that identity can "be established instantaneously between an individual who rapidly passes and the memory of an image."[46] As an identity document, the ideal photograph does not simply offer one view of the subject; it should instead hold all of the possible views or looks related to a specific person. Consequently, the trained agent should exhibit an ideal lens in his memory capable of synthesizing these various views of the subject into a composite image. In this form of identity production, the trained agent should not simply memorize the features of the face, but rather should absorb the whole range of perceptual data related to an individual.

As with E. H. Gombrich's idea of physiognomic forms of perception, which I discuss in the introduction, Bertillon's method recognizes the inadequacy and unreliability of the singular impression or physiognomic constant; as an ideal of critical response, it develops instead an explicit system for the mental production and management of multiple impressions of what are, according to Gombrich, the "various oscillations of the living physiognomy."[47] Similarly, in *The Secret Agent* we can see how this process of critical data production and management informs the narrator's assessments, as well as Conrad's self-professed goal of "render[ing] the highest kind of justice to the visible universe" in order to "make you *see*."[48] In this empathic, utopian fantasy, sensuous detail, as Jesse Matz has suggested, becomes a "solidarity producing concept" constructed around the very likelihood of its failure.[49] Unlike Bertillon, Conrad demonstrates great faith in the "oneness of the impression," but as Matz has observed, the basic impressionist desire to unify the perceiving consciousness with the external world underwrites a "modern predicament," in which impression turns into abstraction, such that the impressionist book narrates "a record of its own undoing."[50] This allegorical relationship, Matz argues, following Paul de Man and Walter Benjamin, gives form to "structural conflict," challenging the impression by reversing the unifying operations of the symbol.[51] Thus, Conrad's relation to the impression is different from Bertillon's mostly in the value he assigns to it. Whereas Bertillon's data management system seems to recognize the problem of the impression from the start, Conrad's basic narrative strategy emerges as a way to deal with the failure of the impression as a utopian ideal of empathic

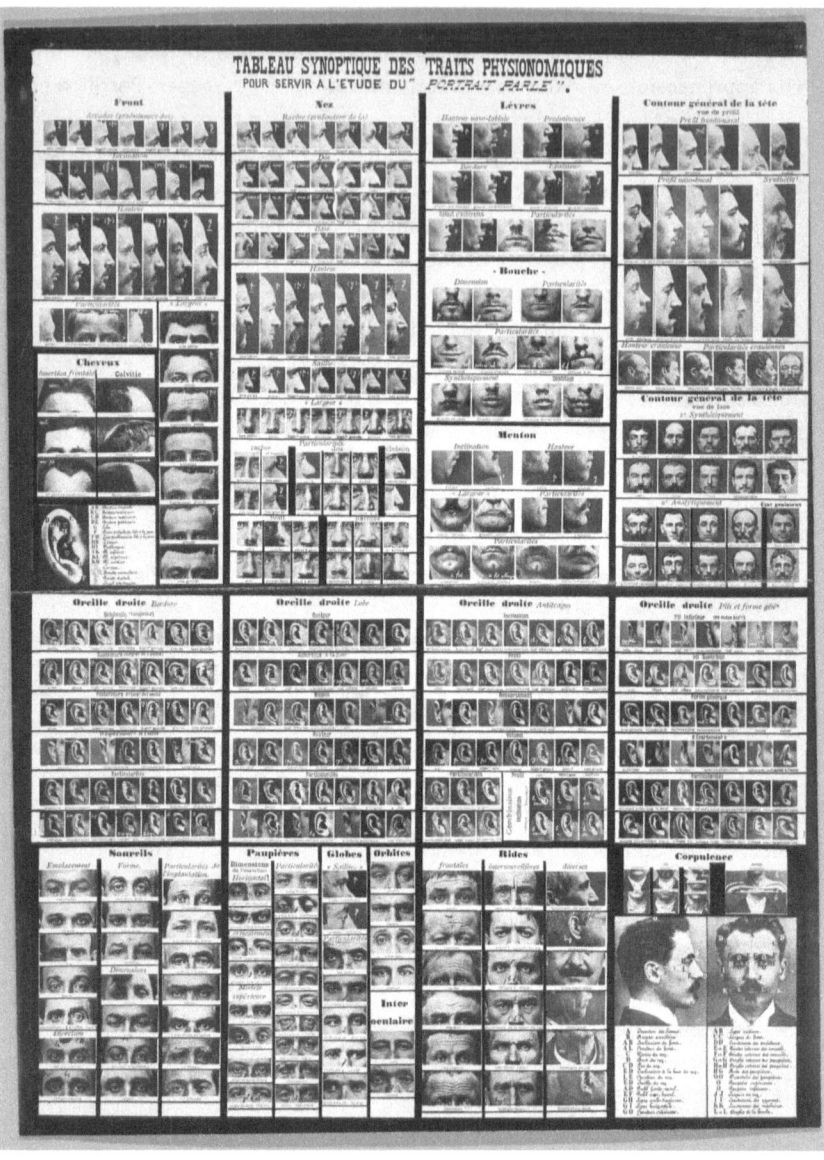

Alphonse Bertillon, *Tableau Synoptic des Traites Physionomiques*, 1909. Courtesy of the Metropolitan Museum of Art, New York, Twentieth-Century Photography Fund, 2009.

perception. Nevertheless, despite Bertillon's distrust of the image, he believes that this failure can be adequately conquered through his archival memory process. Whereas the result of Conrad's impressionism is arguably irresolution, Bertillon's method, like the realist writer's, still idealizes the possibility of instantaneous identification and totality.

Other revisionary accounts of Conrad's impressionism have identified the fracture, the representative void, at the core of an aesthetic that attempts to offer representative totality. For Michael Fried, the face in Conrad reflects the author's relation to the materiality of writing, his struggle with the blank page, such that the reading of the face as a text is an act of erasure, a "marking over" that "renders irretrievable a prior writing."[52] Nonetheless, the face still maintains its ontological certainty by virtue of the "ineffaceable" nature of its capacity for representing depths.[53] In other words, the face derives its certainty from the *act* of representation, not the content it is presumed to represent. It follows from such arguments that impressionist texts are often metageneric, or self-referential, since the act of reading is essential to the meaning of allegory. This is true not only of *The Secret Agent* but also of novels such as *Heart of Darkness* and *Lord Jim*, where the face stands in for a variety of things but most persistently allegorizes the novel or text itself and the various ways that text, as a synthesis, dissolves through the act of reading. In this very function, I am arguing, the face operates as a melodramatic narrative device that represents the fantasy of a totalizing reading characterized by ethical resolution.

Sarah Cole has written that *The Secret Agent* turns toward the melodramatic conventions of the sensational crime drama to make the novel's violence—literalized in the "unendurable reality" of Stevie's fragmented body—comprehensible.[54] What *can* be understood, she contends, is Winnie's ultimate revenge and newsworthy suicide, attached as these acts are to established literary traditions. However important Stevie's body (as well as Verloc's and the Professor's) is to this text, I suggest that the boy's *face* is the most fundamental symbol of melodramatic imagination. Indeed, the rather early appearance of the face as symbol and narrative device in the text suggests instead that the novel does not *turn* to melodrama but employs its conventions throughout. Furthermore, the melodramatic spectacle or impression in the novel does not limit the effects of violence or make it comprehensible. Rather, as its prolonged attention to Winnie's blank face suggests, the novel's melodramatic finale is as impenetrable as the violent incident the narrative obsessively recounts: the decimation of her brother Stevie's impressionistic body.

Melodrama as Physiognomy

As I am arguing, *The Secret Agent*'s staging of melodramatic spectacle aligns the irresolution of the impression as a "solidarity producing concept" with a sense of dramatic opacity that reflects the impenetrability of its subjects.[55] This formulation of melodrama seems to both recognize and depart from what Peter Brooks elaborates in his classic account *The Melodramatic Imagination: Balzac, Henry James, Melodrama, and the Mode of Excess*, where melodrama, characterized primarily by its zeal for complete expression, responds to a loss of tragic vision and ethical consciousness. What emerges as sacred in this worldview is the personality itself, the ego, individual being, and, as in the example of Rousseau's *Confessions*, the "necessity of expressing that being in its totality," particularly as that expression involves the highly gestural enactment of signs that are consequently interpreted, by readers or a reading audience, to "bear the stamp of meaning."[56] Extending from Brooks's account, Agustin Zarzosa underlines a less codified sense of the form, emphasizing the importance of melodrama as a "mode," which, unlike genre, "suggests affinities unencumbered by medium."[57] A mode, Zarzosa argues, is not a "model of reality" or a simple representation of content, but rather a "strategy to solve practical problems of experience" that includes the specific task of "ameliorat[ing] suffering."[58] In doing so, the melodramatic mode stages the "discontinuity" that attends spiritual and moral experience, the "imbalance" that forms the heart of represented aesthetic experiences, "between moral values implicit in the plot and their stylistic articulation."[59]

Whereas classical melodrama exploits the visibility of this suffering and other emotional states, *The Secret Agent* demonstrates the difficulty of seeing into them. In other words, the novel expands a vision of melodrama as a mode in which represented actions "bea[r] the full stamp of meaning" into the form Zarzosa theorizes, marked more radically by the "imbalance" and "discontinuity" of these meanings.[60] In its faithfulness to the ethically "unpardonable" and incomprehensible nature of the bombing, *The Secret Agent* both confirms and unsettles a nineteenth-century mode that "tests the efficiency" of full expression; it explores instead the ethical possibility of "solv[ing] problems of experience" such as "suffering" through the production of illegibility.[61] It does so by engaging melodrama as a physiognomic mode that investigates the idea of "reading" or "seeing" as an ethics, where the ideal of complete expression parallels the impressionist fantasy of solidarity Matz and others have identified. Ultimately, the failure of melodramatic hermeneutics in the novel as a code for reading becomes the means by which *The Secret Agent* reflexively narrates the allegorical redivision of impressionist synthesis. This fracturing is further symbolized in the failure of the face to visually consolidate and make comprehensible the subject's interior, to effectively "bear the stamp of meaning."[62]

In *The Secret Agent*, however, the face is essentially confusing to its readers, who seek in it a melodramatic reification of the individual, ego, and personality. The text engages the face as the symbol of synthesis concepts such as personality promise, but it ultimately disables those concepts, as they posit a readable humanist subject defined by interior, psychological depth. Melodrama thus engages physiognomy as a specific hermeneutic system in which facial features become "signifying elements" that represent "interior qualities."[63] One might be tempted to say, following Ginzburg, that physiognomic logic is semiotic, based largely on the reconstruction and interpretation of signs to find out whatever is "inaccessible to direct observation."[64] While Lombroso's work might be best described as semiotic, because it exploits a range of physically observable characteristics or signs to generalize about types, his appearance in the novel is connected to larger questions about reading. Consistent with Samuels's claim that nineteenth-century fantasies of identification developed around the classification of disability and the "idiot," Ossipon invokes Lombroso and Nordau when characterizing Stevie, engaged in the activity of drawing "a tangled multitude of repeated curves" and circles, as a "degenerate" (*SA*, 40). The irony of Ossipon's attention to Stevie's face and "the lobes of his ears"—as well as his analysis of the boy's drawings—is unmistakable since the scene appears immediately after the narrator's own racialized description of Ossipon's "flattened nose and prominent mouth cast in the rough mold of the negro type" (*SA*, 38).[65] But the acerbic retort of fellow anarchist Karl Yundt puts an end to the matter: "Lombroso is an ass" (*SA*, 40).

As a rather motley assortment, the anarchists themselves disprove the Lombrosian thesis that criminality is indeed readable. As I have suggested, the idea that criminals could be reduced to types might have indeed been laughable by 1908, given the need for more sophisticated forms of identifying them. The Professor especially, who openly broadcasts his intent to bomb at the slightest provocation, turns that claim on its head. Characterizing himself as an "impression," he requires no reading or detection (*SA*, 58).

With his hand precariously on the trigger, he is a "deadly . . . pest" for authorities; he terrorizes in plain sight, "in a street full of men," undermining the very practices that define police work—which seeks not only to recognize the possible terrorist or criminal but also to determine or interpret his "will" (*SA*, 57). The idea that such a "will to use the means" is to be found or exposed by an expert observer or reader underwrites the physiognomic techniques of Lombroso in particular, who connects facial characteristics, not expressions, to innately criminal traits and behaviors and, further, a subject's intention (*SA*, 57). Similarly, the goal of melodrama is to produce just this sort of readability by exploiting the "plastic figurability of emotion, its shaping as a visible and almost tactile entity."[66] The focal point of such figurability is the face, and the resulting visual context, populated by the mute, the disfigured, and the paralytic, not merely is semiotic but involves an excess of signification that incites deep and close reading. As a mode, melodrama hyperbolizes ethical conflict, consistently pressuring the signified for access to the "immediate behind."[67]

Consequently, while a Lombrosian notion of criminal type might have been outdated to a reading audience of 1908, or subject to the scorn of anarchists in 1894, it would conform to melodrama's deeply physiognomic investments. Gunning has observed that as early as 1859 Dion Boucicoult's *The Octoroon* brought photography to the stage, along with the possibility that, in a world of uncertain identity and ethical perplexity, it was now possible to photograph guilty acts.[68] Similarly, Brooks notes that the nineteenth-century novel utilized gesture to "carry a great measure of expression."[69] Works by Dickens, Gogol, Flaubert, Dostoevsky, Lawrence, Balzac, and James, Brooks argues, often elide description "in favor of immediate translation."[70] Gesture, like photography, is not always "operable," meaning that it cannot be executed in such a way as to carry the meanings attributed to it in the text.[71] Consequently, the melodramatic logic that gestures (or photographs) may *mean* something is fictive, for gesture "indicate[s] the intention to mean," belying the belief that bodily or facial expressions, unlike verbal expressions, reveal rather than conceal.[72]

This idea of melodrama as a mode characterized by the intentional revelation of truth or meaning links the various strands of my argument regarding the novel's deployment of physiognomic ideology and criminal typology to Conrad's impressionism, which, I have argued, counters the hypervisualization of ethical certainty. In a modernist vein, *The Secret Agent* resists such reductive typologies of reading by shifting the mode—linking personality to irresolution and illegibility rather than to identity. The novel does not lament the loss of comprehensive representation, as in the realist fiction I discuss in the preceding chapter, but rather, in the style of Kafka, Joyce, and Beckett, strategizes *against* the full disclosure of meaning, where the meaning of the impression cannot live up to its intention, or the different ways in which it is perceived. Given Conrad's attention to these details, we may see how both the history of melodramatic representation and physiognomic inquiry generate primarily ethical questions about our encounters with other faces. Supported by photographic technology, the logic of physiognomic analysis corresponds to the idea that lies and human character traits more generally are observable and can indeed be caught, if not in the instantaneous flash of a camera, then in the creation of bodily records. I have suggested that, as a hermeneutic practice of reading that spans the nineteenth and twentieth centuries, physiognomy is linked to a humanist notion of ethical responsibility that stresses personal and public ownership of one's actions—in other words, the fixing of personality through the process of identification. *The Secret Agent*, however, points toward the possibility of a very different sense of responsibility. More particularly, the question of how we should read in *The Secret Agent* is the question of how we should look at other faces—if to imagine a direct and unmediated face-to-face interaction is to invasively ascribe to speakers' fictional forms of personhood and intention.

Conrad's staging of the visual in *The Secret Agent* is consistent with other modernist texts that engage melodrama to show "characters who see some things and not others."[73] For example, Garry Leonard connects Joyce's own deployment of melodrama to an interest in "strategies of delimitation," particularly in *Dubliners*, where characters are aware of the "struggle" between what they have learned to see and what they have "learned to block."[74] I'll discuss the importance of these strategies as they appear in *The Secret Agent* a bit later. But for now, I use this idea to distinguish between nineteenth-century melodrama as an instructive mode that shows seeing and a modernist version of the form that, as characterized by Leonard, questions the "conditions of possibility that underlie what allows something to be comprehended as 'visual' at all."[75] What we see, according to Leonard, particularly in an environment of "competing visual stimuli," becomes what we notice and later comprehend.[76]

This understanding of the visual as the product of our strategies of delimitation and what they lead us to observe and understand provides an interesting standpoint for gauging the perceptual problem presented by *The Secret Agent*. In fact, what seems important in the novel is that the appearance of the face often exceeds or thwarts characters' various strategies to block it out, disturbing the possibility of a harmonious synthesis of "one's personal environment."[77] I am interested here in how this function of the face, its capacity for being seen or visible among other things that remain invisible and, further, its evocation of both meaning and incomprehensibility, amounts to an ethics in the novel. In light of this question, I turn here to Emmanuel Levinas, whose understanding of the "ethical relation" as it emerges in the "face to face" encounter offers insight into Conrad's own impressionistic use of the face as a site of signification that resists coercion into meaning.[78] Levinas's work stands in contrast to the tradition of physiognomic inquiry I have outlined and the problem of intersubjectivity such a tradition entails. Furthermore, the problem of melodrama, as outlined by Brooks, in which gestural enactment cannot actually carry or produce the meaning it intends, is not, for Levinas, a problem. Rather, for Levinas, a face or expression must only be taken in the pure exteriority of its expressiveness, not in its ability to represent depths or content. "Expression does not consist in *giving* us the Other's interiority," but rather the other "retains his freedom to lie" precisely because his face is not a presentation of his "being."[79]

Admittedly, my book is concerned with the very different model of faciality offered by deconstruction and the notion of prosopopoeia, which, as I will explain in chapter four, similarly dissolves totality and synthesis but can be seen quite differently as an intrusive mode of making the face of another subject in the effort of knowing or controlling them.[80] Nonetheless, my engagement with Levinas seems appropriate here, particularly given his attempt to theorize a face-to-face encounter that is not a defacement or violation of the other; as Levinas remarks, granting the other the "freedom to lie" does not amount to a "neutralization of the other," nor does it enable an ontological "possession" or understanding of the other.[81] Expression itself, whether verbal or physical, as in facial expression, does not presuppose an authentic face. The goodness of the "ethical relation" thus emerges in the failure of will to appropriate or possess the other, where freedom is the ability to "maintain oneself against the other" that develops from the mutual failure of the will to master the other.[82] Given this simultaneous resistance and defenselessness, the "freedom to lie" actually undermines the validity of the concept of lying altogether. Indeed, for Levinas, presuppositions about the "originality" or individuality of face—especially as the subject of psychoanalytic and sociological inquiry—produce moral categories such as "sincerity" and "deceit."[83] Such concepts connect "being" to the presumed "authenticity of the face," further "circumventing" the real "ambiguity" that characterizes the relation between truth and falsehood.[84] Levinas thus faults conventionally held ideals of public responsibility and individual accountability—in which self-disclosure occurs especially through the use of language as an "instrument" or "action"—as in confession.[85] As an alternative, the "ethical relation" occurs when language "renounces" this function and returns to its "essence of being expression."[86] As expression, the "epiphany" of the face is itself a "word of honor."[87]

My point here is not to equate melodramatic inoperability—the failure of expression to match what it claims or presupposes—with Levinasian ethics but to look at some of the ways Conrad's novel, in showing seeing, rewrites the "imbalance" and "discontinuity" Zarzosa ascribes to melodrama.[88] Granting the other the "freedom to lie" means that we accept the "face value" of the other's expression, but not in the manner of Winnie Verloc's blind failure to look into things. For Levinas, Winnie's stance would constitute not an encounter but an evasion of the other that discounts the face altogether. For the face itself *is* precisely this freedom born of the "exceptional presentation of self by self," which is "incommensurable with the presentation of realities simply given."[89] As epiphany, the face appears outside of the circumstances that might define it in one way or the other, as true or untrue, just as it evades the perceptual strategies that produce its appearance. Rather, the face's authenticity is its ambiguity, which contributes to its form.

Much in contrast to a Levinasian perspective, *The Secret Agent*'s characters, particularly Verloc, engage with the face and its failure in fulfilling their presumptions about reading. Vladimir's face indeed continues to haunt Verloc after his meeting with him, even following him, in a scene reminiscent of Mary Shelley's *Frankenstein*, into his bedroom. As Verloc presses his forehead against the window, "suddenly the face of Mr. Vladimir, shaved and witty, appeared enhaloed in the glow of its rosy complexion like a sort of pink seal impressed on the fatal darkness. This luminous and mutilated vision was so ghastly that Mr. Verloc started away from the window, letting down the Venetian blind with a great rattle. Discomposed and speechless with the apprehension of more such visions, he beheld his wife re-enter the room and get into bed in a calm, businesslike manner which made him feel hopelessly lonely in the world" (*SA*, 48). The synthesis Vladimir views between his own traits and their physical manifestation has fully literalized itself, so much so that his face is now "mutilated." Whatever distinction the image originally maintained between face and voice, expression and content, has fully evaporated, such that the voice is no longer witty, but rather the face is. In another scene of bodily parsing, the verbal utterance is now embodied in the visual impression of the face. In this phantom Levinasian vision, the face *is* now the foreignness of the word, and vice versa. The "disproportionately enormous," if not "absolutely monstrous," framing effect of the window mutilates the face as it both limits and magnifies the ways in which it is conventionally perceived.[90] As a disembodied apparition, Vladimir's face is excessively signified; in its totality, it invites Verloc to read but defies his very ordinary perceptive abilities by offering no possibility of content or meaning. The face produces no narrative and, though "witty," is a "pink seal" that cannot be read or detected. Written over in this manner, much in the way the Professor's body literalizes his "will," the face is monstrous in the exaggerated figurability of its impression (*SA*, 58). Verloc, once the overly embodied observed, is now the observer who, "discomposed and speechless," must negotiate the monstrosity of incomprehensible appearance: a framed face without a body, a form without content (*SA*, 48).

Vladimir's face does not narrate the failure of impressionist synthesis, but rather oversynthesizes interior and exterior states. As an apparition, this face further threatens the compartmentalization of Verloc's highly "cultivated domestic virtues"—a life of content—and his identity as a secret agent by bringing together two modes of narrative: the melodramatic mode of excess connected to Verloc's "domestic virtues," and the narrative without content, the "activity" Vladimir demands of the bombing (*SA*, 21). For Peter Brooks, these are the very modes that constitute plot. Following Barthes, Brooks explains that whereas the *proairetic code* concerns the sequence and logic of actions, most evident in the tale of pure adventure, the *hermeneutic code* involves the "questions and answers that structure a story, their suspense, partial unveiling, temporary blockage," and ultimately "the revelation of meaning that occurs when the narrative sentence reaches full predication."[91] Plot, he argues, can be thought of as the "overcoding of the proairetic by the hermeneutic."[92] *The Secret Agent*, however, narrates the failure of both codes. As suggested in the examples of the fatal bombing and the series of violent events that take place at the novel's end, where action is consistently botched or impossible, the quest for meaning is a pointless one.

My intention here is not to apply these distinctions systematically to *The*

Secret Agent but to understand the relation between the face as it appears in the text and these established codes of reading and plot construction; in particular, the hermeneutic inquiry inspired by the face and the novel itself offers no final "revelation of meaning"—no clear ethical outcome. In allegorical fashion, the face then invites its reader to consider the possibility of a narrative that, according to Conrad, can be "laid hold of mentally,"[93] but as it simultaneously resists reading, this face pronounces the meaninglessness of a narrative that cannot center itself in the world of comprehensible appearance, of "distinct, significant, fact(s)" (*SA*, 16). The narrative challenge of the face is also its ethical challenge, since an illegible face confronts the very codes through which we read and generate fictions. That is, to return to the beginning of this chapter, if a face is illegible, then lies and secrets cannot be detected, thus throwing into question an ethical system that attempts to account for the secret recesses of the individual. Indeed, the condition for ethical responsibility in this novel is, to return to Levinas, "the freedom to lie."[94]

The ABCs of Reading

In keeping with the deep sarcasm of the novel, few, if any, characters challenge this freedom.[95] What excites us as readers is not our own quest for meaning but the suspense that builds as the novel's characters misread its developments. Alex Segal has noted that Winnie Verloc's "conviction" that "things don't bear much looking into" signals her own lack of "inwardness" and "depth," so that, despite her fierce maternal love for Stevie, she is ethically vacant, as much implicated in her brother's death as Verloc (*SA*, 149).[96] This charge is rather strong, especially considering the text's implication that looking into things more, reading them and bringing them to light according to a model of public accountability, is an equally futile process. This double bind constitutes plot in the novel, or what amounts to the repeated failure of the hermeneutic code. In its allegorical function as a text within a text, and as an impressionistic oversynthesis, the face also symbolizes the hermeneutic code and its failure. Since reading is often coded as a visual act, this narrative failure underlines the problem of optics as ethics.

I have been arguing thus far that, in its illegibility, the oversynthesized face in *The Secret Agent* allegorizes the failure of impressionist "solidarity."[97] Historically and politically speaking, this face also challenges late nineteenth-century efforts of a crew of "professional readers" to concretize identity and fix personality.[98] In this vision, personality becomes a mere surface manifestation, further intensifying the foreignness of the face as an apparition. This defacement of the face by aspects of the interior it presumably represents is what makes it ineffaceable. Organized in this way, the face, in a rather skewed version of Levinasian ethics, "maintains" itself against the other.[99] In regard to the novel's metropolitan setting, the writing over of this impressionist oversynthesis opposes the abstraction and anesthesia of the metropolis while serving simultaneously as a "protective shield" that "binds" (in a Freudian sense) and anesthetizes the various shocks of urban life.[100] The face, to adopt Freud's lexicon, can be thought of as the "outermost surface" of the shield whose binding energies protect against trauma, the "special envelope or membrane resistant to stimuli."[101] Since most people are acutely conscious of the management of their own faces, the face acts as a defensive guard, and as Christina Britzolakis has suggested, impressionism is itself a response to a "neurological predicament" made most evident in the novel by the extremely sensitive Stevie.[102] Situated as a "metaphorical 'primitive' in relation to [a] metropolitan culture" characterized by the "homogenizing rationality of capitalism," Stevie is a "shock-receptor," unable to bind his protective shield to dispose of excess stimuli.[103] As he absorbs stimuli without disposing of them, Stevie becomes the isolated detail that, for both the reader and the urban spectator, stands out against the mass of other visual influences.

To recast this dynamic, we might return to Leonard and the idea of "strategies of delimitation," which allow characters to block some things from vision and see others, thus imposing some control over the "overwhelming stimulus of urban modernity."[104] Leonard argues that Joyce further builds connections between the successful and unsuccessful implementations of this strategy, as it may produce moments of correspondence between a particular "focus" and a subject's particular emotional state.[105] Similarly, Stevie's intensity as an impression in his own right arises from his extreme impressionability, his inability to successfully delimit his personal environment. This vulnerability, alongside the boy's intense concentration on visual detail, accounts for his neurological undoing in the novel. Stevie consistently oversteps these boundaries by displaying direct and unguarded correspondence between his facial expression and his affect.[106] He was a poor errand boy, likely to forget messages as "he contemplated open-mouthed" the "comedies of the streets" (SA, 7). This unguarded facial behavior is matched only by his verbal outbursts. Drawn by the "pathos and violence" of "fallen horses," he would "sometimes . . . shriek piercingly in a crowd, which disliked to be disturbed by sounds of distress in its quiet enjoyment of the national spectacle" (SA, 7). Unable to manage his bodily and verbal behavior, Stevie also cannot sustain the fiction required for easy participation in human sociality.

In an apparent reversal of Levinasian ethics, however, Stevie's inability to "maintai[n]" himself arguably makes him the novel's ethical center—though an absent, enigmatic one, which must be recounted from various perspectives.[107] But more in line with Levinasian ethics, we can interpret this very defenselessness as a resistance to the pointless intrusions of others. Stevie is the literal embodiment of the novel's critical deployment of melodramatic tropes and gestures; his emotions appear as surface configurations, but in contrast to melodramatic and physiognomic conventions, these emotions do not speak, or find a place in a coherent narrative palatable to human interlocutors. It's not that there is nothing behind Stevie's face, but that his face cannot be read according to the classificatory systems of those who observe it. As the novel's sacrificial lamb, Stevie embodies the hyperbole of melodramatic signification; he suggests a "stamp of meaning" that is at the same time characterized by a "discontinuity" or "imbalance" between the visual representation of his experience and the reality of his suffering.[108] In this sense, Ossipon's remarks about Lombroso notwithstanding, the physical excess of Stevie's embodied emotion invites but does not yield to a reading or interpretation, in which there is meaning behind a face. What might otherwise be read, and consequently narrated, is indeed compressed on the surface of the body into "facts—startling facts" (SA, 21).

In other words, Stevie is not a type but, as Joseph Valente has observed, "an anti-type of the idiot he is supposed to be."[109] Unreadable himself, Stevie does not produce readable writing, but rather draws circles, "innumerable circles, concentric, eccentric . . . a rendering of cosmic chaos, the symbolism of a mad art attempting the inconceivable" (SA, 39). Much like the actual observatory bombing, which could "not be laid hold of mentally," these drawings do not produce a coherent expression but circle chaotically. Valente has elaborated rather extensively on this artistic production, arguing that the drawings engage the tension between the "expression and reactive control of [Stevie's] embodied turbulence" and further link his "neurodiversity" to avant-garde modernist painting.[110] Drawing on "architecture" common to "the discursive construction of idiocy during the modern era" and the "discursive construction of autism spectrum disorder at the present time," Valente argues that the overly passionate nature of Stevie's "social investments" often limits his ability "to process, regulate or express with a normative degree of aplomb."[111] For example, when Stevie and Winnie accompany their mother to her new charity lodgings in a horse-drawn cab, he creates a public spectacle by responding hysterically to the cab driver's whipping of the emaciated horse. His "immoderate compassion" and "convulsive sympathy" for the horse lead him to denounce the condition of the animal as "Bad," "Poor," and a "Shame": "Being no skeptic, but a moral creature, he was in a manner at the mercy of his righteous passions" (SA, 139, 142, 141). Here, Stevie's morality is characterized by an immediate and *felt* relation to events, not an interpretive, narrative, or hermeneutic relation to them.

This immediate relation to expression also positions Stevie as the novel's model aesthete, at least by the standards of high modernism, which, like impressionist aesthetics (if one maintains the distinction), privileges surface over depth. To invoke Pound's *ABC of Reading* and its ideogrammic method, Stevie "KNOWS" without "ANY STUDY."[112] Like the young sculptor to whom Pound refers, Henri Gaudier-Brzeska, he is "accustomed to looking" not into but "at the real shape of things."[113] Accordingly, and as apparent in the horsewhipping incident, Stevie's engagements with the world are not always dialogic, but rather occur as actions, through a series of highly gestural enactments that repeatedly elide the meanings attributed to them. Here, the impression itself—embodied in Stevie's face—results from the subject's inability to adequately filter or delimit the chaotic stimulus of the surrounding urban environment, to construct for himself a harmonious (and normative) visual relation to the world. To return to Brooks, Stevie is part of the "text of muteness," where not only mute but also blind, paralytic, disfigured, maimed, and disabled characters are used to represent "extreme moral and physical conditions."[114] The horsewhipping scene is in effect a pantomime, and Stevie's "sympathy" is indeed "convulsive," excessively physical, much in contrast to his inarticulateness (SA, 139). A melodramatic "overstatement," the scene privileges the primitivism of Stevie's gesture over verbal expression.[115] However, unlike traditional melodrama, there is no real resolution to the moral or ethical conflict staged in the scene. On one hand, the text seems to illustrate Stevie's loss of innocence and faith in the moral order, which he believes to be good. But such a loss of innocence requires that Stevie hold the appropriate disdain for human cruelty by placing blame on the correct person rather than deflecting it. Thus, Stevie believes that the cabman has whipped his horse because he is poor and has children to feed. The guilty party must therefore be the police, who have not adequately protected them. But Winnie stifles the possibility of moral resolution, what might have been overstated in the scene had it been allowed to reach full narrative predication, by manipulating Stevie's moral innocence, assuring him that the police are there not to protect the cabman but "so that them as have nothing shouldn't take anything away from them who have" (*SA*, 144). For Winnie, the implausibility of Stevie's account must not be allowed to persist, even at the expense of saying nothing.

Saying All or Nothing

Rather than "say all," in the Romantic vein of Rousseau and Sade, these characters shut down narrative (Stevie involuntarily and Winnie more willfully) as they make inaccurate moral judgments of others.[116] Verloc's belief in his domestic security accompanies an absolute trust in his wife made possible by her "philosophical, almost disdainful incuriosity," which facilitates all sorts of lies (*SA*, 196). These untruths come to a head during the novel's domestic finale, when Winnie, realizing her husband's responsibility for her brother's death, murders him with a carving knife. She abandons her passive "incuriosity" when faced with the painful necessity of constructing a narrative around the mangled bits of Stevie's body: "Blown to small bits: limbs, gravel, clothing, bones, splinters—all mixed up together" (*SA*, 174). This is not Bertillon's "body of modernity," equally fragmented but expertly parsed and identifiable, but rather a metaphor itself for the inconceivable, what cannot be narrated or reconstructed.[117] Mourning this body, Winnie makes herself unreadable. When Verloc attempts to "face her grief," she shields her face with her hands: "You might look at a fellow," he implores, feeling it "impossible to talk to any purpose with a woman whose face one cannot see" (*SA*, 191, 193). Winnie's face, a "white-washed wall with no writing on it," is, for Verloc, a "blankness to run out and dash your head against" (*SA*, 200, 203). The drama then intensifies when Winnie emerges from her room, veiled in mourning, frustrating Verloc to the point that he "dragged the veil off, unmasking a still unreadable face" (*SA*, 212). Ironically, veils are designed to mask inappropriately readable faces, but Winnie is "in her own house, like a masked and mysterious visitor of impenetrable intentions" (*SA*, 211). In donning this veil, Winnie both conforms to and evades melodramatic representation, as if in conscious resistance to the stage on which she performs, reinforcing rather than resolving the moral inconceivability of her brother's death. Her unreadable, mute face points to her own recognition that any narrative—and Verloc offers her plenty of talk in his attempt to excuse his actions and "face her grief"—will be ultimately ineffective (SA, 191).

Due to this impasse, Verloc is compelled to read Winnie's face, yet he is unable to read it at all. This problem with reading, coupled with his own investment in a domestic stage that is separate but always at risk of public encroachment, underlines his own melodramatic understanding of domestic life. Significantly, Verloc's "happiness" produces this false sense of domestic invulnerability to public exposure. Nonetheless, Verloc also exhibits the melodramatic need to expose, to say all, when the text divulges his desire to confess his deed to his wife at bedtime (SA, 149). Winnie has no use for Verloc's narrative, which rests on the wrongful assumption of mutual reciprocity, even though later she is relieved at having made a "full confession" of her crime to Ossipon (SA, 232). Verloc then fatally errs in his desire to give his wife a voice that might materialize through her obscured face—an intention that she has never possessed. For Winnie, as Verloc admits, was a "woman of very few words" (SA, 203).

Winnie's muteness here recalls the more "primitive" posture of Kurtz's African bride, complete with sounds of "wailing and lamentation," though they exist only in her head (SA, 205). Indeed, critics have linked Winnie's silence, her slide into a primitive prelinguistic past that underlines her genetic connection to her brother's stuttering verbality, to Conrad's endorsement of "Lombrosian regression."[118] Such a connection is clear, but the text looks ironically, even politically, at this atavistic decline into the "deaf-and-dumb sulks" of which Verloc complains (SA, 213). Verloc, significantly, can speak but not act. In contrast, Winnie refuses to speak, such that her impulsive and gestural *act* supplants her voice. She murders her husband with a domestic instrument, the carving knife with which he had been previously slicing meat, which he eats "ravenously without restraint and dignity" (SA, 209). This seemingly melodramatic act paradoxically signals the undoing of melodramatic structure in the novel—as expressed in the failure of narrative and its inability to bring about moral resolution. Winnie's murderous response to her husband's intimate address—made as he reclines on the sofa—exposes the hollowness of Verloc's particular moral belief in "familiar sacredness" and its accompanying narrative (SA, 149). Winnie recognizes this particular narrative failure, as well as the other ways narrative fails in the novel. Unable to account for her husband's deception or to connect her brother's "mangled limbs" to the apparition of his "decapitated head," which "they had to gather . . . up with a shovel," Winnie responds accordingly with an action that is primarily gestural in its irreducibility to language (SA, 215).

In Winnie's murder of Verloc, action trumps narrative dimension and individual psychology, making the "prior writing" behind the face, as Fried claims, "irretrievable."[119] Such an interpretation appears to work against both the operations of melodrama and any sort of "reasoned" memory practice of the type advocated by Bertillon, positing no conclusive correspondence between the inner dimensions of the subject and surface expression.[120] Yet Fried remarks that in Conrad this fundamental "thematic of blankness" is indeed legible.[121] Almayer's face must be "made blank," much in the way that Winnie Verloc's face must be covered with a veil.[122] But in contrast to the other impressionistic faces in *The Secret Agent*, which are, to one extent or the other, written over and oversynthesized, Winnie's face is *really* blank. Consequently, I would suggest that *The Secret Agent* diverges from *Almayer's Folly* in that Winnie Verloc's blank face is not a disfiguring of a "prior" representation but a means of questioning the belief that such representation can ever be read. Ultimately, Winnie's face represents the larger ethical problematic of a hermeneutically based narrative project, the question of how an ethical relation might be understood in the absence of a scheme of readability, or facing, and in the absence of persons, or at least our humanist understanding of them.

As I have suggested, the novel's investigation into these questions accompanies its own reflexive staging of impressionist aesthetics and its rearticulation of melodrama as a mode, one that examines illegibility as an answer to a "practical problem of experience," in particular, "suffering."[123] Given the novel's investment in the history of physiognomic practice, the detection of personal identity, and the conventions of a form or mode, we can also look to this context in determining the novel's historical parameters. This reading, however, is also transhistorical and, in considering the relevance of Levinas's ethics to *The Secret Agent*, demonstrates both the usefulness and limits of such models. However illegible, faces, like most texts, still compel us to read them. In this regard, and as Fried asks of the novel, how might the text's many "unreadable surfaces" signal something more than a "triumph of materiality" characterized by a mere turn toward literary phenomenality without content or meaning?[124] Must we not still read texts and symbols, despite their failure to follow through with their intentions, their failure to mean or express anything? If, as Fried suggests, there is actually a degree of legibility in impressionist erasure, how are we to read?

While the novel experiments with blankness and illegibility in its self-conscious staging as a melodrama—complete with a narrator/physiognomist claiming expertise in the observation of signs—I want to argue that Winnie's blankness is ultimately legible in her turn to action. This is the action for which Verloc's superiors deem him unfit, the action that is seemingly incompatible with content, depths, or voice—that is needed to produce "startling facts" (SA, 21). Facts cannot be read, interpreted, or even narrated. Thus, it is important to note that Winnie's facial erasure here is not the result of her ethical vacancy or of her having been read or "marked over." Oddly enough, Winnie's face is "made blank" by her own intention, not against it.[125] While conforming to the display rules of bourgeois society, Winnie makes herself into an epistemological uncertainty, through a self-inflected act of effacement that connects her own trajectory to that of her brother, the "person unknown," whose dismembered, decapitated body cannot be identified by a face (SA, 74). As with Stevie—recognizable only via a name tag she has sewn on his coat—Winnie's "being," to repeat the Levinasian scenario, does not appear in her face. The "small, tiny fact" of the name tag, the literal manifestation of the "startling facts" Vladimir demands much earlier in the text, metonymically stands in for a face. As the sort of mnemonic device that was central to Bertillon's memory practice, the name tag actualizes a reversal, in which something represents a face, not the other way around. Such a reversal compresses both action and content in the narrative, much in the way the story of Winnie's eventual suicide is contained within a paragraph in a newspaper (SA, 21). After the murder, she meets Ossipon, who recognizes her and agrees to accompany her to France, but later abandoning her when he jumps off of a moving train. Significantly, he invokes Lombroso while gazing "as no lover ever gazed at his mistress's face," simultaneously analyzing its resemblance to her brother's (SA, 245). As a seeming penance for this desertion, he literally carries the paper scrap of her narrative in his pocket. "Menaced by this thing," this fact, he reads and rereads its last sentence compulsively (SA, 253).

As a proairetic overwriting of the hermeneutic, Winnie's "impenetrable mystery," "pulsating wrongfully to the rhythm of journalistic phrases," represents a reversal of conventional plot (SA, 256); the novel does not so much do away with ethical concepts like intention and motivation as align them with action rather than content. And so Ossipon—in a final fight against the metonymic abstraction of Winnie's story into nothing more than "a small tiny fact," a piece of newspaper, much like the label on Stevie's coat—attempts, quite like a Bertillon-trained detective, to "lay hold mentally" of a dying woman's face, from the perspective of onlookers; "by what they could see of her face she seemed to them to be dying" (*SA*, 254).[126] Perhaps this compulsive reading and rereading of the blank face, of a "person unknown," as an action that yields no conclusive narrative thread constitutes an ethics and politics for Conrad. This is not a "surface reading," with its focus on what is "apprehensible" in a text, nor is it a "symptomatic reading," which seeks to expose a latent truth that the text does not make explicit.[127] However masochistically, Ossipon has embraced the discomfort of reading a blank face, in recognition of the impenetrability and foreignness of the other. Such an ethics, which accepts the essential discomfort of illegibility and nondisclosure, contests the Freudian project of "making conscious the most hidden recesses of the mind" in favor of the *act* of reading and looking closely.[128] To a degree, this action resembles a Levinasian ethics, but one that operates within the historical parameters of impressionist fiction—which, in aiming to make one "see," is itself a theory of reading. The face cannot be read, and yet the project of reading it is a necessary defense against the overwriting of narrative, its constriction to pure action.

4 Modernist Prosopopoeia; or, Making Faces

> He had been a remarkably handsome man; still was, on one side of his face. If anything, his injuries threw the beauty of his remaining features into sharper relief. He reminded her of some of the "fragments" they used to draw at the Slade, where so often a chipped nose or broken lip seemed to give the face a poignancy that the undamaged original might have lacked. It disturbed her, this aesthetic response to wounds that should have inspired nothing but pity.
>
> —Pat Barker, *Toby's Room*, 2012

> Though I have seen my head, grown slightly bald
> brought in upon a platter
> I am no prophet—and here's no great matter.
>
> —T. S. Eliot, "The Love Song of J. Alfred Prufrock," 1917

T. S. Eliot's "The Love Song of J. Alfred Prufrock" (1917) is a specifically modernist commentary on prosopopoeia, the lyrical act of face making that, in its most basic function, confers voice onto a silent or absent entity. Indeed, Prufrock's famous admission, that "it is impossible to say just what I mean," attends an anxiety about his face as it articulates "what [one] mean[s]," generating the famous lines of false assurance: "There will be time, there will be time / To prepare a face to meet the faces that you meet."[1] He also stresses the likeness of this predicament to the beheading of John the Baptist, observing his severed, aging head, "brought in upon a platter," as it represents his inability to speak or prophesy with authority.[2] In this case, decapitation is a sign of impotence and failure; one must "prepare" a face that withstands the damaging gaze of other faces. Since the face is a primary means by which we recognize others as individuals and "personalities," this literal beheading is a testament to the subject's (and the poet's) loss of authority. But as Eliot elaborates in his essay "Tradition and the Individual Talent" (1919), this erasure does not compromise the poetic vocation but instead contributes to its success. In advancing his well-known doctrine of "impersonality," Eliot asserts that the "progress of an artist is a continual self-sacrifice, a continual extinction of personality."[3] However, it's the state of Prufrock's head, looming about him as a lost, even abject, object, that underlines the difficulty of such an "escape from personality."[4]

As seen through the story of John the Baptist, "The Love Song of J. Alfred Prufrock" also highlights the potential violence of prosopopoeia. Anyone who has seen Giovanni di Paolo's fifteenth-century depiction of the apostle's decapitation, *The Beheading of John the Baptist*, known for its shocking physiological accuracy, will find themselves unable to look away from the site of the wound spurting jets of blood, as well as the realistic, haloed head of the executed, fallen with precision on its gold plate. This chapter is concerned not only with this violence but also, as it relates to more literal models of facial construction, with prosopopoeia's more restorative function of "mobiliz[ing]," much in the tradition of art forms like caricature or portraiture, a *view* of other subjects, of other faces.[5] I suggest here that Prufrock's anxiety about "facial loss" is common to a modernist facial imaginary in which the retreat from the face's figuration—itself an "escape from personality"—compels a return back to the face toward an expressive ideal of likeness that mediates what we can or cannot view in another subject, or another face.[6]

In this chapter I follow this tension—between refacement and defacement, the making of faces and the horror of their loss—as it appears in explicit modernist pronouncements about the aesthetics of facial construction and in the experience of facial injury and disfigurement that helped define the "social and cultural legacy" of the First World War.[7] The war generated, as Suzannah Biernoff has observed, a "fantasy of repair," inscribing the face in novel and shocking ways into the terrain of modernity.[8] Indeed, the sheer numbers of men with facial injuries—sustained en masse because of the conditions of trench warfare and new innovations in weapons technology—prompted a "design response" that, as Katherine Feo has argued, reflected the "implicit belief" in the necessity of "hiding or covering" their injured faces.[9] Feo sees this rehabilitation effort as socially conservative, fueled by the fear that men with severe facial mutilation would be economically dependent on the state. Julie Powell has argued similarly that the impetus for producing prosthetic facial masks, like those designed by American sculptor Anna Coleman Ladd in her Studio for Portrait Masks, which opened in Paris in 1918, actually reflected a normative ideal of masculinity in which French veterans—seen through an aesthetic backdrop of Graeco-Roman statuary—were aligned with "the myth of a stable, essential France."[10] The inflexible copper masks, Powell contends, attempted both to recover a soldier's original face and to verify its maleness, signaling a "quality of pastness" while simultaneously endeavoring to shroud the real visual marks of "destructive change."[11]

These claims about the conservative nature of facial restoration and its relation to traditional masculinity notwithstanding, I offer here a quite different frame for considering the wounded or disfigured face. As David Lubin has observed, though the determination to use prosthetic masks as a way of hiding facial disfigurement or the disfigured themselves coincided in many ways with the interest in masking that would come to occupy so many modernist writers and artists, including Eliot, Pound, and Picasso, it seemed "out of step with the strong modernist spirit of candor that arose at the end of the war."[12] Indeed, the inflexible, uncomfortable masks—which were also laborious and time-consuming to produce—offered only a slight contribution to the overall problem of facial disfigurement in a war with millions of casualties.[13] Furthermore, as inanimate devices designed to be worn on a live face, the masks quickly became obsolete as the recipients' actual faces changed with age.

With Lubin's observations about masking in mind, I reframe this problem of likeness within the context of modernist statements about the face, more specifically as they appear in Mina Loy's *Auto-Facial-Construction* (1919) and in the critical context that formed around the construction of Henri Gaudier-Brzeska's sculpture *The Hieratic Head of Ezra Pound* (1914). With both cases, I examine the practice of prosopopoeia and the more general critical context of face making to articulate a different set of questions that are relevant to our viewing and valuing of the wounded face. More particularly, I ask what aesthetic principals and ethical considerations are at work in the representation of disfigured faces, in their reconstructions, and, furthermore, in our looking at them. By moving between a more detailed elaboration of the concept of prosopopoeia as it appears in deconstructionist criticism from the 1980s and 1990s and close analysis of the surgical and visual record of facial restoration during World War I, I recast a critical binary that inadvertently concretizes the authenticity of the war-damaged face against what is seen as a normative, if not dishonest, effort to reconstruct it. This schema,

I argue, excludes many of the existential realities that typically characterize our relation to our own faces and their social, emotional, and expressive functions. Highly relevant to these issues, and as indicated in the example from Pat Barker's 2012 novel *Toby's Room*, is the question of how a damaged anatomy might display a deep structure of aesthetic expression, or form, as well as the ethics of our viewing of it.

While I will return to the subject of Ladd's portrait masks, I discuss in more detail Harold Gillies's pioneering surgical work, which radically changed the way surgeons approached facial wounds and, in the spirit of the prosopopoeia I invoke, involved visualizing the wounded face in every conceivable way. This work developed at the same time that the "public visual record of the war" attempted to exclude veterans with facial disfigurations.[14] An amateur painter himself, Gillies brought art to plastic surgery and saw it as an aesthetic enterprise, viewing the face and skin in their sculptural and tactile dimensions, as having both interior and exterior surfaces that come together in a precise, structural arrangement. Regarding Gillies's process, *Toby's Room* has likely made more familiar the story of his collaborator, Slade Professor of Fine Art Henry Tonks—who had trained as a surgeon—and his wartime charge of drawing the faces of facially wounded soldiers at Queen Mary's Hospital, Sidcup. Even though Tonks, the esteemed teacher of well-known modernists such as Augustus John, Paul Nash, and Wyndham Lewis, produced work that was considered old-fashioned and methodologically out of line with the aims of avant-garde modernism, I consider his viscerally shocking pastel drawings, as well as Gillies's own writings about plastic surgery, most notably in his influential tome *Plastic Surgery of the Face* (1920), in light of the same aesthetic concerns about likeness and expression that, I argue, motivate Loy and Gaudier-Brzeska.

My argument about this commonality centers on Loy's concept of "facial integrity"—a totalizing ideal that values what the face expresses and its presumed faithfulness to the subject.[15] In their modernist examples of prosopopoeia, both Gaudier-Brzeska and Loy recharacterize the meaning of likeness, what it means to look like oneself or be seen as oneself, as it relates both to the actual knowledge of presumably unique individuals and to the expressive scripts that determine personality types, whereby one person may seem more like another. Originally circulated as a pamphlet advertising her exercises for harmonizing the contours of one's personality with one's face, *Auto-Facial-Construction* advances a modern "beauty culture" that consolidates an individual organized around categories of personality and subjectivity (*AFC*, 165). I pair Loy's treatise with an example of literal facial construction, Gaudier-Brzeska's sculpture *The Hieratic Head of Ezra Pound*, completed in early 1914, only a year and a half before the young French sculptor's death in the trenches of World War I. While the sculpture precedes the First World War, I suggest that Gaudier-Brzeska's own critical vocabulary—in particular, his ideas about "sculptural feeling" or "ability" as an "organizational" process—coincides with Gillies's explicitly articulated approach to the "strange new art" of plastic surgery.[16]

These questions about representative figuration and likeness are also crucial for thinking about the ethics of both viewing and reconstructing a wounded face, and this chapter indeed underlines affinities between medical advancements in facial restoration and modernist aesthetics during the First World War. Aaron Sheehan has offered a similarly motivated analysis that attempts to read Ladd's production of portrait masks within the historical contexts of vorticism and surrealism, underlining Ladd's own casting of herself as a dealer of "material and . . . spirit" as evidence for an undeveloped Bergsonian view.[17] Given that Ladd left little to no written evidence of having engaged with aesthetic trends or avant-garde movements, I would suggest that Ladd's self-assessment reflects more broadly her training as a portrait artist than any specific philosophical outlook. As I will elaborate, the goal of fusing "material" with "spirit" is essential to traditional portrait production, and this aim, regardless of how each artist sought to reformulate it, also binds the articulations of avant-garde modernism I discuss here. As Hugh Kenner has noted of Lewis's painting, vorticism attempted to move energy into "conjunction" with form, attending to "an unaccountable array of elements, all interacting."[18] And while I do read Gaudier-Brzeska's artistic statements within the context of some of the aims of vorticism, as well as through the filter of Pound's, and later Kenner's, characterization of both the sculptor and the movement, Gaudier-Brzeska's actual sculptural vision cannot be equated with vorticism outright. Like Loy's regime for "facial integrity," it attempted to arrange discordant and exaggerated elements into sensuous totality, a form, or likeness, of something or someone (*AFC*, 165). I thus argue that common to the more radical aims of each artist is a more traditional value for figurative representation and verisimilitude that was likely an essential part of their training and experience as artists.[19]

The basic idea of likeness as a pliant form of surface expression—capable of being stretched, deformed, distorted, and refigured, but "caught" nonetheless—is essential to the account of the modern face that I construct in this book.[20] In the case of late nineteenth-century images of Oscar Wilde, I have argued, caricature, itself a portrait form, operates by deforming likeness to the extent that the subject is potentially no longer recognizable outside of what is known about their "expression." The question of how one is like oneself, one's face, or one's photograph also motivates the plot of Dreiser's *Sister Carrie*, inspiring a particular form of gendered labor that, I have suggested, abstracts the subject and disfigures the face, but certainly not beyond recognition. At the back of each of these claims is the idea of portraiture, which, as Catherine Soussloff observes, was understood to be a social genre and upheld "the idea of the singular individual in relationship to others for whom recognition is essential."[21] Furthermore, portraits are iconic in that there is a "projection of interiority onto the depicted person."[22] In earlier portraits the "identity" depicted in a portrait was a matter of "individual virtue," but this was replaced in more modern portraiture, Soussloff argues, by the concept of "personality."[23]

Sarah Blackwood also characterizes portraiture as a "method" of representing "surface likeness" that sought to "make metaphysical qualities visible," providing "everyday people" with "new ways of imagining themselves, and the characters that portraits conveyed, as subjects with interiority."[24] Crucial to this formulation of the portrait, I would add, is its projection of a fundamental notion of identity based on a subject's perceived recognition of their own or other's faces. As I have argued of Wilde's *The Picture of Dorian Gray*, Dorian obsessively rereads his portrait for an indication of his intentions and motivations and, further, to understand what his emotions "feel like."[25] As Silvan Tomkins has argued, our identification with our emotions and affects, understanding what they "feel like," is key to our "awareness" of our own faces and those of others.[26] In the texts I examine here, this same concern for "facial awareness"—regarding the myriad ways reconstructed faces might reveal a likeness to the more inchoate and often intangible aspects of human emotional and expressive experience—motivates a prosopopoeia that also reimagines the portrait form.[27]

Mina Loy's *Auto-Facial-Construction*

As with examples in the previous chapters on Wilde, Dreiser, and Conrad, I situate the works I examine here within a history of physiognomic inquiry that, to return to François Delaporte, divided the interior and exterior of the human subject to engender a new "psychological and physiological complexity," a new subject: a humanist individual constructed around the project of reading the presumed connections between the "soul's emotions" and "their bodily signs."[28] Such a physiognomic reading project also galvanized traditional portraiture and its attempt to forge in an image a sense of likeness to a recognizable person, and the more modern instruction Loy provides in *Auto-Facial-Construction* about how to most accurately perform an idealized portrait of one's self is no exception. Loy's program for the rejuvenation of the face not only reflects her effort to promote and capitalize on her system of facial exercises but also advances her belief that the face can be manually stimulated against the distortion of aging and, further, managed to solicit a more or less accurate reading from others. The more radical premise behind *Auto-Facial-Construction*, however, is that we look most like ourselves when we are not ourselves, naturally—and that, through manual stimulation, both women and men can guard themselves against the potential loss of energy that accompanies their own face-work, their labor to be equal to their own faces.

With this claim, I return to Lois Tyson's argument that women in naturalist fiction, in particular Edith Wharton's Lily Bart, are "wasted" by their own "transcendental project," their "labor to escape existential inwardness through self-reification" and "self-aestheticizing."[29] Loy engages this same problem of self-production and self-aestheticization in *Auto-Facial-Construction*, promoting the face as a sculptural ideal, an aesthetic arrangement of planes and surfaces, subject to willful management, hygiene, and revitalization, that guards itself against the exploitative reading of others. This work, however, does not "waste" the face, but rather stimulates a more transparent, harmonious relationship between the work a face does and one's feelings about it. To take Gaudier-Brzeska's terms, articulated most forcefully in *Blast I*, Wyndham Lewis's paean to the vorticist movement, "sculptural feeling is the appreciation of masses in relation."[30] Sculpturally speaking, then, the face also brings the various parts of the human subject—the feeling parts and the speaking parts—into a surface relation that, like a portrait, verifies an individual with specific qualities and virtues to a viewing audience. For Loy, it does so, to quote *Auto-Facial-Construction* more fully, by reframing the parameters of personality so that one can "look like" oneself:

> The face is our most potent symbol of personality.
>
> The adolescent has facial contours in harmony with the conditions of his soul. Day by day the new interests and activities of modern life are prolonging the youth of our souls, and day by day, we are becoming more aware of the necessity

for our faces to express that youthfulness, for the sake of psychic logic. Different systems of beauty culture have compromised with our inherent right, not only to "be ourselves" but to "look like ourselves," by producing a facial contour in middle age, which does duty as a "well preserved appearance." (*AFC*, 165)

The literal technique of bodily reform and innovation Loy advances in the pamphlet reformulates the basic premise of Wilde's *The Picture of Dorian Gray*, where the youthful beauty of Dorian's anatomically real face transcends the tainted squalor of his soul. In contrast, Loy contends that our faces must keep pace with the "youth" of our souls, which has been prolonged by "the new interests and activities of modern life" (*AFC*, 165). This is Loy's concept of "facial integrity," a "basic principle" that reflects her "understanding of the human face," developed from "years of specialized interest in physiognomy as an artist" (*AFC*, 165-66). Explicitly promoting "reconstruction," Loy's argument hinges on an ideal of seamless expression that is literalized in the idea of the portrait, where the body exteriorizes the soul into a recognizable, individualized identity.

In Loy's program, however, these signifying elements are overtly subject to artificial manipulation and mediation. This facial management is not "preservation," which offers "at best, merely a pleasing parody of youth," but is rather more radical, in that the "subtle element of the ludicrous inherent in facial transformation by time, is the signpost of discouragement pointing along the path of the evolution of personality" (*AFC*, 165). Loy's practice of auto-facial-construction is a bodily intervention that, as Tim Armstrong has noted, reflects the desire to "render [the body] part of modernity by techniques which may be biological, mechanical, or behavioural."[31] Given the insistence of Loy's entreaty against aging gracefully, her seemingly enthusiastic embrace of "modern life" as it prolongs the soul's youthfulness is not without ambivalence. If people have no "power to communicate" or express their actual feelings, what does modernity offer them? While attractive, the "new interests and activities of modern life" exacerbate the fragility of "facial integrity" and its claim to an unmediated relation between the soul and its bodily expression. Loy asks more directly, "For to what end is our experience of life, if deprived of a fitting aesthetic revelation in our faces? One distorted muscle causes a fundamental disharmony in self-expression, for ... if the original form of the face (intrinsic symbol of personality) has been effaced in muscular transformation, they have lost the power to communicate their true personalities to others and all expression of sentiment is veiled in pathos" (*AFC*, 165). Loy's thought here reflects that of an aesthetician like Diderot, who argued that, in painting, "displacing a facial feature even by as much as a hair [could] make the difference between beauty and disfigurement," as well as Simmel's later claim that the "aesthetic effect" of the face is ruined "by the disfigurement of only one of its elements."[32] Loy's vision is similar: as the "muscular transformations" of aging efface the "original form of the face," depriving "men and women" of harmonious "self-expression," they can no longer "communicate their true personalities to others and all expression of sentiment is veiled in pathos" (*AFC*, 165). In actuality, modern life and "partially distorted muscles" have disempowered these subjects, weakening their personalities and softening "the original form of the face" (*AFC*, 165). As a remedy, Loy urges women and men to "become masters of their facial destiny" through a series of willful, mechanical movements aimed at revitalizing the muscular attachments of the face (*AFC*, 165).[33]

Loy views aging as both a literal and metaphysical disfigurement but does not really specify how such changes to the form of the face may be viewed differently in women than men. There is the further indication that an aging face could become a caricature of itself, producing only the slightest if not "ludicrous" glimpse of the subject's actual "experience of life" (*AFC*, 165). For Loy, and for Eliot's Prufrock as well, aging catalyzes the loss of expressive power and, consequently, personality—making "facial integrity" less viable. In this case, personality is related to the power to amplify and project oneself both vocally and visually.[34] Both Christina Walter and Carolyn Burke note Loy's explicit preoccupation with F. W. H. Myers's *Human Personality and Its Survival of Bodily Death*, published posthumously in 1903, and its claim that personality could transcend the body. Myers's work represents an increasing cultural fascination not with the success or authority of personality but with its superficiality and likelihood to fail as a mode of self-presentation. Asserting that such personality failures are productive, Myers argues that human personality is by nature a "much more *modifiable* complex of forces than is commonly assumed."[35]

Prosopopoeia; or, Face as Defacing

This idea of personality as both weak and strong, inherently "*modifiable*," links the current discussion more clearly to the concept of prosopopoeia.[36] Beyond its most basic function—which is to give voice to an absent or deceased entity—the actions of prosopopoeia become rather difficult to generalize. James Paxson, for example, examines the exclusively female prosopopoeia in classical and medieval personifications, where the often misogynistic trope of "the talkative woman" was the "literalized manifestation of prosopopoeia's lexical character," linking woman to "riot, chaos, and uncontrolled speech."[37] Given this history, Paxson asserts, "prosopopoeia involves making not only artificial humanoid agents out of abstractions, but the insistent making of *speakers*."[38] Loy's manifesto literally reinforces this function of prosopopoeia, advertising the willful reconstruction of the face as an artificial and "humanoid" means of outwitting nature and resisting the abstracting powers of age. And while Paxson's commentary allows for a reading of *Auto-Facial-Construction* as a deliberate response to this "talkative woman," Loy's address to both "men and women" (*AFC*, 165) suggests that she is appropriating prosopopoeia in the more general project of taming and disciplining speech, a means of restructuring the personality to create effective speakers and make talk more powerful by saying "just what I mean."[39]

The point of Loy's prosopopoeia is also to recover the "original form" or outline of the face as a means of resisting the formlessness that attends age, the lost power to "communicate" our "true personalities to others" (*AFC*, 165). Conjured into being through various forms of mechanical stimulation, this "form," I have argued, promises increased vocative strength and, consequently, a new form of personality made possible through the performance of the face as a living portrait. It is important to remember that Loy's pamphlet is, quite literally, an advertisement. In contrast to a poem such as "The Love Song of J. Alfred Prufrock," *Auto-Facial-Construction* broadcasts its mission with unwavering confidence. The boastful, actively articulated declarations in the piece—"I will instruct" and "I understand"—solidify the speaking "I" (*AFC*, 165). There is no need to call to an "other," as in apostrophe, to help constitute that "I." As a result, Loy's prosopopoeia counters the general tendency of the trope to create relations of insecurity, even paranoia (as with Prufrock).

Such insecurity arises because prosopopoeia, as Paxson describes it, is "the linguistic image of the mind's projective tendencies."[40] Paxson follows Paul de Man's account of the term, as do most contemporary discussions of prosopopoeia, crediting him with transforming "what was once an isolated trope" into a "universal cognitive modality."[41] Adequately summarizing the argument de Man advances in *The Rhetoric of Romanticism* is a rather difficult undertaking. Indeed, almost all of the essays in the 1985 special issue of *Yale French Studies* devoted to "The Lesson of Paul de Man"—including those by

Barbara Johnson, Jonathan Culler, Shoshana Felman, and Michael Riffaterre—commit themselves in some capacity to this task. The most oft-quoted description of the term appears in the essay "Autobiography as De-facement," where prosopopoeia is defined as "the fiction of an apostrophe to an absent, deceased, or voiceless entity, which posits the possibility of the latter's reply and confers upon it the power of speech. Voice assumes mouth, eye, and finally face, a chain that is manifest in the etymology of the trope's name, *prosopon poien*, to confer a mask or a face (*prosopopon*)."[42] Within this fiction, the face is a "totalizing power," establishing a relationship between the internal and external dimensions of a subject; it arranges its component parts—mouth, eyes—into a coherent whole.[43] But this coherence is contradictory, in that giving voice to something absent, lost, or deceased is, to follow de Man's analysis, simultaneously an act of effacement, of "disfiguration," in which the promise of "preservation" and individual distinction recedes in the weight of the face's "undo[ing] of its own claims."[44] How does the face "un[do] its own claims?" For Loy the totality of "psychic logic" between the face and soul is so precarious that its loss amounts to an undoing, a diminished power "to communicate [one's] true personalit[y] to others" (*AFC*, 165). Any such "disharmony" between the interior and exterior creates friction, so that one does not seem "like" oneself, and thus actualizes the face's, and the personality's, undoing. The contradiction here is that Loy's remedy for this problem, the restoration of "psychic logic" through her method of "conservation," is itself a fiction, an artificial undoing of the face's natural state in exchange for its "original form" (*AFC*, 165).

For de Man, as for Loy, the contradiction of prosopopoeia reflects its role as a "'*speaking* face,' the locus of speech, the necessary condition for the existence of articulated language."[45] In de Man's account, this imagined face also consolidates a speaker, a subject. De Man's reading of Wordsworth's *The Prelude* examines this totalizing power of the face as it first gains meaning through the inscription of the eye, which displaces the mother's breast as the object of the infant's gaze and as the medium for establishing kinship and human discourse: "man can address and face other men, within life or beyond the grave, because he has a face, but he has a face only because he partakes of a mode of discourse that is neither entirely natural nor entirely human. The encounter between mind and earth (or heaven) is therefore not itself a dialogue or even . . . a listening . . . but a mute scene of looking, the mind gazing upon a speaking face."[46] In Eliot's "Love Song," Prufrock's terror arises from this "mute scene of looking," a prosopopoeiac making of a face that is explicitly "not . . . a dialogue."[47] Both Wordsworth's and Eliot's speakers fixate on the power of the eye as it establishes a linguistic relation but simultaneously disables the speaker's ability to define and narrate that relation. In the well-known lines from "The Love Song"—"And I have known the eyes already, known them all— / the eyes that fix you in a formulated phrase"—the invasive eyes accompany a face, and consequently a voice, that formulates the speaker's own face linguistically as a "phrase."[48] Because there was not sufficient time for self-making, "to prepare a face to meet the faces that you meet," the faces that he meets apostrophically will his own face and, consequently, voice into being, usurping his ability to articulate what he "means."[49] In other words, the speaker's inability to verbally articulate his "meaning" as a subject leads to his visual reduction and formulation as an object. In contrast to *Auto-Facial-Construction*'s urgent call that people become masters of their facial destiny, the face or "eyes" in this poem do not so much consolidate a speaker as underscore the fragility, even impotence, of voice. Indeed, the poem stages the dilemma of "face-making" as it disfigures and effaces, rendering the living dead and dumb. This dumbness haunts Prufrock's perpetual "indecisions" and "revisions," his inability to authoritatively claim his own face before others have made it a linguistic object and surface, "formulated," "sprawling," and "wriggling" on the wall.[50]

In de Man's account of prosopopoeia, the speaker's gaze animates its object, essentially asking for its reply, which, in return, silences the speaker, striking them "dumb."[51] J. Hillis Miller examines the ethical questions surrounding these chiasmatic shifts in his 1990 study *Versions of Pygmalion*. For Miller, prosopopoeia, most paradigmatically illustrated in Pygmalion's love of the statue he has made, also characterizes the act of reading; necessary for storytelling, it is essential to what the author, narrator, and reader of a text do. Anytime someone reads a text, they create a "seemingly living person(s)" out of dead words.[52] Such a performance of reading occasions "fragmentation," "mutilation," and "dismemberment," as prosopopoeia does not project the "wholeness of a self . . . but fragments that stand for a whole."[53] Prosopopoeia is thus intrinsically violent and artificial, presupposing, as in "The Love Song of J. Alfred Prufrock," the loss of whatever it resurrects. The ethics of prosopopoeia are therefore complicated, and Miller returns to these questions throughout the book. In reading, as in the act of prosopopoeia, there is the ethical work of potentially "getting the text right" and taking responsibility for it, but there is also the capacity for violent forms of duplicity in our invention of persons.[54]

Henri Gaudier-Brzeska and *The Hieratic Head of Ezra Pound*

The modernist sculpture to which I now turn, *The Hieratic Head of Ezra Pound*, is a monumental prosopopoeia that, I argue, guards the living from death and other forms of violent invention by divesting the face of the language that would undo it. As a deliberate misrecognition, the constructed face still seeks to project a form of expressive likeness to its subject. As with Loy's program for the artificial rejuvenation of the face, where one looks most like oneself when one is naturally not oneself, Pound both praised and defended the finished sculpture not as it reproduced his face but as an expression of his character. In his account of the sculptor's life and work, *A Memoir of Gaudier-Brzeska*, which, first published in 1916, is part homage to the fallen soldier as victim of the "war waste" and part fervid articulation of his own vorticist theory of art, Pound writes, "A kindly journalist 'hopes' that it does not look like me. It does not. It was not intended to. It is infinitely more hieratic. It has infinitely more of strength and dignity than my face will ever possess."[55] Gaudier-Brzeska had earlier affirmed his intentions to Pound: "You understand it will not look like you, it *will . . . not . . . look . . . like you*. It will be the expression of certain emotions I get from your character."[56] Critics have typically framed Gaudier-Brzeska's declaration in terms of the heavily masculinized rhetoric and aims of the vorticist avant-garde, in particular, Pound's own interests and anxieties, even though, as I note earlier, Gaudier-Brzeska's actual relationship to vorticism was more tenuous and more likely corroborated by Pound and the sculptor's literary contributions to *Blast*. Nonetheless, this has generally been the preferred reading of Gaudier-Brzeska's famous sculpture, taken in its unmistakably phallic manifestation as a monument to Ezra Pound, priest and poet, in expensive Greek Pentelic marble.[57] Indeed, Pound asked Gaudier-Brzeska to make the sculpture "virile" and later wrote to his intended, Dorothy Shakespear, saying, "Brzxs column gets more gravely beautiful and more phallic each week."[58] Lisa Tickner argues that the phallic head reflects the anxiety that "art as a pre-dominantly masculine activity was being feminized and domesticated," as it reinforces a grammar of "brutal energy: opulent maturity, fecundity, destruction and fear."[59] Despite this ostensible reading of the head, she suggests that we view it from another angle, where the term "hieratic" is necessary to maintain the sculpture's status as "*phallus*, with or without a Lacanian gloss—signifier of atavistic potency and plenitude—rather than just any old dick (Tom's or Harry's)."[60] Here, Tickner points to the possibility of slippage

Henri Gaudier-Brzeska, *The Hieratic Head of Ezra Pound*, 1914. Courtesy of the National Gallery of Art, Washington, DC.

between the head as phallus and the head as penis, which seems rather ironic considering Pound's serious contention that the work has "strength and dignity" because it does not look like his own face.[61] Indeed, Pound's reference hinges on the distinction between his own "face" in its anatomical reality and his "head" as a work of art. Thus, one could argue quite humorously that the meaning of *The Hieratic Head* turns on the slippages of the analogy it sets up: face is to penis as head is to phallus. This kind of reading, which opens the possibility that the head was some sort of joke Gaudier-Brzeska played on Pound or at least a piece of avant-garde propaganda, has been, to some arguable degree, corroborated by Pound's and Gaudier-Brzeska's contemporaries.[62]

Regardless of Gaudier-Brzeska's actual relationship with Pound or his personal intent in sculpting the head, the finished product does accord with many of Pound's stated aesthetic imperatives. Jon Wood argues that the bust challenged the traditionalists who valued the sensuality of Greek sculpture. Instead, Wood asserts that *The Hieratic Head* is an "outdoor, large-scale, phallic work to be seen from a distance."[63] For Wood, the sculpture offers a playful avant-garde challenge to the sensualist position, provocatively asking, "who wants to stroke Pound's head?"[64] Wood's analysis also points to the possibility that the phallic bearing of the head might slip into the territory of anatomical reality: the penis. In this relationship, the body, in its mortality, gives the "head" a purpose. That purpose, according to Wood, is to create a monument to Pound's genius that pairs "de-capitation" with self-renewal, that is, the real body's metamorphosis into a "self-generating and self-sustaining entity," a face into a head.[65]

Whereas Wood, like Tickner, argues that *The Hieratic Head* operates as a mask, I read the sculpture not merely as a disguise but as a building of a face that participates in its own effacement and disfiguration. Rather than corroborate individual identity, as in a portrait, this construction does not coordinate the exterior and interior dimensions of the human subject. Nevertheless, Gaudier-Brzeska apparently called the sculpture a "portrait" and complained that Pound's physical presence during its construction was annoying and prevented it from "coming along."[66] To the extent that this "portrait" is also a mask, disabling verisimilitude, the work disrupts "physiognomic perception," but not in the service of disguising the subject.[67] Rather, as Gaudier-Brzeska indicates, the sculpture strives to recreate in stone something more essential about its subject—something "like" its subject, an "expression" of "emotions" that are ascertained from "character."[68] Significantly, the mouth of the sculpture is sealed, silent, as are its eyes; elongated slits, they do not gaze openly in direct address, suggesting that the poet is squinting, straining to see. As a monument, the head does not call out or ask for an address. In this reversal of de Man's version of prosopopoeia, the artist, by making their subject mute, allows it to speak, to "say just what [it] mean[s]."[69]

Sculpture separates "expression" from the linguistic dimensions of the lyric, fusing it with pure matter, stone. As Hugh Kenner observes of Gaudier-Brzeska's work, "shape ... manifests psychic intent," such that "all shape was eloquent."[70] In Kenner's account, which is in reality an evaluation of the sculptor's work that reflects Pound's value for it, *The Hieratic Head*'s "bleak masses," "unadorned plains," and "narrow eyeslits" that gaze "without pupils" represent the belief that "whole civilizations" could be read in their orientation toward "masses and planes"—"the very equating of civilization with stone."[71] Certainly, this equation represents Gaudier-Brzeska's modern primitivism, or at least as it was received and later publicized by Pound, and the sculpture casts Pound as both idol and shaman.[72] But how do we read such a surface? If the face is the "locus of speech" and shape itself is "eloquent," then the point of this particular disfiguration is to efface speech and, further, any attempt to represent or redescribe it.[73] In its mute eloquence, the head is indeed hieratic, as the word's definition implies—hieroglyphic or ideogrammic in essence, as meanings compound without explicit conjunction or explanation. Perhaps we can make sense of this contradiction in light of Pound's imagism, particularly his call for "direct treatment of the 'thing'" and, in *ABC of Reading*, his elaboration of his ideogrammic method, where he addresses poetry as a "verbal manifestation" that is not interpreted but "KNOW[N]."[74] Here, Pound idealizes precisely the mode of uniform vision that E. H. Gombrich and Ernst Kris attributed to fascist propaganda, which they believed valued event over ritual and fusion over critical reflection. Rather than the sort of immediate apprehension they associated with "physiognomic perception," Gombrich and Kris valued forms like caricature, which they connected to distortion, regression, aggression, and, as Louis Rose argues, "shifting distances" of viewing.[75]

In terms of this politicized schema, *The Hieratic Head* presents itself to be seen or "known," not read. As a surface totality, it is constructed to inspire "shifting distance of viewing it" and to resist totalizing efforts to ascertain it. As a prosopopoeia, *The Hieratic Head* registers the tension between Pound's admiration of expressive totality and its subsequent disintegration, sustained first by the possibility that through speech or expression the face gains the status of a linguistic object that, like Prufrock's face, may ultimately be fixed in "a formulated phrase" or perception.[76] Unlike Loy's idealized face, the various parts of *The Hieratic Head*—the crooked nose, the heavy block of hair, the frown, the imperfect stone—come together in tension, not totality. However, the sculpture still reflects a more traditional physiognomic ideal of expression that is consistent with Loy's ideal, in which the expert reader recognizes or sees "character" in the features of the face. Charles Darwin, writing in 1872 in *The Expression of the Emotions in Man and Animals*, defines physiognomy as "the recognition of character through the study of the permanent form of the features."[77] Gaudier-Brzeska's observation that the sculpture of Pound's head "will be the expression of certain emotions which I get from your character" similarly aligns the idea of "character" with the physiognomic form of the exterior but, in contrast, posits some existing idea of "character" that emerges in spite of itself—and Gaudier-Brzeska's emotions about it—as a source for the expression.[78] He articulates a sculptural vision in which human emotions appear by way of the "SURFACE" in his letter "Written from the Trenches," when he writes that "I SHALL DERIVE MY EMOTIONS SOLELY FROM THE ARRANGEMENT OF SURFACES."[79] Eliot would expound on a similar view in "Tradition and the Individual Talent," where he contended that, in poetry, emotions should "not happen consciously or deliberately" and were neither "recollected" nor "expressed."[80] Similarly, in the case of *Auto-Facial-Construction*, the revitalization of the face beyond its natural contours reflects a feeling about oneself that is made possible by surface and shape. If, for Loy, this face reflects a new subject that is artificially "humanoid" rather than humanist, to use Paxson's terms, the poet all the while advocates a humanist ideal of "psychic logic" that promotes likeness and recognition (*AFC*, 165).[81]

This is a logic of expression that links Loy's and Gaudier-Brzeska's modernist experiments to the more traditional aims of portraiture, as well as to a physiognomic ideal that, as elaborated by Delaporte, one could "possess in one's anatomy and in one's physiology a structure of expression."[82] The idea of an embodied expressiveness also sheds light on Pound's assessment that Gaudier-Brzeska's sculpture of his head "has infinitely more strength and dignity than my face will ever possess."[83] Writing in May 1911 in response to the death of the artist Aristide Delannoy, Gaudier-Brzeska affirms this view in one of his quite lengthy letters to his lover Sophie, whom he addresses as "little mumsie":

> Dearest, the mistake you make is to confuse "expression" with the successive appearance of the face. Expression, as I tried to say, is the sum total of the vices and virtues of the whole [inner] life which shows in the aspect of each individual. I might no doubt say that one person has more expression than another if his enthusiasm, his anger, his passions are more lively in his face, if there is more sarcasm or gaiety in his laughter and more sadness in his tears; but that laughter and those tears are mere accidents caused by nervous excitements, in the course of which the whole expression is not changed, but coloured, or, if you like, veers toward a note of gaiety or sorrow. . . . A loathsome personality—like that pupil of yours for instance—can laugh, make pretty faces, or work herself up as much as she likes, her *expression* doesn't change, you still see her filthiness show through

her coarse lips, her vileness through her low forehead or her ill-shaped nose, her stupidity and malice through her eyes.[84]

This physiognomic analysis, certainly immature, sheds some light on the sculptor's vision for *The Hieratic Head*. While the head did not look like its subject, it expressed the subject's "whole" life. In doing so, the individual features of a live face are eclipsed by the formalization, or expression, of a person's character. Gaudier-Brzeska thus echoes a more traditional nineteenth-century belief that facial expressions, such as pain or sorrow, are constant and identifiable, subject to formalizations that both reflect and override their connections to real "nervous excitements" and stimulations. At the same time, his aestheticized view of human character as it appears in expression is anti-psychological; personality traits such as "filthiness" inevitably become visible through the student's "coarse lips" and "vileness through her low forehead or her ill-shaped nose," not the other way around. This formulation of expression reimagines the portrait form, retaining an idea of character and "individual virtue" that appears not through the window of an imagined interior but in the shape of the face itself.[85]

Harold Gillies, Henry Tonks, and the Future Face

A good style will get you through.

Harold Gillies and D. Ralph Millard, *The Principles and Art of Aesthetic Surgery*, 1957

For Gaudier-Brzeska, shape creates an energy and agency, molding the soul. In his "Vortex" manifesto, the sculptor indeed wrote that "THE PLASTIC SOUL IS INTENSITY OF LIFE BURSTING THE PLANE."[86] Gaudier-Brzeska's declaration seems future facing, as if anticipating Mike Nichols's 1967 film *The Graduate* and the "great future in plastics" promised to its young protagonist.[87] In this context, however, plastic describes more generally a pliant material capable of being molded and then fixed, a catalyst of radical spatial rearrangement. This meaning is highly relevant to my discussion of Loy's and Gaudier-Brzeska's various pronouncements about likeness and expression, where likeness is perhaps minutely but continuously recognizable in an expression of a person that may in fact be deformed (by the sculptor or artist) from the original source. As I suggest here, such ideas coincided with the onset of World War I as a stage for the development of a "strange new art" that Harold Gillies called "plastic surgery of the face."[88]

As an amateur painter, Gillies wrote copiously about his own work and employed a discourse similar to Loy's and Gaudier-Brzeska's to frame his art of reconstructing faces as a matter of beauty and form.

While Loy was interested in physical culture and bodily reform, I cannot document what knowledge of plastic surgery she or Gaudier-Brzeska could have possessed when they were authoring their treatises on facial construction and sculpture. Loy's reference to "facial contours," however, and the rhetoric of *Auto-Facial-Construction* more generally reflect the discourse that appeared in many publications on both facial repair and plastic surgery at its inception in the teens, twenties, and thirties (*AFC*, 165). Ladd's prosthetic facial masks were inspired by the earlier work of Gillies's colleague, F. Derwent Wood. Trained as a sculptor, Wood saw his work as corrective and aesthetic, and he explicitly articulated his aesthetic intention of restoring to a man a seamless relationship to his old face.[89] The process of reconstructing soldiers' faces placed a high value on aesthetics, such that medical rehabilitation came to resemble an artisanal or "craft process" with "outcomes."[90] Consequently, there was an idea that artists were necessary to "finish" what surgeons had started.[91] Ladd and Wood studied photographs of the men's original faces, and when photographs were not available, they attempted to infer from other physical features the overall shape of the face. In her papers, Ladd explained that she sought in her "study of all the features of the man" indications of his "character and personality."[92]

The work of reconstructing an animate, expressive face was quite different, however, than that of constructing prosthetic facial masks. For Gillies, as he writes in *Plastic Surgery of the Face* (1920), the definitive published record of his work at Queen Mary's Hospital, Sidcup, an "adequate diagnosis" of what the injured face has lost can only be made after thorough and precise study, whereby a sculptor, working in plaster, models the missing contours of the original face.[93] Gillies understood that "external contour" was not simply an empty form, but rather should reflect "deep structures" or "sub-structure" of the face.[94] The answer to a more agreeable appearance was not to mask the mutilated parts of a face, but rather "re-arrangement," a process whereby, as Gillies writes in another article, "displaced tissue should . . . be replaced to its normal plane."[95] Successful surgery meant that the surgeon must attend to the face not simply as a surface "re-arrangement" but as a multidimensional structure with interior and exterior surfaces.[96] In order to plan a patient's future face, the loss of facial tissue must be carefully assessed and can only be replaced by a consideration of the entirety of the face's composition, where "all lost tissue should ideally be replaced in kind—skin for skin, bone for bone, etc."[97] This approach to the face in its totality was a response to the crude visual outcomes of treatments for facially wounded soldiers during the war. As Andrew Bamji has noted, Gillies's surgical theater was experimental, as the "pool of knowledge" regarding existing techniques for facial repair and their relevance for individual patients was rudimentary at best.[98]

Gillies was explicitly interested in recreating a patient's looks, and he saw such reconstruction as a means of restoring to them their humanness. When two thousand men arrived at Aldershot, Cambridge Military Hospital, after the Somme offensive of 1916, Gillies described them as "men without half their faces, men burned and maimed to the condition of animals."[99] Rather than using fillers or heterogeneous grafts, Gillies refined techniques for reforming the face by stretching skin from other parts of the body, tubes of living tissue, which would increase blood supply to the grafts and thus decrease the chance of infection or rejection of the tissue. Gillies kept detailed pictorial and visual records of his work, of which Tonks's pastels are an example, and spent significant time attempting to project the outcome of his operations; this meant visualizing the face in every way possible, through photography, sculpture, drawing, and painting as a means of forecasting a successful outcome that was somehow in harmony with the person or subject of the surgery. He would also enlist a sculptor to create a plaster model of his projections about his patient's future face.

Of course, Gillies was clearly concerned with whether the new face he designed suited the patient personally. Writing in 1963 to Gillies's biographer, Reginald Pound, Horace Sewell, a patient who underwent at least twenty surgeries, calls Gillies a "godsend to thousands of men of war," stressing his satisfaction with his nose and describing the process of its selection. Claiming that he was not "fussy," he deferred to the surgeon's choice of a roman nose, which he "never regretted."[100] The affectionate and even humorous tone of the former patients' letters corroborates the idea that Gillies's goal was to aid in the recuperation of a soldier's humanity by attempting to restore his face's practical functions—including his ability to chew and swallow food—and by offering the most aesthetically pleasing reconstruction of his face possible. Gillies's own writings about his work demonstrate his understanding that a face is a reflection of a totality, a personality, and emphasize his controlling role in its outcome. Writing much later in a second tome, *The Principles and Art of Plastic Surgery* (1957), Gillies claims that "surgical

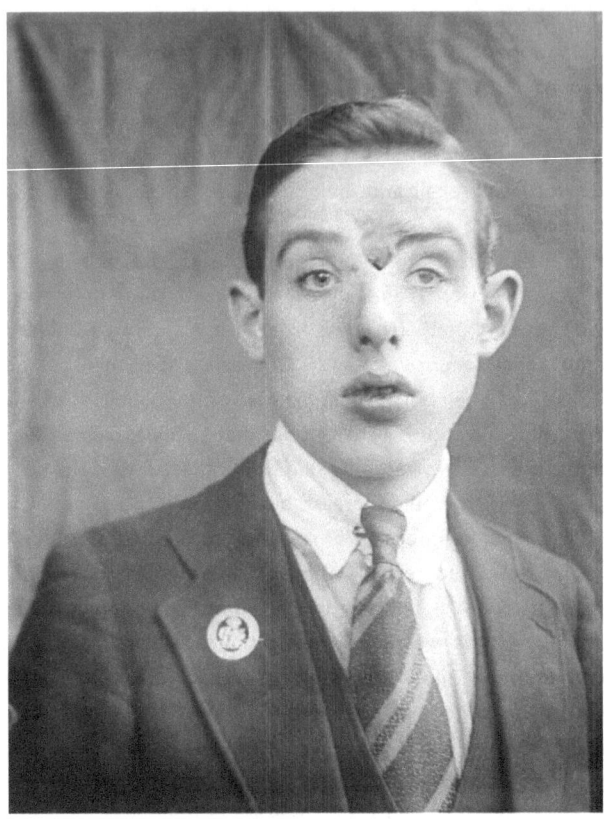

Photograph by Horace Nicholls, circa 1916. Courtesy of the Imperial War Museums.

style is the expression of personality and training exhibited by the movements of the fingers; its hallmark—dexterity and gentleness."[101] Gillies is suggesting here that a finished face will reflect the style or personality of its maker, not its wearer. Nonetheless, a surgeon must not be crude but must exercise "dexterity" and "gentleness" in creating the characters of individuals. In another lecture from 1934, given at Northwestern University in Chicago, Gillies gestures at the potential for plastic surgery to go politically awry, against humanness toward the erasure of the individual. Essential to plastic surgery, he argues, is a "habit of style," in which faces may bear the "stamp of the hand that moulded them," to the point that one may recognize a surgeon's style in a lip or an eyelid.[102] The problem here is "type," which can, according to Gillies, reflect an "element of impressionism" in its best form

Modernist Prosopopoeia 137

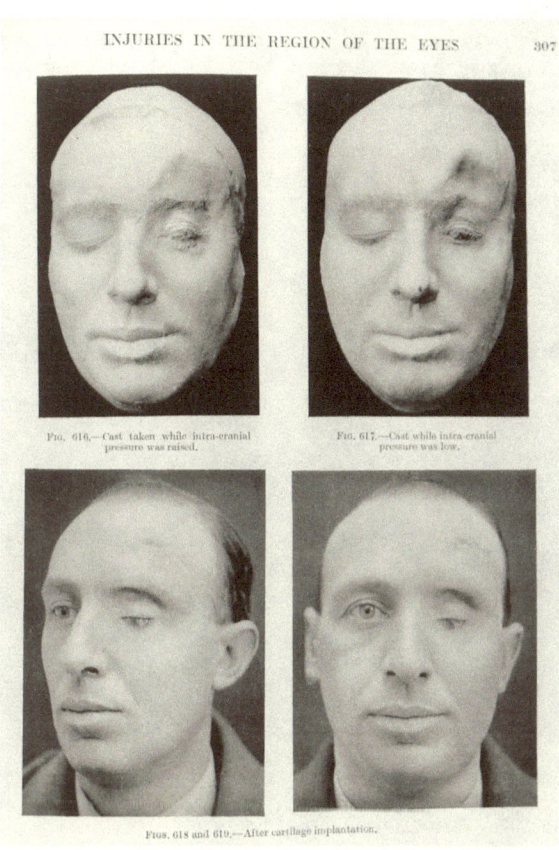

From Harold Gillies, *Plastic Surgery of the Face*, 1920. Courtesy of Wellcome Library, London.

and an "element of cubism" at its worst.[103] The worst scenario for Gillies, however, referencing "the dictatorship governments of the world," is that insistence on a "perfection of form and uniformity of physique" will lead to a "uniformity of facial outlook."[104]

Here, Gillies elaborates an ethics of surgery that, in the 1930s, counters an imminent fascist preference for physiognomic and aesthetic uniformity, which he considers a potential political problem of plastic surgery. A quick perusal of all of the recent plastic surgery or "bad" plastic surgery websites would suggest that his projection is now a reality. While these more recent faces may have form, like the prosthetic masks that quickly grew obsolete

138   The New Physiognomy

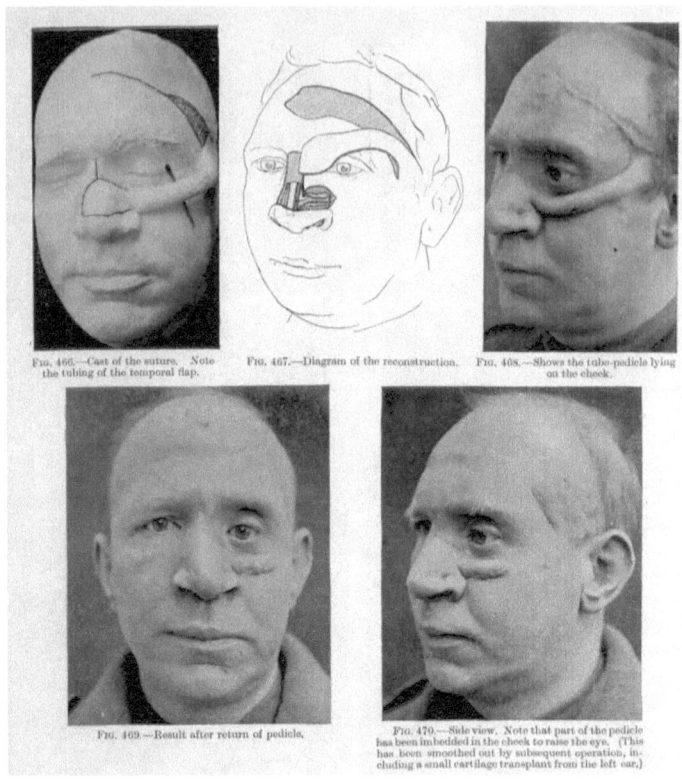

Fig. 466.—Cast of the suture. Note the tubing of the temporal flap.   Fig. 467.—Diagram of the reconstruction.   Fig. 468.—Shows the tube-pedicle lying on the cheek.

Fig. 469.—Result after return of pedicle.   Fig. 470.—Side view. Note that part of the pedicle has been imbedded in the cheek to raise the eye. (This has been smoothed out by subsequent operation, including a small cartilage transplant from the left ear.)

From Harold Gillies, *Plastic Surgery of the Face*, 1920.

as a veteran aged, they lack what Gillies calls, in *Plastic Surgery of the Face*, "vitality," which develops from careful and thoughtful consideration of all aspects of the patient's facial transformation.[105] In that same text, Gillies describes a process involving a collaboration of artists. Once a plaster cast of a face is made, a sculptor "models the missing contours."[106] In line with Loy's and Gaudier-Brzeska's sculptural vision of the face, this face is significantly modeled as form before surgery is performed. The masks, too, are surface expressions but placed at a further remove. They are in essence prosthetic, formal, and, regardless of material, plastic devices used to reimagine and rehabilitate a face and, consequently, a person. What is interesting about the mask here is its pliability, as well as the work by the sculptor of erasing the temporal distinction between the past face and the future face.

Along with the plaster casts, Gillies's method included extensive before and after photographic documentation of his patient's faces. A day spent looking at the photographs is a viscerally unnerving experience. One's eyes are persistently drawn to the wounds, but the photographs say little about the person in them. They rather illustrate various types of injuries and procedures—"injuries of the lower lip and chin," for example, or "repair of the cheek"—and through the vast catalog of photographs one loses sight of the patients as individuals, who are not referred to in the text as such.[107] While the "after" faces are formed by the surgeons' hands, the photographs, particularly the close-ups of eyes and other parts of the face, invite objective analysis and comparison. Gillies's highly detailed method of projecting a future face highlights the surgeon's or artist's ethical relationship to the person whose face is being made, including the responsibility of making something that "feels like" the patient's original face.[108] In linking these aesthetic projections to the dynamics of prosopopoeia, I am not suggesting that Gillies, or any other figure in this chapter, knew of the term. I am rather interested in how the structural dynamics of prosopopoeia may help us understand both the ethical and aesthetic dimensions of Gillies's work and Tonks's record of it. An aesthetically pleasing face, capable of integrating the facially wounded soldier back into society and human intercourse, would, as surgeon Archibald McIndoe remarked later in a 1958 lecture, "enabl[e] the owner to take his normal place in society without comment."[109] As part of a normative body, the successfully reconstructed face is not remarkable and does not inspire a second look; the disfigured face, however, does inspire looking, if not "pity" or "horror."[110]

My interest here is in the visualization process required to reconstruct a face, in particular, how a surgeon may witness in an anatomy damaged beyond logical comprehension a kind of "deep structure" of expression or form that is also consistent with patients' feelings about their own faces.[111] This kind of visualization is also the work of portraiture, which seeks to exploit recognizable expression and, as a method of giving faces, is also a prosopopoeia. Miller's account of prosopopoeia demonstrates how this very sort of reconstruction is ethical because in creating a person we identify our responsibilities to that person. My sense is that facial disfigurement presents a special case for ethics, since the very project of reconstructing a face in this context implies the surgeon/artist's acceptance of an ethical responsibility in returning the subject to the sort of personhood that is implied by having a face. This is not simply a project of normalization but an aesthetic project of creating a face that takes into account a subject's own "facial awareness" of what it "feel[s] like" to have a specific face or expression.[112]

François Delaporte has elaborated on some of these "problems of identity" in his recent book *Figures of Medicine*, where he emphasizes the right of those with "severe disfigurement" to "normalize their lives" as a way of "saving a life."[113] Delaporte argues that before and after pictures of facial transplant procedures stage surgery as an act of liberation, but they do not erase the problem of what it is like to live with a face that is not one's own, the complications for which there are no psychological precedents or resources.[114] He thus asks whether such a particular "problem of identity" should be "approached solely via the detour of one's self image," when identity "belongs to the imaginary" and is "also the representation of a being one wants to remember."[115] Indeed, the idea of facial reconstruction as a necessity takes as truth the idea that the facially disfigured person is socially dead, although many of Gillies's patients were accepting of their initial surgical results and did not return for further surgeries.[116] To this extent, because the surgeries were experimental, there was no way of knowing what justice to the actual person such face making could offer, or if the new face was actually a plastic defacement that offered no likeness to the "being one wants to remember."[117] Insofar as Gillies measured the outcome of a surgery in terms of its justice to an individual, and not simply as a normative procedure designed to consolidate a sense of traditional masculinity or an imaginary self-image, his detailed patient files show that he would honestly assess the surgical results, and in some cases he deemed the "cosmetic result" of a surgery "very poor" or expressed doubts about the face's functionality.[118] In the worst-case scenarios, soldiers later died of infection or even on the operating table in the process of undergoing a series of surgeries. One well-known case was that of Henry Lumley, who, as detailed by editor Samuel JMM Alberti in the beautiful edition of reprints of Tonks's portraits *War, Art and Surgery: The Works of Henry Tonks and Julia Midgley*, died in 1918 of infection a few weeks after his final operation for severe petrol burns at the age of 25.[119] Having undergone two years of operations that attempted to repair what is perhaps the most extreme case of injury detailed in Tonks's catalog of drawings, Lumley's case in particular literalizes a crucial ethical dilemma—a "fantasy of repair" that in fact may cause more damage than good.[120]

In addressing what is at stake in this "fantasy of repair," I turn more specifically to Tonks's drawings, which, as records of damage done to correct damage, are formally medical illustrations, likely not seen outside of medical contexts until their exhibition at University College London in 2002. Indeed, Tonks saw the drawings as inappropriate for public display, writing to the government's propaganda office that they were "rather dreadful subjects for the public view."[121] Biernoff argues that while Tonks's pictures "bear witness to physical and psychological trauma" and "violently disrupt the cultural ideal of embodied masculine subjectivity," they still, though in complex ways, reflect the specific conventions of medical and military illustration.[122] Perhaps Tonks considered it a betrayal of his subjects to publicly link their disfigured faces to this "symbolic anatomy" of the "military body," with its connection to personal characteristics such as "valor, heroism, patriotism," and "courage."[123]

In evading this symbolic link, the drawings may be considered, as Biernoff has argued, "antiportraits."[124] Rather than consolidate identity in any normative way, she contends, they "stage the fragility and mutability of subjectivity" through the shocking "abyss" of the injuries.[125] Tate Britain museum curator Emma Chambers also addresses the drawings in relationship to portraiture, which, she argues, draws on the concept of "likeness."[126] Diverging from Biernoff, Chambers suggests that the portraits are physiognomic, such that the external characteristics of a face, or signs, offer suggestions of the sitter's "inner emotional state," going beyond "external appearance" to consolidate the identity of the subject.[127] She is interested in how facial disfigurement influences the viewer's construction of the subject's identity, arguing that the pictures essentially "pee[l] back" the "layers of the face . . . to reveal its interior structure," showing the viewer a "physical hierarchy of skin, muscle and bone."[128] The result is to produce "detailed and medically authorized knowledge" for the viewer while establishing "the normative structure of the face."[129] Unlike traditional portraiture, these "surgical portraits force the viewer to come to terms with the bodily materiality of the sitter" and push the concept of "'likeness'. . . to its limits," through the persistent "mismatch" between "ruptured" skin and the face's "intact" features.[130]

But what exactly, I ask, do the faces' intact features convey? Perhaps they preserve at least the ideal of recognition that supplies a portrait with its form, as it were. Indeed, we might return here to Soussloff's remarks about portraiture, which identify in it the artist's "projection of interiority" and "personality" onto the depicted person.[131] Chambers's recreation of the conditions of portrait production, in particular the relation between Tonks and his sitters, offers significant insight into this dynamic as it applies to Tonks's drawings. While Tonks's use of pastels—as opposed to paint or watercolor—would allow him to work faster, he still would have had somewhat intimate and lengthy contact with his sitters. The sitter—who would likely be extremely self-conscious of being looked at—would be aware that he was the object of the artist's vision. Chambers writes that the artist must "look intently and dispassionately at his subject for an extended period of time," seeking to create a "'likeness' both through the illusionistic representation of physical appearance and the suggestion of the inner presence or personality of the sitter."[132] Yet in Tonks's works, as Chambers notes, the immediate visibility of what is "physically beneath" the skin "unsettles" the very projections of the viewer that characterize the dynamics of portraiture.[133] The pathological view past the skin's surface disrupts the portrait's and the viewer's projection of the sitter's personality.

It is in part the pastel medium that allows for this, problematizing a comprehensive account of the work's surface. Unlike photography or even watercolor, pastels allowed Tonks to capture the gradations of skin tone and the actual dimensionality of the wounded flesh. As has been noted by numerous critics, the drawings simultaneously juxtapose the intact, normative features of the soldiers—complete with immaculately groomed hair and newly shaven skin—to the viscerally shocking manifestations of extreme violence, what Biernoff calls the "abyss" of the wound.[134] But what of the wounded face's capacity for expression and, further, the viewer's tendency to endow it, as in the spirit of portraiture, with a form of interiority? In the Tonks portraits and in the surviving photographs, the men's eyes are especially haunting, conduits of the subject's "expression," at the same time that the face's expressive capabilities are disabled by its injury. There is in them the promise of prosopopoeia and, further, of personality—the way in which, to return to de Man, the sitter's "voice" might "assum[e] mouth, eye, and finally face" but ultimately does not.[135] The face does not function as a "totalizing power" but still gestures at the possibility of its coherent "re-arrangement," inviting us to read it, however futile that exercise.[136] The damaged face still contains within it the "fiction" that prosopopoeia supports, of the very return of an "absent, deceased or voiceless" entity.[137] Our relation to the portrait is not necessarily marked by "separation" as Biernoff has argued, nor do we find recognizable identity in the drawings.[138] In the case of the drawings, inasmuch as they promise something, the very idea of a return has been replaced by the fiction of a future predicated on the literal death and damage of the subject's past identity.

The drawings offer the viewer elements that render the subjects expressive at the same time that the visual representation of the wounded flesh denies the idea of an interior that is more than just flesh. Whereas the physiognomist attempted to read signs that were already present in the expressive structure of the face, Tonks's pictures provide an immediate entrance to what's behind the face when its destruction limits the possibility of this reading. When viewing the pictures, one's vision feels conflicted. Due to their fragility, the pictures have been framed in arrangements of four; the presentation, as in Gillies's book *Plastic Surgery of the Face*, encourages one to generalize about the nature of the various injuries and about the soldiers themselves. At the same time, one is attracted to individual faces. The eye zooms and retreats to a face that looks especially young, or to a particularly serious wound, or to eyes that seem more expressive than others. Among the pictures, however, there is one drawing that cannot be considered a portrait—a close-up detail of a reconstructive procedure. Grouped among the pictures of faces, the wound—which cannot be identified as a specific part of the face—is abstracted from a face that is not visually present or immediately identifiable. In the drawing, the outer layer of the skin is literally peeled back and held in place with some sort of suture, while the various layers of the face's interior are distinguished through the tonal gradations of the pastels. What stands out is the dimensionality of the facial tissue; the pastels seem to glisten and highlight the ways in which the wound's material structure extends infinitely inward.

This wound, abstracted in its materiality from the whole face but seen In the presence of so many faces, highlights what the other, damaged faces do to project a subject's identity, as well as their relation to a recognizable field of expression that is in part established by normative facial features. The injuries in the portraits both eclipse and highlight the most sociable of expressions, such as a smile. Regardless of Tonks's intentions, we see expression in them that both normalizes the sitter and restores to them their humanness. The expression itself, then, or at least the hint of it, invites the viewer's prosopopoeia. The portraits are thus pathological only inasmuch as they gesture at a recognizable norm of expression that the viewer might synthesize into a personality or type. As in our readings of facial expressions, one has a very clear sense of the meaning one is looking for in the first place. This again confirms Delaporte's account of facial pathology—in which expression exists only when it can be situated within a coherent visual field. Based on Gillies's comments about types of faces, it seems clear that early

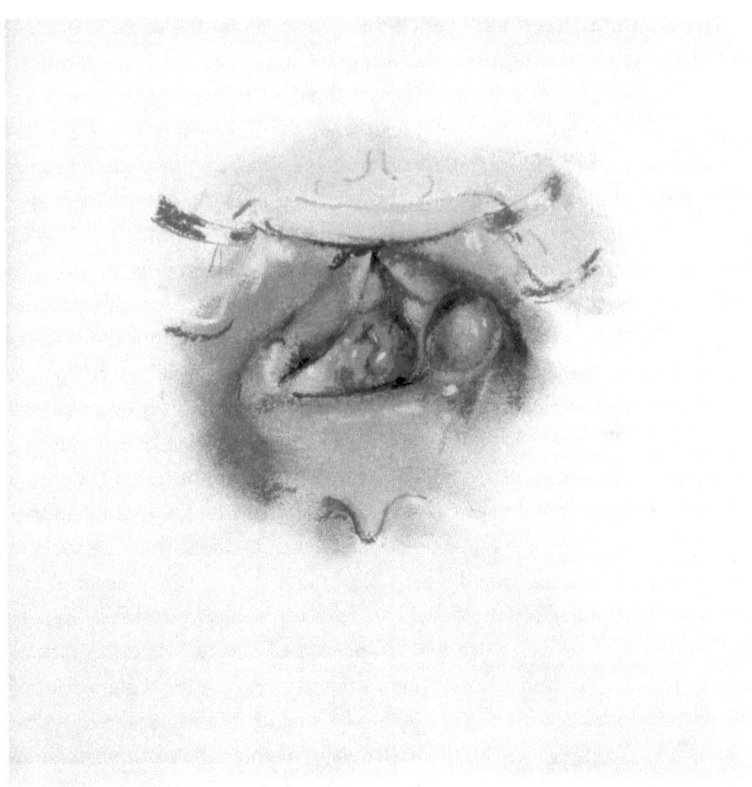

Illustration by Henry Tonks, 1916-18. By kind permission of the Royal College of Surgeons of England.

plastic surgeons had this field in mind as they attempted to assess the success of their results, but unlike physiognomists, who typically analyzed intact faces, they were not working with a consistent set of protocols or procedures.

These surgical subjects were thus distinctly pathologized, and Tonks's portraits offer no exception, as the soldiers' disfigurements, even in the "after" illustrations of reconstructed faces, push shockingly at the norms of recognizable facial expression. Chambers's argument that the portraits encourage a "switching of vision," between the medical and the aesthetic, can thus also be linked to Canguilhem and the visual registers of the normal and pathological expressive fields.[139] Tonks's own writing about the portraits is rather sparse, but he offers an assessment of his work in a letter to Dugald

Sutherland MacColl, which has been quoted by Chambers, among others: "I have done some . . . rather fine pastel *fragments*! One, I did the other day of a young fellow with rather a classical face was exactly like a living damaged Greek head as his nose had been cut clean off just where noses of antiques generally are cut off. . . . It is capital practice, and I feel I am having *excellent* practice in drawing."[140] What strikes me about this seemingly callous evaluation, adapted by Pat Barker for her novel *Toby's Room*, is Tonks's characterization of his work's relation to form. The "results" are not possible without an understanding of the likeness between the soldiers' damaged faces and what Eliot would call the "existing monuments" that determine a work's formal relation to the past.[141] For Tonks, the new damage to a patient's face cannot be recorded without reference to what Chambers terms "an iconography of art-historical prototypes," which positions him as an alien and impersonal observer of his subjects, removed in a sense from the immediate context of the portrait's production.[142] At the same time, Tonks sees his work as an opportunity to hone his drawing skills. For both Tonks and Gillies, the hospital was a theater for experimentation and the construction of new forms. Gillies, as Bamji has noted, saw the work for its use value as an "educational resource" given the general absence of knowledge about facial reconstruction techniques.[143]

Tonks's pastels and Gillies's self-constructed archive of surgical knowledge thus literalized the ethical dynamic of prosopopoeia that Miller identifies, where to make a face means not only to take responsibility for that face but also to use the other it signifies for an aesthetic or practical end. Biernoff's analysis of the production of the portraits, while framed in different terms, corroborates Miller's account of this prosopopoeiac practice. While one may be tempted to regard the pastels as portraits, she reminds us that "the conventions of portraiture are at odds with the condition of being a patient."[144] While portraits are invested in the "legible signs of character and emotion," medical illustration, she argues, following Foucault, "delineates and treats the condition, not the individual," privileging a "'clinical gaze' capable of abstracting the disease from the patient," or the wound from the face.[145] But Tonks was trained as a surgeon and as an artist, and as Biernoff notes, the drawings are characterized by both gazes, clinical and aesthetic. Tonks's "fascination with the underface" is matched by his attention to the patient's hair and eyes.[146] Unlike the photographs of the patients, in which the facial wounds often look like black holes leading to a total inner abyss—as if one can look straight through the body—Tonks's drawings show

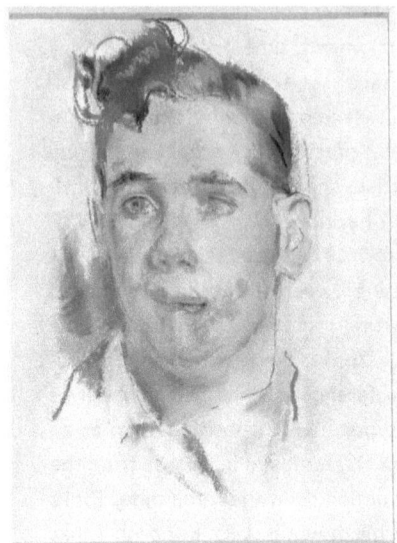 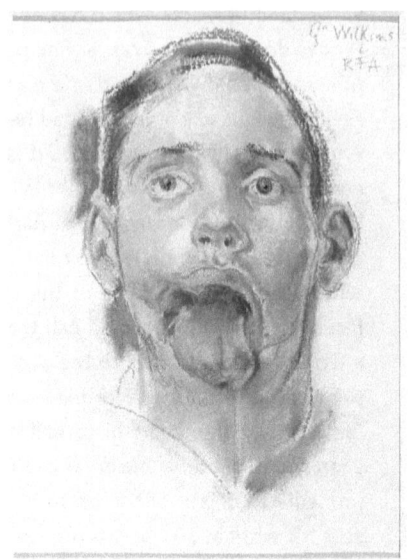

Illustrations by Henry Tonks. *Left*, Private C. H. Morris. *Right*, Private Gunner Wilkins. By kind permission of the Royal College of Surgeons of England.

us the dimension inside of the body while simultaneously organizing seemingly legible persons.

 What stands out in the pastels is Tonks's ability to capture the relative ages of his sitters in the tenderness of the many boyish faces, their soft bloom of skin, juxtaposed to terrifying wounds. When viewed alongside the patient files and other records left by Gillies, one can begin to construct a life narrative for many of these patients. It is not only the drawings but also the archive of materials that influence our gaze as viewers. The successful surgical result might accompany a successful reintegration of the wounded into society, where a patient might take up his work as a tailor or machinist. There are also the stories of the patients, like Lumley, who died of infection from the surgeries and even on the operating table. As records of damage, Tonks's drawings, as well as the accompanying details of these patients' lives, seem to ask us to know them. This call for intimacy, I am arguing, reflects the dynamics of prosopopoeia, where the subject is endowed with a voice that cannot be usurped or formed by the projective gaze of the viewer, but at the same time encouraging that gaze, that reading.

 Tonks's portraits thus invite the possibility of an ethical model of viewing in which the very seeing of these pictures is a form of valuing. This viewing is in fact a prosopopoeia, an act of facing, that in some sense always gestures at its own failure, especially in this context, where the fantasy of a fully integrated subject is impossible and has been all but eviscerated by war. One cannot get one's face back. We might then use the word "witness," following Allen Grossman, as a reference to the intelligibility of what we are able to see in other faces.[147] While Grossman does not use the term "prosopopoeia" in "The Passion of Laocoön: Warfare of the Religious against the Poetic Institution," he asks what "can be invested in a face and perceived by looking at a face," particularly in regard to the question of what poetry is.[148] In this essay, Grossman takes the sculptural faces of the Laocoön—the Trojan priest who was attacked by either serpents or his sons, for knowing too much—and the blind Homer as examples of the ways in which the "sculptural image" of the face becomes the "'supreme' case of human construction."[149] For Grossman, these stone faces encourage our "imaging" of them, a form of seeing that he links to the act of poetic making and "building" and that he also argues "specif[ies] the value of a person."[150] The "science of this 'building' and 'distribution,'" he claims, "is poetics."[151] The construction of the face is thus central to the act of making poetry, and poetry, as Grossman defines it, is the act of making faces. This is in fact a critical explanation of why we deem some people's faces to be, quite literally, poetic. The face of Homer or of Laocoön, he argues, "demand[s] a text."[152]

What do we do when we give a face a text? As Grossman notes, we value persons when their experience is intelligible to us. When that experience "ceases to be intelligible," it produces instead "its own image for inspection."[153] Our text is our reading, or imaging of that image, that face, in which we see the "*eidos*" of the person—which Grossman defines as "the own image of the person both particular and general, *but subject to scarcity*."[154] This "scarcity" is "the moment of poetry," the point where our imaging must do its work of making and the moment where the self that is witnessed in a face both retreats and gains clarity.[155] The *eidos* both supplies the human form of the self and situates the self as other to that form. Grossman notes the blind face of Homer, with its mutilated "dead eyes" and "beautiful but devastated head."[156] There is "represented destruction" in this face that bears "witness to *a catastrophe of a particular sort*."[157]

There is indeed a voice in the damaged face's very witness to destruction. We may think about the ethical considerations at work in our viewing of damaged or disfigured faces, like those in Tonks's portraits, precisely through this understanding of *eidos*, as it supplies human form or self to a face while also locating that self as something other, something distant or scarcely intelligible, a visual expression of unbearable harm. This is a way of reframing the problem Barker articulates in *Toby's Room*, through the viewpoint of art student Elinor Brook, who is disturbed by her aesthetic response to the task of drawing a wounded face, her finding in it a "poignancy" that "the undamaged original might have lacked," where the actual "injuries" throw into "sharper relief" the "beauty" of the subject's "remaining features."[158] As if directly sensing her conundrum, her instructor, Henry Tonks, responds, "It's worrying, isn't it... when it makes them more beautiful."[159] Here, Tonks describes the problem of imaging a face, which is also the problem of prosopopoeia. We may indeed image these faces in a way that gives them form, attributing to them personhood, even giving them personality, through our making and, further, valuing of them. It is their damage—their "witness" to unimaginable *"catastrophe"*—that encourages us to participate in this poetic action that humanizes the pictures as portraits and simultaneously situates them as other to the forms of readable identity portraits seek to create.[160] This face—this witness, according to Grossman—becomes the speech of a person, in a way that is not "communicative but constitutive of the human world."[161]

As I have attempted to illustrate, this "facing," in Loy, Gaudier-Brzeska, Gillies, and Tonks, is also the work of a novel portrait form—a living portrait, a stone portrait, a medical portrait—that still aims to corroborate a sense of likeness between a portrait and its subject, all the while reconfiguring the kind of voice that can be linked to the viewer's "projection of interiority" onto the portrait's subject.[162] While recognition is essential to portrait's project of placing "the singular individual in relationship to others," this reformulation of the portrait places value on the idea of the subjects' identification with their own faces and expressions and what those expressions "feel like."[163] In Tonks's work in particular, this sense of "facial awareness" ascribes value to the wounded or disfigured face without inviting the sort of intrusive projections that would diminish the subject's voice.[164] If we think of voice as "constitutive" rather than "communicative," following Grossman, we may indeed be able to reformulate the problematic ethics of the projective gaze through a prosopopoeia that does not deny humanness, but rather reorients our *view* of a subject against a uniform mode of viewing that would seek to undo it. As a discourse of restoration and as a model of imaging, this particularly modernist take on prosopopoeia "de-

Modernist Prosopopoeia

prives and disfigures to the precise extent that it restores."[165] It also reflects the "fantasy of repair" that, as Biernoff has argued, characterizes the "social and cultural legacy of World War I."[166] With disfigurement at its core, this prosopopoeia allowed modernists such as Gaudier-Brzeska and Loy to erase the temporal distinctions—between a past and future face—that create obsolescence, guarding voice against its diminishment by the reading eyes of others. Prosopopoeia, I have suggested, need not be thought of as a projective hallucination that silences the voice of the other. As a way of looking and as an art form, and as it characterizes the work of Henry Tonks, prosopopoeia offers instead a startlingly real indication of our own vulnerability, our "constitutive" desire to witness, read, and value the wounded faces of others.

5 Unreadable Persons
The "Face-Scape" of Old Age

> At 50, everyone has the face he deserves.
> —George Orwell, *Collected Essays*, 1968

> No vanity's displayed:
> I'm looking for the face I had
> Before the World was made.
> —W. B. Yeats, "Before the World Was Made," 1933

> All are limitory, but each has her own
> nuance of damage.
> —W. H. Auden, "Old People's Home," 1970

When Christopher Isherwood remarked that W. H. Auden, at the age of sixty, seemed "monumentally" old, he meant it literally, adding that his face "really belongs in the British museum."[1] Like Oscar Wilde's, Auden's appearance provoked a sizable amount of commentary. By late middle age, the poet appeared to be aging at an accelerated pace, his face's deep geological folds inciting his own well-known assessment that it resembled "a wedding cake left out in the rain."[2] Hannah Arendt lovingly saw the same countenance through the lens of traditional physiognomy—"as though life itself had delineated a face-scape" that made "manifest the 'heart's invisible furies.'"[3] Another observer, arguably David Hockney, who drew Auden, spared all sentimentality when he reputedly asked, "if that's his face, what must his scrotum look like?"[4] While casual commentators have connected Auden's appearance of advanced age to his smoking, amphetamine use, drinking, anxiety, and squalid living conditions, the poet actually had a genetic disease, called Touraine-Solente-Golé syndrome, the major symptom of which

W. H. Auden, 1971. Photograph by Jane Bown. © Guardian News and Media Limited, 2023.

was the thickening, furrowing, and clubbing of his skin and digits.[5] Nonetheless, one's immediate response to seeing this face is, like Arendt's, physiognomic. It asks us to read it, disclosing its ravaging by the poet's life itself, in particular, the late-life "unhappiness" and "misery" Arendt saw in it.[6]

Hockney's insensitive claim suggests that Auden's nether regions also showed the ravages of time, or at least were deeply connected to the general damage age rendered to his face. This link between face and scrotum—or genitals, more generally—will figure significantly into the later portions of this chapter, as it does in my earlier discussion of Ezra Pound's "head." I pause on it only briefly here. Hockney's fantasy is that a marvelously grotesque scrotum is the undisclosed counterpart to Auden's extreme facial furrows. The poet's "balls" are the secret portal of old age, the symbol of something hidden and inscrutable. But in contrast to the idea that one's age can be hidden or disguised through plastic surgery, exercise, cosmetics, or apparel—to be read or deciphered more consistently with one's presentation of self—the fantastically distorted scrotum is the very secret that the face inevitably betrays. While Auden does not look his age, his years are not concealed in the way we would have imagined, but rather hyperexposed, exaggerated in an unreadable, if not damaged, form.

W. H. Auden's "Face-Scape"

With Auden's face, I return here to a tension I outline at the start of this book, between the face's potential for synthesizing degrees of feeling into recognizable forms and readable expressions and its capacity for disturbing that harmony, as elaborated by Georg Simmel in "The Aesthetic Significance of the Face" (1901), where he argues that the smallest "disfigurement" can convert the face's "aesthetic affect" into something "aesthetically unbearable."[7] As if anticipating Mina Loy's *Auto-Facial-Construction*, his vocabulary evokes age and other forms of debility as grotesque pathologies that disrupt the aesthetic, further linking the "stretching and spreading of the body" to the kind of mental disintegration that is seen as a characteristic of old age.[8] Simmel's account suggests that the "aesthetic effect" of the face is lost with age, when form does not "embrace its parts and hold them together."[9] Such a face, unable to successfully synthesize feeling with expression, becomes unreadable. What, then, are we to do with Auden's face? Given that Auden's face is still a face, what does this "face-scape" tell us about aesthetic form more generally?

These questions follow from the examples of the preceding chapter. In the case of Gaudier-Brzeska's sculpture *The Hieratic Head of Ezra Pound*, Pound's desire to have his face cast as a deliberate misrecognition of himself refutes in many ways the terms of intelligibility through which we confer onto others the status of persons. While Pound's well-known anxieties about masculinity are evident in his request that Gaudier-Brzeska make the sculpture more "virile" and in his praise for its "phallic" form, his remarks point to a corresponding anxiety about age and its damaging effect on the "hieratic" nature of the head as a readable script or kind of writing.[10] A similar ageism appears in Mina Loy's 1919 pamphlet *Auto-Facial-Construction*, with its mechanical program for fending off the distortion of personality that accompanies aging, seen as a literal "disguise" of one's face—or in, for example, Wyndham Lewis's and Pound's reverence for a "virile" version of modernism that connects anti-sentimental "hygiene" to the clarity and "straightness" of expression.[11] As I have suggested elsewhere in this book, through my analysis of examples ranging from caricatures of Oscar Wilde to portraits of soldiers with blasted faces, this ideal of legibility, based on "logic" or "facial integrity," underlies a notion of facial pathology that is tied to a crisis in observation, the way we attribute personhood to others, as well as to subjects' feelings about or identification with their own faces (*AFC*, 165).

I need not stray too far from Auden's own poetry to illustrate this point. Consider "Doggerel by a Senior Citizen," from May 1969, in which Auden comically defends his own artistic obsolescence. Claiming that "I cannot settle which is worse, / The Anti-Novel or Free Verse," Auden interrogates a periodized sense of artistic production that distinguishes young from old, innovative from stale: "Though I suspect the term is crap, / If there is a Generation Gap, / Who is to blame?" "Me alienated?" Auden writes, "Bosh."[12] This confident "skirmish" with alienation gives way to the more depressing vision of "Old People's Home" (1970), where "all are limitory, but each has her own nuance of damage" (*CP*, 861). Whether Auden means "limited," with the correctly spelled "limitary," or is coining his own neologism to characterize the condition of old age, he taxonomizes the "Old Ones" into a number of types: those who are "intelligent of what has happened," those "muttering Limbo," those "terminally incompetent" who "sully themselves," and ultimately those "stowed out of conscience as unpopular luggage" (*CP*, 861). "We all know what to expect," Auden writes darkly; with old age comes a condition of facelessness and diminished social worth. Indeed, while sitting on the subway, Auden laments that he must "revisage" the person he is going to visit, "who she was in the pomp and sumpture of her hey-day / when week-end visits were a presumptive joy, / not a good work"; he concludes by acknowledging his wish for her "speedy painless dormition" (*CP*, 861).

In Auden's poem, old age elicits a crisis in observation for the speaker, who is cast as the observer or reader of the poem's aging subjects. The poem enacts the speaker's own strategy for negotiating this crisis, which involves the mental technique of refacing an unreadable person. To quote Yeats, this "looking for a face" could refer to the act of writing poetry, where one calls into being—in an action typical of prosopopoeia—younger faces to "revisage" an unreadable, damaged anatomy.[13] In this chapter, I continue with the question of what it means to "face" damage, as I attempt to think through some of the ethical problems related to the tension that appears in Auden's poem between the aesthetic violence and destruction involved in viewing—of "revisag[ing] or refacement"—and our valuing of others. As such, I refer both to the kind of damage to another that may result from the action of facing and to the idea of a face, as it stands in for a text, or even a work of art, as a damaged form that solicits that facing. In the case of "Old People's Home," it is impossible for Auden to "revisage" his subject, obviously a valued friend, without also thinking about her death.

By referring to the idea of "damage," I do not aim to corroborate the same modernist ageism I attribute to Loy or Pound, but rather intend to view it as an "aesthetic formulation" that links the intelligibility of persons to the question of aesthetic form.[14] I explore this connection more explicitly in the final section of this chapter by elaborating on the term "defacement."[15] Elsewhere in this book, I use the term "prosopopoeia" similarly to refer to the at once destructive and restorative mode of facing that connects modernism and its aftereffects. I thus begin this chapter by attempting to consolidate some of the strands of thought that emerge from these frames of analysis, in particular, various examples that thematize the production of legibility as it relates to an aging face. We might return, for example, to Lily Bart's encounters with an ill-lit room and a mirror in *The House of Mirth* (1905). Psychologically wedded to her face-work, Lily's desire, like that of Eliot's Prufrock, is both to maintain her "face" and to guard it against the intrusive readings of others. The result, however, is unsightly: the start of "two little lines near her mouth," "faint flaws" that are unalterable.[16] Lily's face cannot be changed. Much like the aging portrait of Dorian Gray, the literalized image of Lily's lined face exceeds its connection to the "face" Lily wants to maintain for the reading eyes of others.[17]

But in the story my book tells, aging is not so irreversible. With plastic surgery or the right kind of facial exercises, one could quite possibly have a new face. As Orwell proposes in this chapter's first epigraph, one really can have the face they "deserv[e]."[18] I have argued thus far that in aesthetic modernism the idea of the face shifts from a nineteenth-century ideal that values *what* the face expresses to a notion of the face itself as a manageable surface expression defined by the parameters of the body. Indeed, Orwell's seemingly hopeful conclusion—penned in his notebook from 1949—is usually taken out of context, especially since he was to die soon from tuberculosis and never saw his fifty-year-old face. The famous last words are actually a rather sarcastic indictment of modern life and the seemingly contradictory obsession with "softness & luxuriousness," on one hand, and "improvement in health & physique, continuous supersession of athletic records," on the other.¹⁹ Orwell's commentary and his own ill health provide an ironic backdrop through which to consider the modernist pursuit of a body that could be radically improved and thus saved from "decline"; this "ideology," according to age studies theorist Margaret Morganroth Gullette, locates in the slackening body a diminished potential for creativity.²⁰ Inspired by the intersecting fields of geriatrics, endocrinology, and sexology, both female and male modernists attempted to fortress themselves against decline and the claims of age. The desire to engineer the body as a means of creating and maintaining a "logic" between interior and exterior dimensions of a readable self is consistent with a view of modernism, as Tim Armstrong has argued, "characterized by the desire to *intervene* in the body; to render it part of modernity by techniques which may be biological, mechanical, or behavioral."²¹

Yeats in particular connected more literal forms of bodily alteration to the rebirth of sexual vitality and expressive authority. He had read surgeon and sexologist Norman Haire's *Rejuvenation* (1924) and elected, along with thousands of other men, to undergo the procedure developed by Viennese biologist Eugen Steinach. Yeats credited his Steinach operation, performed in 1934 by Haire, with a "resurgence" of sexual energy and dramatically increased artistic productivity.²² The surgery itself was basically a vasectomy designed with the intention of redirecting bodily "energy" from the "production of semen to the production of hormone," activating, as described in Peter Schmidt's *The Conquest of Old Age* (1931)—which Yeats owned—a fictional "puberty" gland.²³ The fascination with Auden's scrotum acquires new meaning in this context. The testicles, whose declining function and ravaged form are seen to incite the aging process, may be surgically remade into the repository of youth. To rejuvenate one's genital region is the equivalent of getting a new face. To re-form oneself literally means to surgically excavate one's existing form to create a new legibility based on being or feeling, in one way or the other, more like oneself.

In this fantasy of self-identity, legibility appears in a new, unwrinkled face, either in its original form or as an adequately "revisag[ed]" product (*CP*, 861). As I note in the preceding chapter, in the case of injured war veterans, faces that are seen to be "damaged" almost always appear against a normative, temporal representation of the original form of a person's face. In the cases I discuss here—which include the geriatric sciences developing within the modernist period; a midcentury film about the problem of age and masculinity, John Frankenheimer's *Seconds* (1966); and finally, Cindy Sherman's photographic portraits of herself in the personae of women from Hollywood's golden era—aging is explored from a number of vantage points, but most commonly as a socially threatening form that disturbs the idea that we can always know persons and thereby connect with them on the basis of that legibility. More productively, as it thwarts medical efforts to describe it through mimetic and physiognomic assessment, an aging form can be understood in terms of its challenge to the taxonomic structures created and sustained in the project of reading it. As Michael Pettit has demonstrated, "physiological research" in the early twentieth century galvanized "speculative fantasies about . . . techniques to reverse the aging process" and the legibility of a "glandular self" or psychology that was pliant and receptive to bodily interventions whose "claims resemble science fiction."[24] Such fantasies, as well as the construction of youthful legibility that emerges from them, stretch into the more explicit cultural fictions and fantasies of the midcentury, where the fear of an aging, unreadable subject extends, to quote Scott Herring, modernism's "long term aesthetic effects."[25]

Herring asks how the "embodiments" of old age—in particular the perceived "frailty" and "fragilization" of the elderly—might "supplement our understandings of modernism's pacing alongside its revised timelines."[26] Since I have been arguing that the representation of faces and facial types—pretty, wounded, pathologized, caricatured, and so on—underwrites a modernist preoccupation with the reading and writing of legible texts, the aging face offers another specific type of embodiment through which to consider modernism's extended temporal scope. As the most striking and available visual form through which we can think through the relationship of embodiment and legibility, the face is also the form whose loss—whether through war injury or age—occasions the social death of the unreadable person. Heather Laine Talley has more recently examined the problem of legibility in what she aptly coins the "disfigurement imaginary," where facial disfigurement is seen to occasion "social death" or the "cessation of social viability."[27] Talley argues that the rhetoric of facial repair—in examples such as "extreme" makeover, facial feminization surgery, and the transnational effort to repair cleft palates—"reduces the experience of facial difference to one of suffering" and consistently "implies that the life that endures is hardly life at all," thus staging surgical intervention and repair as a lifesaving necessity.[28] As a particular form of embodiment that elicits both social anxiety and corresponding fantasies of repair, I reflect on the aging face as a form that, in the discourse of early geriatric medical theory, is characterized as an unreadable, disingenuous, and unstable form, a threat to easy interaction and social order.²⁹ More specifically, I ask, how might we read old age? Can Auden's face be read, or is it an irrecuperably "damaged" form?

This is not to pathologize Auden's face. Aging faces are not actually less readable than young ones. I incorporate the idea of "damage," however, as a particular aesthetic category, one that counters a construction of legibility centered on the new or youthful face. In the examples I analyze here, such a logic underlay a developing pathology of aging bodies and, accordingly, supported a decline ideology focused on repair and rejuvenation. Indeed, as Armstrong recounts it, the popularity of the Steinach operation drew on specific cultural fears of "masculine decline" by promoting an "internalized eugenics in which reproductive potency was sacrificed for greater energy."³⁰ The vasectomy prevented aging men from fathering children, but the idea that they "inseminate and father only themselves," Armstrong argues, fueled Yeats's later "dream of self-creation" and incarnation.³¹ Judging from before and after pictures that appear in Schmidt's tome, which show "'healthy' weight gain suggestive of pregnancy," Armstrong identifies the "overtones of what we could call the transsexual-pathogenic."³² Yeats indeed, as Armstrong notes, equated his exile into old age with an overly compartmentalized masculinity that sabotaged his interest in a more androgynous imaginative identity. Significantly, Armstrong suggests that the surgery impacted Yeats's *feelings*, his renewed energy, his sense of self-recreation, and, quite crucially, his interest in "possess[ing] a woman's sexual identity."³³ Regardless of Yeats's psychological or emotional sense of transformation, Schmidt's photos and illustrations, his proof of male rejuvenation, are visual and bodily. They present this renewed masculine energy as evident in physically observable characteristics such as weight gain and in the rejuvenation of the wrinkled, sagging face into a smoother, fuller surface. The rejuvenated male subject cannot simply *feel* more energetic and vigorous but must be physically readable as such.

With the example of Yeats in particular, Armstrong demonstrates how closely aligned the fields of geriatrics and sexology were in producing the legibility of the aged person in the early twentieth century, especially through the discovery of the endocrine glands and their connection to the presumed legibility of a person. *The Conquest of Old Age* demonstrates quite clearly the interconnections between gender status and age; the study not only considers experiments aimed at the rejuvenation of aging men, involving the xenotransplantation of testicular tissue and hormones from others species, but also discusses the "transformation of sex" with regard to "natural and

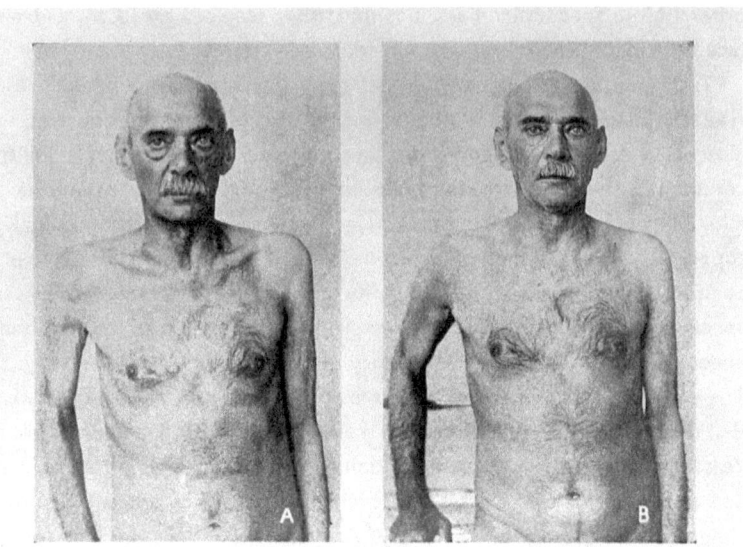

(a) SEVENTY YEAR OLD PATIENT BEFORE THE STEINACH OPERATION
(b) TWO MONTHS AFTER THE STEINACH OPERATION
(*Ufa Steinach-Film*)

From Paul Kammerer, "Rejuvenation and the Prolongation of Human Efficiency: Experiences with the Steinach-Operation on Man and Animals," 1923, reprinted in Peter Schmidt, *The Conquest of Old Age*, 1931. Courtesy of Wellcome Library, London.

artificial hermaphrodites."[34] According to Schmidt, "hermaphrodite[s]," "eunuch[s]," or "persons castrated in early youth" do not have "properly" functioning "reproductive" or "puberty glands."[35] They are in many ways, Schmidt elaborates, not fully male or female and thus show many of the physiological signs, such as the excessive accumulation of body fat, exhibited by those in advanced age.[36] Despite this sense of gender indeterminacy, Schmidt believes that the isolation of the "reproductive gland" as either male or female—since *"what makes a man is the male puberty gland"*—is crucial for rejuvenating aging men and, for those affected by gender intermediacy, the acquisition of a stable gender identity.[37]

Given this definition of *"what makes a man,"* as well as Schmidt's photographic catalog of the visual, observable outcomes of masculine rejuvenation, it follows that those males displaying typically feminine characteristics demand even closer scrutiny on the part of the observer. In guinea pigs Schmidt notes that the "feminized" male's "mammary glands were strongly developed, but its male genital organs remained atrophic," which leads him to deem such animals "homosexual" in their impulses.[38] While Schmidt uses the term "homosexual," he is actually describing what would have been more accurately called "inversion." In *Second Skins*, Jay Prosser takes great pains to distinguish between the two terms, arguing that inversion was often represented in sexology as a "corporeal mistake, a cross-gendered condition caused by a deceptive body."[39] In these accounts by Krafft-Ebing and Karl Heinrich Ulrichs, among others, the bodies of inverts were, for the sexologist, considered "unreliable text[s]" in their failure to speak accurately for their "true gender."[40] As Emma Heaney has observed, this body was critical to an "individualizing form of the diagnostic" in which "men of science" reduced the varieties of "trans feminine experience" into a "single entrapped figure."[41] This sexological model, Heaney argues, catalyzed the expansion of surgical and scientific knowledge, including gland transplantation and the "sex change," that sought to explain and clarify "gender nonconformity."[42]

Schmidt does illustrate how confusing situations could be surgically fixed and therefore rendered more legible through the isolation and transplantation of reproductive glands. Transformation of sex and rejuvenation were thus closely linked through the literal idea that reproductive glands—which were more determinate of gender than the appearance of one's genitals—could be surgically isolated, transferred, and transplanted from one human being to the other. Historian Chandak Sengoopta has called the 1920s the "decade of the testicle": "From *Good Housekeeping* to the *Journal of the American Medical Association*, there was no escape from the latest news and debates on the secretory functions of the testicles."[43] While Eugen Steinach had begun experimenting with sex change and testicular transplantation in guinea pigs by 1912, leading to the development of his Steinach operation, Serge Voronoff began performing monkey gland transplants on the aging rich in 1922. Roisin Kiberd has called these xenotransplantations examples of early "body-hacking," a "cosmetic" scrotum surgery that carried with it "cachet and . . . status" available only to the wealthy.[44]

Yeats's Steinach operation would have been one form of this body-hacking, and Norman Haire, who performed it, actually wrote the introduction to the first English translation of Niels Hoyers's *Man into Woman*, the 1931 account of the surgical transformation of artist Einar Wegener into Lili Elbe, most recently popularized through the successful film *The Danish Girl* and the 2015 novel by David Ebershoff.[45] Haire was part of an international network that included famous sexologists such as Magnus Hirschfeld, founder of the Institute for the Study of Sexual Sciences in Berlin, where Elbe's surgery was performed. Apart from the questions about identity arising from Elbe's story, Armstrong's interest, as well as my own, is in the surgery itself. For Armstrong, obvious advances in plastic surgery and prosthetics following World War I led to the possibility of the surgery, but more important was the work of such interventions in "declar[ing] the body to be in crisis."[46] In other words, modern surgical interventions offered a new definition of both the aging body and the queer body as bodies that *needed* to be saved by surgical methods.

Readable Types: Early Geriatrics

In the outline I am constructing, the surgical and discursive production of legibility was a shared enterprise in the confluence of geriatrics and sexology—one that produced old age as a physiognomy, or face. While the first fellowship in geriatric medicine was created in 1966 at City Hospital Center in New York, a Mount Sinai affiliate, the practice of modern geriatrics is generally dated by historians to 1866 and the work of French psychiatrist Jean-Martin Charcot, who studied a group of women, mostly over seventy years of age, in Paris's Salpêtrière Hospital and later collected his observations in *Clinical Lectures on the Diseases of Old Age* (1881). In good general health, these women had been abandoned or disposed of as diseased, thus inciting the physician's effort to distinguish between pathology or disease and old age as a distinct period of life. Concurrent with the developing discourses of physiognomy and criminal anthropology, with Charcot the aged body became its own system of signification, capable of being read, analyzed, and examined by an expert, where "visible signs" were taken to conceal "inner states of disorder."[47] As Stephen Katz observes in *Disciplining Old Age: The Foundation of Gerontological Knowledge*, however, Charcot created a methodological problem by giving pathological status to healthy bodies simply because of their age. The challenge consisted in distinguishing old age from normal states of the body. Charcot, through his observations of the women in the Salpêtrière Hospital, claimed that "textural changes which old age induces in the organism sometimes attain such a point that the physiological and pathological states seem to mingle by an imperceptible transition, and to be no longer sharply distinguishable."[48] Here, Charcot characterizes the aging body as a body in transition; its signs are no longer "distinguishable" as the result of pathology or physiology and are confounded by the diagnosis of a set of degenerative diseases related to the visible signs of old age—wrinkled and dry skin, gray hair, loose teeth, and stooped posture. For Charcot, aging is accelerated by "textural changes" that both are essential to the aging process and disguise it by creating a perceptual physiognomy, or face. Even the trained observer may find a person's age imperceptible, or the signs of aging may not be "distinguishable" from the signs of health.

As we know, the ability to see or perceive age is difficult. And we are less likely to pick up on a person's aging if we see them regularly. Affirmations like "You look great!" often underline the ellipsis of time in the mode of observation of the subject. Similarly, the subject of aging occasions a crisis in the idea of the observer as expert, for the more closely an observer inspects an aging body, the less perceptible it becomes—the physiognomy of old age becomes less clear.[49] As Katz points out, Charcot's *Clinical Lectures* "articulated the power/knowledge relations" that would define the new physiology of old age, but it also contributed to a "pronounced irony" that would come to trouble the developing fields of geriatrics and gerontology: "The more the clinicians and physicians distributed diseases through the aged body and probed its surface to discover the signs of senescence and degeneration, the less able they were to deter their pathological effects."[50]

Consequently, as geriatrics became a more therapeutic study, there was an increasing understanding of the aged body as one that betrayed the very signs with which it was visibly identified, in other words, one that disabled the kind of immediate or codified reading that is produced by a physiognomy. For example, in *Geriatrics: The Diseases of Old Age and Their Treatment* (1914), physician I. L. Nascher counts dissimulation as a primary characteristic of old age even though he also advances the idea that this is not pathological, but rather reflects a distinct phase in an individual's normal development. While the imagined readability of the subject motivates Nascher's geriatric enterprise, the four-hundred-page *Geriatrics*, like Charcot's *Clinical Lectures*, formulates in the aged body a radical idea of personhood based on its lack of intelligibility. Nascher saw aging as a process of cellular and tissue degeneration and, most interestingly, drew connections between the cellular turnover of the individual and the concept of personality. Because the aging process entails the continual "waste and repair of tissue," new cells differ so radically from earlier, childhood cells that "the aged individual is in fact an entirely different individual from the one who was formed from the ancestors of the late cells."[51] The only "connecting link" between these two individuals is the "personality, modified by intelligence education and the acquisition and suppression of traits."[52] Whereas the aging process is physiologically inevitable, personality is inherently flexible and influenced by environmental factors such as education and socialization. In contrast to the personality, the aged body itself reveals some "continuation of activity ... maintained by retention of sentience in the original cells" but resembles an "old vessel which has been repeatedly repaired until not a splinter of the original timbers is left," so that only "the individuality and the name remain."[53] Regardless of Nascher's identification of the "personality" as a potentially static (but modifiable) stabilizer of personal and social identity, this concept of aging imagines an unrecognizable subject, physically distinct from the person they once were, and therefore irreducible to an inherited, genetic code or explanation. What remains open to observation is the subject's "personality" or "individuality."

One wonders how Nascher or Charcot would have viewed Auden's aging face. Would it have simply been interpreted as one physiological example of aging within a spectrum of faces affected by cellular degeneration, or as an example of pathology? Nascher resorts to nineteenth-century physiognomy in his description of the "appearance of the senile individual" as "repellent to the esthetic sense."[54] While a child's appearance "arouses sympathy," old age is marked by a "disagreeable facial aspect" that exacerbates our feelings of "repugnance" and "irritability if not positive enmity" toward the "economic worthlessness" and "helplessness of the aged."[55] In addition to the "loose" and "lusterless" skin filled with "coarse and fine wrinkles," the "waste of muscles" appears in the lips, nose, ears, eyes, eyebrows, and the "so-called weak chin of the physiognomists."[56] There are also changes in the "anatomical relation of the bones to the face," external modifications in the individual that Nascher ultimately traces to alterations in the patient's "mentality."[57] For Nascher, old age is a "face-scape" that, as a distinct cellular pathology, externalizes specific mental traits such as "overwhelming interest in self," a "stubborn unreasoning perverseness," impaired memory, "suspiciousness," and "lessened interest in the events of the day," among others.[58] Nascher reiterates again that the most "noticeable" indicator of these mental fluctuations is a "change in facial expression."[59] He significantly retains an ideal of physiognomic constancy as an indicator of "senile mentality," despite his diagnosis of the profound and unpredictable bouts of unreason, loss of emotional control, and even "irrepressible sexual fury" that characterize the condition.[60]

As Nascher's *Geriatrics* indicates, geriatrics was a physiognomic enterprise devoted to establishing its practitioners as expert interpreters or readers able to distinguish the signs of old age from actual diseases. Yet as I am arguing, the very project of rejuvenating the aged body complicated the task of the observer by giving rise to new notions of personhood structured around transition and illegibility. Whereas Nascher employs physiognomic methods to produce the apparent readability of aging bodies, glandular theories of rejuvenation and transplantation actually sought to diminish the observability of old age, thus generating a new set of ontological problems related to the nature of persons. In discussing "Reactivation in the Male" through "heteroplastic methods," Schmidt, in *The Conquest of Old Age*, articulates the central problem of transplantation. Since most healthy men were unwilling to donate their testicles, recourse was made to either "executed men" or "men killed by accident." Would the transplantation of a criminal's testicles "transmit criminal proclivities to the receiver?"[61] The question exposes the specific fear that a face or a body may not explicitly manifest the internal degeneration inherited from the testicles of a criminal. Indeed, the greatest fear of eugenicists, as Schmidt attests, was that "elderly men would procreate children of poor quality."[62] While the explicit fear is that such offspring would not be of good enough quality, the underlying fear, I would suggest, is that they actually would, such that healthy children would not visibly reflect the low social worth of their deteriorating parents. It would, at least, make inherited traits and similarities less readable.

"Bartleby" and the Helplessness of Old Age

In the texts I am examining, the unreadable person occupies a space of "negativity" that, as Lee Edelman writes, cannot be identified with the "conservation of human community."[63] Edelman analyzes the Occupy Wall Street movement and its ironic appropriation of Herman Melville's famous scrivener, Bartleby, as a "face" around which to build a collective movement. Though "Bartleby, the Scrivener: A Story of Wallstreet" was published in 1853, I offer a brief reading of the story here given its connection to the physiognomic history I outline in this book and its facialization of old age as an unreadable text. The narrator reveals his physiognomic investments early on in the story, having hired Bartleby with the belief that "a man of so singularly sedate an aspect" would balance the "fiery" and "flighty temper[s]" of his other copyists.[64] The eldest of these, Turkey, is known to the lawyer by his face, which in the morning hours exhibited a "fine florid hue" but after the noon hour "blazed like a grate full of Christmas coals" ("BS," 19). In these later hours of the day, his business activity became more "strange, inflamed, flurried and flighty," resulting in "incautious" work that he defends with the following response: "True, . . . but with submission, sir, behold these hairs! I am getting old. Surely, sir, a blot or two of a warm afternoon is not to be severely urged against gray hairs. Old age—even if it blot the page—is honorable. With submission, sir, we are *both* getting old" ("BS," 20). Aging as well, the lawyer is to some extent able to see himself in Turkey, thereby positioning himself as an expert reader of a person he claims as a readable subject. The ironic humor of this readability is clear; old age "blot[s]" the page, making important writing unreadable.

Consequently, Turkey, who, in contrast to Bartleby, refuses to stop working for the man, is given the least important papers to copy and thus performs the most inefficient work. Regardless, he wants to keep working precisely in order to avoid going the way of Bartleby, of turning into a "blot" that is itself unreadable. He thus flatters the lawyer with an appeal to the legibility of his person, drawing attention to his "gray hairs"—not his alcoholism—as the reasonable explanation for his mistakes. The lawyer's own age, apparent in the story's first sentence—"I am a rather elderly man"—is also important here ("BS," 17). Advanced age and experience should of course cement the lawyer's narratorial authority, but always looming is the prospect of narrative failure—which he predicts at story's outset, lamenting that his lack of "materials for a full and satisfactory biography of this man . . . is an irreparable loss to literature" ("BS," 17). More specifically, the "irreparable loss" of Bartleby's narrative will accompany the "irreparable loss" of its elderly speaker to humanity. Near the story's end, just as Bartleby's refusal to quit the office has allowed the landlord to have him arrested and sent to the "Tombs," the lawyer, fearing the landlord, goes "fugitive"; he absents himself from Manhattan (making a temporary home in New Jersey), "surrender[s]" his business to the copyist Nippers, and "almost lived in [his] rockaway for the time" ("BS," 50). His "rockaway" is his carriage. Consequently, the narrator's appeal to common humanity at the end of the story, his attempt to claim Bartleby as a readable person, is also an attempt to incorporate his own aged self into that humanity.

While "Bartleby, the Scrivener" is ostensibly about the irrecuperable singularity of the scrivener, it is no less about the unassimilable nature of the narrator, who is desperate to save his own aged body from the "irreparable loss" of being not much more than a "blot" on the page ("BS," 17, 19). In the morning, Turkey's work is "valuable," as he "accomplish[es] a great deal of work not easy to be matched," but the quality declines so much as the day progresses that the lawyer's overall investment in his employee does not pay off ("BS," 31). "Bartleby, the Scrivener" corroborates the narrative of old age, to return to Nascher, as a condition of "economic worthlessness" and "helplessness."[65] In terms of the story, old age offers no viable or useful product, and the narrator himself is also eager to defend himself from this veritable uselessness. The story thus anticipates many of the concerns about the intelligibility of aging bodies that underwrite geriatric study in the early twentieth century. And despite Loy's particular message about aging gracefully, it further characterizes rejuvenation as a specifically masculine preoccupation focused on the social and economic worth of men. In his infamous "Fixed Period" speech, given upon his retirement from Johns Hopkins University in 1905, Dr. William Osler claimed that men over forty years of age were useless and that men over the age of sixty "perpetuate" unconscious "evils" through their various professional mistakes and social misdemeanors, such that it would be an "incalculable benefit" to society for them to stop work.[66] He further caused public outrage by referencing Trollope's dystopian novel *The Fixed Period*, in which older men were euthanized by chloroform. Laura Hirshbein has argued that many have taken Osler's remarks out of context and that the idea of age-based retirement at the beginning of the twentieth century was unusual given that men only retired when they were financially secure enough to stop working.[67] Regardless of the controversy Osler's speech inspired, "the fixed period" became a code phrase for the social menace that old age presented to the future of America. In general, and even from the standpoint of those seeking to make old people young, the idea of increasing numbers of elderly men in the workforce was provocative. The physician A. S. Blumgarten, for example, writing in 1923 in the introduction to George F. Corners's treatise on the Steinach method, *Rejuvenation: How Steinach Makes People Young*, calls rejuvenation a "problem," drawing attention to the unexpected social effects of prolonging the period of man's "vigor" and "youth."[68] For Corners the potential capitalist fantasy in which everyone continues working to increase the national wealth may lead to "economic war" between older and younger generations over pension funds and "disability clauses."[69]

Trading Faces in John Frankenheimer's *Seconds*

While the concept of an age-based retirement was a novel idea in early twentieth-century America, the idea of a "fixed period" of productive life for men incorporated itself into the American imaginary with ease, as Katz has argued, through an "interdisciplinary circulation of stereotypes" in which the nonscientific "discursive fashioning of old age" shows us the conceptual limitations of science.[70] If twentieth-century science, according to Katz, "arbitrarily rework[s]" and "borrows" from dystopian fiction of the nineteenth century its "often secondary or inconsequential metaphors and narratives," these now-dominant metaphors and narratives progress further into fictions of the mid-twentieth century to the threat of a body not merely "rejuvenated" but totally overhauled, showing few physically observable signs of the actual transition.[71] The antagonist of Aldous Huxley's satirical indictment of the empty commercialism of Hollywood culture, *After Many a Summer Dies the Swan* (1939), for example, is an aging California millionaire, Mr. Stoyte, whose private doctor specializes in longevity. One of his sources of income is "THE PERSONALITY CEMETERY," an apparent parody of the famous Forest Lawn Cemetery in Glendale, which is also the subject of Evelyn Waugh's 1948 novel (and the film on which it was based) *The Loved One*. Stoyte's cemetery advertises itself as a mortuary experience that is "DIFFERENT"; its "external architecture" is filled with various mock-ups of great monuments and sculptures, such as Rodin's *Le Baiser* and Shakespeare's tomb at Stratford upon Avon, and organ music is "broadcast by concealed loudspeakers all over the cemetery."[72] Regardless of this effort to convert death into an attractive and artful package, the moneyed Mr. Stoyte receives testosterone injections in his buttocks to enhance his diminishing sexual potency. Hormone treatments for men, along with Voronoff and Metchnikoff, are topics of discussion in the novel, where total rejuvenation is seen as an impossibility. In this novel, the male body in particular may be redirected only temporarily from its inevitable moral and physical "decay."[73]

Huxley's account of the futile and immoral search for total overhaul anticipates another dystopian fiction, situated further into the century, John Frankenheimer's disturbing 1966 film *Seconds*, based on the 1963 novel by David Ely. A blend of horror and science fiction, the film follows aging banker Arthur Hamilton (only in his early fifties and played by John Randolph) as he visits the headquarters of a shady unnamed "organization"; ultimately under coercion, he agrees to fake his own death and is then reinvented through extreme plastic surgery into the sexually robust and beautiful artist Antiochus "Tony" Wilson, played by Rock Hudson. In his commentary for the Criterion Collection edition of the film, David Sterritt writes that *Seconds* "is both Frankenheimian and Frankensteinian, carrying Mary Shelley's concept of a 'Modern Prometheus'" to "the industrialized domain of midcentury

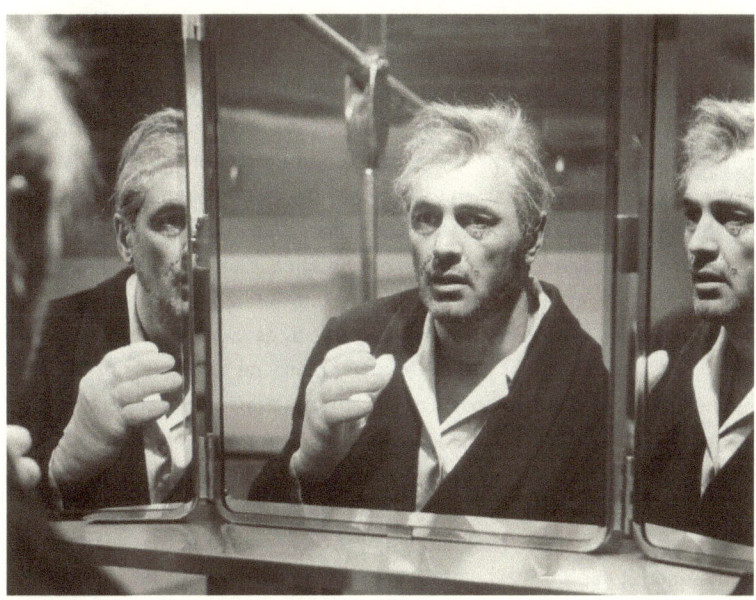

Rock Hudson in *Seconds*, by John Frankenheimer, 1966. © Paramount Pictures. All-star Picture Library Limited/Alamy Stock Photo.

America, where people are personnel . . . and *processed* personnel, to boot. Arthur will be processed into Tony the way pink slime is processed into hamburger."[74] The metaphor here is undeniably apt, as Arthur is routed through a meat processing plant on his way to the shrouded company headquarters. The processing produces a subject in perpetual transition, a condition that is concealed by his appearance as product. Unable to adapt to his new and more exciting life as an artist in a Malibu community of other seconds, in which he feels controlled and manipulated by the "company," Wilson returns to the headquarters and asks to be remade once again. Since he refuses to "sponsor" another possible "second," he is instead executed by lethal injection.

The film is in many ways the imaginative literalization of Osler's "fixed period." The company preys on this masculine anxiety about productivity and work, and its scheme reflects a more general anxiety about aging in the 1960s, the decade in which Medicare was introduced, geriatrics became an acknowledged medical specialty, and the United States began to wonder about how it would it care for a population that was living into advanced age. Frankenheimer indeed remarked in an interview that the film was a response to "all this nonsense in society that we must be forever young, this accent on youth in advertising and thinking."[75] The ugly underside of this emphasis was a corresponding anxiety about the social effects of aging, and a developing sociology of old age concerned itself more specifically with questions regarding the self and identity of the elderly individual, as well as his integration into society.[76] As a passing narrative, the film examines these questions about aging while playing on the same issues of intelligibility and identity that underlie the earlier geriatric studies I have examined.

Indeed, Tony Wilson is billed by the company as its surgeon's "best work," meaning that he passes as a much younger man; the "seconds" or "reborns" he meets in Malibu are obviously not as attractive. In initially supplying their client with a new face, the company also gives him a new signature, by literally altering the ligaments in Arthur Hamilton's hand. While Arthur Hamilton dabbled in watercolor, Tony Wilson is an established painter with a mark, a signature style. The company provides paintings that corroborate Tony's identity as a painter—hung precisely in his new Malibu studio—but he is told that "in time you will perfect your own style." The decision to make Tony an artist engages the problems of claiming a face and, further, a sexual identity that is not one's own, neither of which were ever, in the first place, fully *felt*. The art lies about who Arthur/Tony is; it is not an extension of its maker's hand, but rather represents the alienation Tony feels in his new body.

Seconds underlines the apprehension about what it means to wear other faces, in particular, the faces of younger men, because to wear the face of a younger man does not mean that one *is*, sexually speaking, a younger man. When Wilson becomes uncontrollably intoxicated at his party, his behavior discloses his insecurity about his claim to his product. When a guest asks about his method of painting, he answers that he paints naked, as it's "the only way to get to the truth." In Tony Wilson, Arthur Hamilton has developed a defiant sense of humor, keen to broadcast the truth to his guests, who, unbeknownst to him, are also seconds. And like the older people they once were, there is no world for them outside of the society they are so eager to make for themselves, so they are to an extent not unlike the other old folks who have congregated in retirement villages. Arthur/Tony's concern here is that he cannot claim himself in the paintings, which he did not paint. This is the angst surrounding the forgery of his signature, and its balm is Arthur Hamilton's absent face. Each time Wilson looks into a mirror and touches his pretty face, it as if he is trying to remember another face.

The issue of disguise and the corresponding problems of legibility it poses fall in line with the two earlier films in Frankenheimer's paranoia trilogy, *The Manchurian Candidate* (1962) and *Seven Days in May* (1964). In particular, to revisit Sterritt's remarks about the film, what is a person, post-processing? As it explores the sociology of aging, *Seconds*, like Huxley's novel, suggests that aging persons do experience specific issues related to self and identity, as well as social integration, that cannot be reconditioned through bodily intervention. While the face of Rock Hudson is transplanted onto Tony through a surgical procedure, he achieves his new six-foot-four body through months of exercise and rehabilitation. The film does not offer any evidence that there is a magic hormonal key to this younger body except for rigorous physical conditioning that miraculously does not have to be maintained after Wilson moves to Malibu. The promise for Tony Wilson seems to be that the reconstructed body itself can rejuvenate its mental and emotional fibers to match its claims. John thus gently pushes Wilson to throw a cocktail party in order to meet the neighbors, but Arthur/Tony replies that he is not ready, affirming again the stereotype of the aged as socially reclusive, disinterested in social integration.

The aging Arthur Hamilton was also socially estranged, as is later corroborated in Arthur/Tony's own visit to his former wife, who claims that he was not interested in sex and was disengaged from familial life. The company thus plants its employee Nora, played by Solome Jens, in apparent hopes that she will reawaken Tony's sexual desire and consequently his motivation to pass as a second.[77] They meet and return to Nora's beach house, where Arthur/Tony tells her that "you don't know anything about me really." "Yes, I do," Nora replies, "It's all right there in your face." She touches his new face, murmuring that "the good things always happen with the real." Nora's analysis, staged as it is, plays ironically on the idea that a newly constructed man can be read as "real," that his fabricated life will indeed authenticate itself as the asexual and asocial tendencies of his advanced age dissipate and as he becomes happily rejuvenated through new social and intimate connections. Arthur/Tony's participation in this fantasy is required so that Tony will no longer be Arthur and will in fact become the "stud bull" his surgeon has destined him to be. Nora thus brings him to a Bacchic Santa Barbara gathering in which he is encouraged to jump naked with countless strangers into a large barrel full of grapes. Farber counts the scene, filmed at an actual festival, as "very bad," especially as it attempts to represent "the break down of Hamilton's inhibitions."[78] While Arthur/Tony is actually abashed by the intimacy with strangers, Nora, exhilarated, strips and jumps into the vat. As Arthur/Tony attempts to stop her, he is stripped by the revelers and forcibly thrown in, dunked, and slathered with pulp.

Arthur/Tony now understands what it means to behave appropriately as a second, or to pass, even though he is surrounded by people, we find out, who know he is passing. In the next scene, the hoped-for cocktail party materializes, the place to socially validate his relationship with Nora and to confirm his new sexual freedom. But the freedom is portrayed as a joke. In one conversation, a woman informs him that she belongs to a "special kind of group." "Nothing subversive, I hope," Arthur/Tony replies, to which she responds,

> GUEST: Oh, good heavens, no! We change sects!
> WILSON: I beg your pardon?
> GUEST: Oh, no, no. Good heavens. You thought I meant. . . . Sects. S-E-C-T-S.
> WILSON: Oh, sects! . . . Well, Thank God!
> GUEST: We change every month. Right now, we're in Aztec. Huitzilopochtli, Quetzalcoatl, virgin sacrifice and all.

As Sean Easton has claimed, the scene reveals the "shared discourse underlying the worldviews of both the outwardly countercultural and corporate, institutional agents in the film."[79] Through this confluence of countercultural and corporate fantasy, the humor in the scene also draws attention to the connection between this decidedly heterosexual society of "reborns," or the rejuvenated and reconstructed old, and those who have undergone similar transformative surgeries on different parts of their bodies. However, at this moment the film seems to omit the possibility that one might sell one's life in order to come back as an entirely different sort of person with a new gender or, in this case, genitals. Arthur Hamilton just wants to be younger and more exciting. Nonetheless, the uncomfortable humor is exacerbated by the fact that the audience must now have an inkling that the party guests are in fact other reborns, who know that they are all reborns, and thus surgically transformed persons.

To the extent that Arthur has transformed himself into the more dynamic Tony, he has seemingly mastered a new, more aggressive style of social banter, but this cavalier speech, with the help of alcohol, is soon to out him, particularly after he demonstrates too much familiarity with Harvard, Arthur Hamilton's alma mater, and golf, the hobby of an aging man, not a decadent artist. Whereas Arthur Hamilton's identity was professionally compartmentalized in a way that became increasingly meaningless, thus motivating him to undergo such a perilous rebirth, the company encourages him to cultivate the various lifestyle pursuits that would make him equal to his face. One might indeed overlook the most basic but radical premise on which the film is based, that the chance to start over is the chance at having a new face and, further, the chance of living a life that is equal to that face. In the film, Hudson's face, symmetrically inexpressive and even dull, seems to acknowledge the failure of Arthur's rebirth as Tony. The company indeed admits to its high percentage of failures, but it avoids the question of how men with empty affective lives can forge the kinds of experiences that will corroborate their new faces.

Accordingly, at the beginning of the film, the viewer is shocked by the visual mutilation and parsing of the banker's face, made even more disturbing by the 9.7 mm fisheye lens used by Frankenheimer's director of photography, James Wong Howe.[80] This grotesque dismantling of a face finally morphs into a bandaged face that is later unmasked as Hudson's in front of the mirror. Hudson's fine features are the antidote to the dread and terror of this disfigurement, but all of the images take for granted the question of what a face does in corroborating an identity. Ely's novel mentions that Arthur/Tony looks at his face hundreds of times in a day, amazed at how surgeons had transformed "a face that tended to be rounded, florid and a bit jowly, and had somehow made it lean and long and hard, with prominent cheekbones and chin."[81] Unlike the text that could be seen as an important antecedent for the film, Oscar Wilde's *The Picture of Dorian Gray*, in *Seconds* the terror of having a new face derives from the fact that there is no portrait of Arthur Hamilton's face aging hideously in the attic—no "memento" to remind Arthur/Tony of what he once was or even is. Arthur/Tony's suffering is the cost of capitalist fantasy, where modern identity production is literalized as a business that trades in the production and consumption of faces. In becoming different from himself by literally consuming another invented identity and maximizing the promises of capitalism, Arthur Hamilton becomes a man with a mark—a "signature" that corroborates his identity as a painter.

There is no question in the film of a mere rejuvenation of Arthur Hamilton through something like testosterone therapy or a skin graft. Rather, in this fantasy, the livable life requires a total overhaul of the person, but at the expense of individual freedom. Taken in conjunction with the earlier geriatric studies I have examined, the film brings up the question of how we might reimagine the limits of our own bodies outside of the mechanisms of capitalist power production and the operations of the state. This is also, I would suggest, a question about art, since the film aligns the capitalist production of bodies with the production of art. The new face of Tony Wilson is the surgeon's "finest work," and its "real" readability is posed against the illegibility of Arthur Hamilton's old face. However, in attempting to produce itself as a readable and thereby nonthreatening subject, the new face of art uses itself up, or participates in its own defacement.

The logic of defacement has been most beautifully and elliptically explored by Michael Taussig in *Defacement: Public Secrecy and the Labor of the Negative*, which is essentially a study of the ways in which power is maintained through concealment and public secrecy. Part of the "violence of daily life," defacement "catches us unawares."[82] What is this violence, Taussig asks, and how does the human face become the form through which we can ideally think about this type of violation? The answer to this question lies in the nature of the "public secret," that which is "generally known but not spoken," or what we know not to admit that we know.[83] This sort of dissimulation, according to Taussig, maintains the social structure and its attendant models of selfhood. Despite the basic prohibition that enforces such concealment, there is in the public secret an incitement to betray the secret, which is produced in having a face; Taussig mentions the "tenderness of face and of faces facing each other, tense with the expectation of secrets as fathomless as they seem worthy of unmasking."[84] This desire to unmask the secret amounts to a kind of surplus that "(dis)establishes the real," a fantasy made up by the state designed to justify its own power; it is a form of "contrived illusionism" presented as "cultural truth," an effacement of the "noncontractual elements that underpin the workings of the social contract."[85]

My summary here may not do justice to the complexities of Taussig's argument, in particular the philosophical grounding of his theory of the negative and his ethnographic accounts of the effects of Zapatista and Selk'nam unmasking. My account does, however, allow us to consider what the idea of defacement can tell us about old age in *Seconds* and, more particularly, what it is about a person—and faces—that cannot be concretely regulated, registered, or read. In the film, Arthur/Tony is slow to understand the "secret" of his society of reborns who pretend they are not reborns; in fact, he is horrified and distraught when he understands that his love object Nora is an employee of the company. The "public secret" of this openly deceptive social organization is especially evident at the cocktail party, where Arthur Hamilton begins to show himself, consequently unmasking Tony Wilson's secret that he is, in many ways, still Arthur Hamilton, revealing the negative personality traits that characterize the "senile mentality," the "stubborn unreasoning perverseness," the loss of emotional control, and even the "irrepressible sexual fury" that prevent a happy form of socialization based on the willingness to conceal the open secret.[86] The party is also where Tony misunderstands his guest's reference to changing "sects" as changing "sexes," a slippage that openly broadcasts the possibility of another form of defacement—and establishes parallels with the defacement of Arthur Hamilton by Tony Wilson by Arthur Hamilton, who is also the subject of the company's defacement—and the defacement of genitals by other genitals. One's genitals, of course, are not one's face, but Taussig, interrogating the "links between secrecy and nakedness of the human form," argues that the genitals are a core part of the logic of defacement.[87] As such a perfect work, Tony Wilson inspires this defacement. Like some statues, which have a "strategic, built-in desire to be violated," defacement "is already inscribed within the object," just as, in the film, the beauty of Rock Hudson / Tony Wilson cannot be contemplated outside of the grotesque images of Arthur Hamilton's perspiring face.[88]

In *Seconds*, Tony Wilson is significantly clean-shaven and unweathered, but the play on "sects" and "sex" suggests that his face—as opposed to the aging, fleshy face of Arthur Hamilton—also incites the unmasking of his new sexual virility, just as Auden's wrinkled face, for Hockney, motivates the revelation of his similarly lined scrotum. Thus, Arthur/Tony watches in horror as Nora strips naked and jumps into the vat of grapes with the revelers in Malibu. While the body may be rejuvenated and refined through reconditioning and exercise, to what extent is Tony Wilson a *total* reconstruction of Arthur Hamilton? The genitals, given the humor that circulates around them in the film, may be the one part of Arthur Hamilton's reconstruction that the film does not address. Nonetheless, it's Tony Wilson's face that incites the damage occasioned by the genitals of an older man. This initial surgical refacement of the person, in Taussig's terms, invites further defacement in the form of the viewer's unmasking, or the viewer's perceived unmasking of an individual—resonant with Hockney's speculation about the revealed truth of Auden's nether regions.

Cindy Sherman's Modernist Aftereffects

Instead of a totally overhauled person, Arthur/Tony becomes damaged goods, and he even seeks a do-over by requesting another identity that might coherently meld his own wishes with the company's desires. He wants a "new face" and a "new name" but admittedly desires to "do the rest." His hope is to be equal to his new face, but for him this kind of coherence requires agency from the company and the fantasy of identity it sells. By refusing to sponsor a new client, however, he fails to adhere to the company's terms and is consequently deemed a damaged product, ineligible for a new name or face. I suggested earlier, in the case of Loy, Yeats, and Auden, that such an idea of "damage" can be seen as an "aesthetic formulation" that counters the fantasy of total identity that is represented by the new and younger face.[89] My use of this term reflects Jennifer Ashton's analysis of Ben Lerner's *10:04: A Novel* (2015), which, she argues, offers instruction regarding the separate but related meanings of "total" and "totaled" in the case of damaged art. Midway through the novel, the narrator's friends hatch the idea of creating "The Institute for Damaged Art," a place for collected works by artists that, due to damage, have been "formally demoted from art to mere objecthood" and banned from circulation.[90] Moving from the distinction between "total" and "totaled," she credits the novel with the idea that no work can be "totaled" without a "concept of the *total* work"; furthermore, a work of art may be classified as such by way of the idea that any damage renders it "totaled." Extending from these claims, she suggests that the novel advances an understanding of the work of art in its "willing subsumption of damage," such that damage becomes "a matter of the intended form of the work" and its project of visualizing crisis as something "we can look at together."

In his response to Ashton's article, Theodore Martin questions Ashton's pinning of the novel's capacity for resistance on its intentional strategy for doing so, its having willingly recorded its "market concessions" and "economic compromises," and expresses doubts about the actual difference between damage and "repair," "damaged art" and "redeemed art," or dystopia and utopia. The "contradictory form of *10:04*" remains "at best," he argues, "a reflection of the contradictions that structure life under capitalism." My point in outlining this argument is not to elevate one reading of Lerner's novel over the other but to connect this discussion of damaged art as both a political and aesthetic formulation to the models of illegibility and deface-

Unreadable Persons 175

Cindy Sherman, *Untitled #565*, 2016, dye sublimation metal print. © Cindy Sherman. Courtesy of the artist and Hauser & Wirth.

ment that emerge from the examples I have examined here: Auden's face, Yeats's Steinach operation, the discourse of early geriatrics, Melville's "Bartleby, the Scrivener," and the total overhaul of Arthur Hamilton in *Seconds*. I conclude this chapter by adding another name to this list, Cindy Sherman's, whose work's "willing subsumption of damage" probes the problem of longevity and ageism on numerous levels. I reflect here only briefly on the recent series of portraits of Sherman posed and costumed as aging film stars from Hollywood's golden age, which I saw in 2016 at the Metro Picture Gallery in New York. The portraits in their faded glamour feature women's haunted faces, and they are doubly perplexing because of our knowledge of Sherman herself; it's not clear whether Sherman is impersonating the physiognomic forms of another era or the women that inspire them are posing as her. If the face must do work to appear like the self one wants to claim or remember, who is being claimed in these pictures? The faces in the portraits also open questions about longevity that are not just literal but stylistic. They seem to acknowledge that faces, like texts, stand in for "aesthetic effects" that persist but may have aged out of relevance to the contemporary moment.[91] As with Auden's "Doggerel by a Senior Citizen," with which I began this chapter, this staging of obsolescence, as well as the probing of one's life as an aftereffect, is also a critical reflection on the role of the artist.

At the time that I saw them, I had not yet aged enough to feel a strong identification with the photographs, but as the years have unfolded in the writing of this book about faces, I've become more disconcerted by the way the photographs, as well as Sherman's subsequent Instagram artworks, both document and "confront what aging means to a woman."[92] Sherman's photographs offer a visual exploration of Mina Loy's unsettling question, "For to what end is our experience of life if deprived of a fitting aesthetic revelation in our faces?" (AFC, 165). If, for Loy, "facial integrity" means fashioning a facial legibility that projects the "youth of our souls," what kind of face is Sherman constructing and what "esthetic revelation" does she seek (AFC, 165)? Sherman's work is technical and involves largely herself. She has also characterized her photographs as "fantasies" in which she manipulates her own body and image as she would a mannequin.[93] However, the more recent photographs use sets and costume to experiment with temporality; they place aging women not only in an earlier era but also in a dated photographic genre, the publicity shot, which almost always featured younger women. In a departure from an earlier stylistic impersonality, the photos are Sherman, and yet they are not. Sherman has indeed acknowledged her own feeling of relation to the photographs. They convey "pain," as she puts it, yet the women are "looking forward and moving on."[94] Placed within the conventions of genre, the pain interrupts the more readable Hollywood image the stylized conventions of pose and clothing seek to convey. The eerie faces of the women, faces that play on the conventions of portraiture, are thus "like" Garbo's or Swanson's or Stanwyck's but also "like" Sherman's. As with the caricatures of Oscar Wilde's face, we catch something in them that brings to mind a known face. But Sherman's portraits draw our eyes in two directions: toward our image of the artist, Cindy Sherman, and separately toward our vision of the screen sirens who are the ostensible subjects of the portraits. This discordance, I suggest, accounts for the pain we witness in the picture.

Rather than self-portraits, these are "performed portraits" that look back reflexively at the modernist era.[95] My own mind returns to Lily Bart's staging of herself in a gauzy white garment for observation in a rich person's home, where her offering of herself as a legible product is followed by her subsequent humiliation in the face of a mirror. She doesn't intend to be read through, but instead as one kind of person rather than another. Sherman's portraits seem to acknowledge this problem of the work, as well as the ensuing pain involved in the construction of oneself as a legible aftereffect. The images exaggerate the rupture that occurs through the ellipsis of time, and the viewer recognizes a face that is not the subject's own, but rather Sherman's masked face, marked by her own pain. More exaggerated are the photographs that Sherman began posting on Instagram in 2017. Unlike the more elegant portraits, they are bizarrely rescaled faces in the tradition of the "close-up." Though not as formalized as the earlier golden-era portraits, they have been read as a defiant commitment to women's "ugly beauty" and as commentary on the cultural narcissism of the "selfie."[96] The result of Instagram's own filters and facial manipulation technology, the photos also explore the formal work that a face does despite the very specific kinds of damage and distortions that only aging women know about, the secrets that inevitably threaten to betray us even on our best days. As Simmel so unkindly observed, sagging and furrowing disrupt the face's aesthetic effect, its ability to "embrace its parts and hold them together."[97] The faces are—in the tradition of caricature—just barely held together by their figurative likeness to Sherman's own face. But the real draw is the way the images broadcast little secrets and thus participate in their own damage or defacement. Quite a few of the images showcase women's unkempt facial hair. One woman has grown a beard. Faces are not just wrinkled but pocked, scarred. Pores are crudely visible. The women incompetently manage their own efforts at defacement. Unfortunate makeup choices are both the dated aftereffects of an earlier era and the result of poor application skills. These women are out of style or have bungled style. Sherman images the vulnerability of inexpert self-styling in an era where YouTube videos teach women how to expertly contour their faces with features they do not naturally possess.

Such images reaffirm a Baudelairean account of caricature; they require a modern, self-conscious viewer who must acknowledge their own sense of superiority in recognizing the "bad taste" on display in the photos. At the same time, the portraits channel a fear and vulnerability that relates specifically to aging women and the modern technologies of rejuvenation that haunt their own making of faces—which range from specialized makeup techniques to injectable fillers to camera filters. These interventions in the aging process, like Botox, a neurotoxin that literally paralyzes facial muscles, both deface the face and underwrite the face as form. At the moment that Sherman's photos highlight and respond to facial deformation, even pathology, they simultaneously operate as portraits, documenting the face's capacity to form even the most distorted physiognomies. Unlike Rock Hudson's clean-shaven and symmetrical face, which is itself the product of rejuvenation, a work of art, these faces do not invite damage or violation, but rather give face to the damage that is involved in making a face. They invite our viewing of the tension that exists between the face's potential for synthesizing degrees of feeling into recognizable forms and readable expressions and its capacity for disturbing that harmony. Unlike the other examples I have discussed in this chapter, Sherman's faces do not seek to produce their subject's readability as one specific kind of person or the other.

In the other contexts I have elaborated, the readable subject is an artificially or surgically constructed subject, built with the consciousness that one's being in the world is the result of being read as one thing or another, that in order to be a person in the first place, one must have a particular kind of readable form. In *Seconds*, the "new face" of a person represents the constructed form of legibility produced by market capitalism. For Taussig, however, there is autonomy beyond capitalism, but it lies in illegibility, what we cannot discern. And what we cannot discern and what, as readers, we cannot simply describe is what is behind the damage. This unseen is the "surplus" that, as Taussig remarks, incites us to look harder, to read deeper, into the unknowable abyss of other beings and other forms. This looking, as Taussig illustrates, is always an action of defacement. In the tradition of prosopopoeia, to read another face—which is, for Taussig, also a text—is to reface it and thereby cause more damage. To reface something, as Taussig claims, is to "recuperat[e] a surface," a live face, that has been previously unmasked, whether that action be on the part of the state, in its own interest, by "photo-ID state certifying portraits," or on the part of the victim as a means of transgressing the state that has unmasked it.[98]

For Taussig, this dance—between defacement and refacement, masking and unmasking—is related to the face's "allegorical proclivities" and its place in the *"history of reading."*[99] To illustrate these claims, Taussig imagines a reading child who suddenly encounters "a picture in the midst of the text, a depiction of the written."[100] Following Walter Benjamin, Taussig argues that this allegorical image, most often seen as a figurative or literal face, "reconfigure[s]" the work of reading as a negotiation of image and text, exposing both the "prohibition of transformation" and the "possibilities for transformation," or, through "mystery," the emergence of "something new."[101] This idea of the visual of the face as an allegorical image that both masks and incites damage complicates a one-dimensional understanding of what a readable surface is and, further, the work of giving an "accurate accoun[t]" of it through our "reading" practices.[102] Extrapolating from Taussig's argument, any reading of a work resurfaces it, very much in the way a picture or image in a book, in the tradition of allegory, compels a reading that both refaces the words and does damage to them.

Seconds offers a rather grim portrait of a dynamic that may otherwise be, as in Taussig's outline, a source of "mystery," agency, or play. The newly rejuvenated body of Arthur/Tony cannot master its contradictions to fulfill the "possibilities for transformation" offered by refacement—of developing a fully integrated identity in which one can become equal to one's face, as Mina Loy would have it, or, in the case of Yeats, even equal to one's desire or feeling about oneself. In the examples I have outlined, the aging individual brings to the forefront the rupture that elicits a crisis in reading—in our ability to construct an account of the surface—as well as the loss of face and social death that presumed illegibility implies, when everything in the capitalist power structure seeks to produce easy, finished identities and to manufacture legible, unthreatening subjects. Admittedly, an aging face is no more legible or illegible than a younger face. However, when set against an ageist construction of legibility built around the "new face," we may look at Auden's face or Sherman's Instagram posts as representing a particular form of illegibility that inspires the kind of close looking inherent to the function of the face as form (*AFC*, 65).[103] We may not be able to see what is in the form, but it inspires the action of reading it nonetheless. To return to Taussig's formulation, which addresses the ethical dimensions of our sometimes invasive desire to know others, faces are tender, especially when they are "facing each other"; their very "tense" and expectant engagement makes their secrets "seem worthy of unmasking."[104] Taussig's emphasis here is not on what is unmasked, or the unmasking itself, but on the agency of the face as it compels us to know it. Thus, Taussig's logic of defacement ultimately demonstrates how human community may in fact be built around the bodies of persons, worthy and tender in their illegibility, who simultaneously evoke our desire to know them. We might see the aging form as a model of resistant aesthetic engagement based on that act of encountering the "tenderness" of other faces, especially those faces, like Auden's, Simmel would dismiss as "aesthetically unbearable."[105] We liberate ourselves by facing damage, in our continued desire to know what we will never know.

Epilogue
"Getting Out" of the Face

> The body image is dominated by the face image. If it were possible to amputate the face and for the subject to continue to live, we would predict a phantom face of much greater longevity and resistance to deformation and extinction than in the case of phantom limbs following amputation.
>
> —Silvan Tomkins, *Affect, Imagery, Consciousness*, 2008

> This is my face but I am not this: I exist behind and yet beyond it.
>
> —Jonathan Cole, *About Face*, 1999

The last words of this book were written not without the help of a sun-filled sabbatical in southern Spain, interrupted by the onset of a global pandemic. As my family and I prepared for our emigration, we were advised to bring enough passport-sized photos for the numerous cards that would verify our identities during the year (to become three) of our stay. They were required for everything from school matriculation to joining the local soccer team, and, as expected, we soon ran out of the precious miniatures. After spending the better part of a week searching for a machine that might spit out a few dozen of these jewels, I applied for a municipal library card, dutifully submitting not one but two face shots: that appearing in my photocopied passport, and a new and glossy *carnet* with white background.[1] When I returned two weeks later to retrieve my new card, my picture was not on it. "Está en el archivo" (It's in the archive), the librarian said. Annoyed about the waste of a perfectly good photo, I began to wonder about my lost face.

Was it scanned for use in some database, or, more likely, filed away in some municipal attic?

What does it mean to lose one's face? Over the past few years, most of us have become accustomed to masked facial interactions and to conversing with black squares. I tend to move my face closer to the square as if I can see the person there. I lean in. I smile. The face-to-face interaction directs even our most blind exchanges; we may no longer register the contradiction that, for Jenny Edkins, attends our consciousness of face: between its potential disappearance into "a world of digital images and the post-human" and our simultaneous sense of its "endur[ance] as an emblem of political personhood."[2] For Edkins, following Deleuze and Guattari, the "face is a politics" produced by specific political systems that see it as a "necessity."[3] In this view, where virtual experiences of facing are purely replicative, the face is a trap we cannot escape. Edkins's analysis draws on a fascinating selection of photographs, ranging from the posters of missing persons that appeared in Manhattan after the 2001 attacks to Robert Lyon's catalog of the survivors of Rwandan genocide to Suzanne Opton's billboard portraits of Iraq War veterans. Despite the dynamism of these forms, Edkins announces her "suspicion" that a "politics that makes a face is a politics that produces a person as object," bypassing the possibility that the portraits' formal qualities may actually produce images, or at least "spark[s]," to return to Walter Benjamin, that evade objectification.[4] As I have argued, a face may produce both a sense of aesthetic remoteness—of "mystery," to return to E. H. Gombrich—and a familiar "impression of life."[5] In his famous essay on Garbo's face, Roland Barthes addresses this same dynamic when contrasting the "individualized" effect of Audrey Hepburn's face—which, he argues, displays a "specific thematics (woman-as-child, woman-as-cat)" distinguished by "her person"—with the "conceptual" and "essential" beauty of Garbo.[6] Notwithstanding the animal references, Barthes suggests that the viewer's familiarity with the personality of Hepburn herself produced an "infinitely more complex" face that was not a product of unilateral objectification.[7]

As with the numerous examples I have discussed in this book, which range from celebrated figures such as Oscar Wilde and W. H. Auden to unknown soldiers, I have argued that the person or personality is both a distorting lens and a conduit for reading a face. At the same time, form itself is intimately connected to our experiences—our familiarity with a person or personality. As an example of portrait photography, which may range from the mug shot to the selfie, the passport photo, as a form, seeks to limit what

Epilogue 183

Discarded identification photos.

Hepburn's face and Wilde's face encourage, the distortion of one's apparently objective appearance by the form or expression of the person—the personality.[8] At eleven, my son has endured enough of these sittings to know that he must work to project a "neutral" expression. When my then-five-year-old daughter infected her pictures with a defiantly snarled lip, we had them retaken for fear that they would be sent back. Behind the requirement of expressive neutrality—which curtails earrings, eyeglasses, and unmanaged hair—lies a more basic fear that a person's image may be marred by form, rendering identification cards and documents useless or, in a perhaps worse scenario, purely procedural, as suggested by my doubts about the location of my own unused portrait. Something feels wrong these days about a face that is not used up.

Form is essential to our reading of faces, but it may also mask a face; this problem, I suggest, underlies the state-driven demand for neutral and expressionless photographs that seek to image a "real" or authentic face. At the same time, as Hans Belting observes, the process of self-representation, realized in the portrait form (of which the passport photo is no exception), represents "the withdrawal of life from the face," its "stiffen[ing] into a mask."[9] This evisceration of face is an effect of other forms of portraiture, such as the selfie, as well as our obsessive efforts to form or transform the face. As evidenced by the ads that fill my social media feed, Botox and other fillers are now marketed to an ever-younger demographic of men and women as part of their regular beauty routines; the most recent news is that injecting neurotoxins into the face paralyzes its musculature, thus preventing expression lines from forming in the first place. In this common scenario, the face becomes a literalized display of the portrait's function of divesting "life from the face." As Josh Cohen has observed in his manual *How to Read Freud*, antiaging creams and procedures "appear to be unambiguously on the side of life," but they really demonstrate "the death-drive at work," or the "collective phantasy of erasing the fact of having *lived*."[10] Placed within the history of expression I have outlined, artificial interventions into the aging process attempt to produce a "changeless, *lifeless*" face.[11]

Perhaps the "*lifeless*," Botoxed face is the twenty-first-century manifestation of the sort of "facial integrity" and "psychic logic" Mina Loy imagined just over a hundred years ago.[12] The desire to construct an expressionless face is one form of the many kinds of the "self-aestheticizing" interventions that, in the early twentieth century, motivated Lily Bart's "transcendental project," directed against the kind of self-abstraction—or, expression itself—that produces lines on a face. The cultivation of an ageless face may be seen—as goes the current popular argument about the "provocation" of Madonna's new face, or the "good work" apparently performed on Martha Stewart's face—as a defensive front to the inevitability of self-abstraction,

Epilogue

ageism, and facial loss, a response to an anxiety about faces that, as with my photo, do not get used, are no longer desirable, resist or are denied circulation, or have been quietly harvested for use in some database.[13] In the digital age of social media and selfies and instant photographic replication, these are the thousands of faces that we delete in our quest for the perfect image or the ones that linger unseen, receiving embarrassingly few "likes." These are the faces that remain, like the faces of the old or disfigured, unread.

The fear of obscurity in a digital age invested in the endless replication of images surely matches our worries about the reckless use of those images. This is the slippery slope of "facing," of contemporary interventions like Botox and camera filters, or, as Hans Belting puts it, "expression that devours the face."[14] That is, the problem of having a face is also the problem of misidentification, or, as is evident in the shock expressed over Madonna's face, of not being equal to one's face. This contemporary predicament also has a precedent, I have argued, in visual images of Oscar Wilde, in the photographic style of American realism, in the pseudoscientific construction of criminal physiognomies, in the glandular account of human personality, in literal practices of modernist face making, and in the first efforts to construct the aged body as a scientific object of study, among other examples. Beyond Frankenheimer's *Seconds*, a host of midcentury and contemporary films extend these "aesthetic effects," fictionalizing the horror of losing one's face while speculating about the plight of acquiring the wrong one.[15] Released the same year as *Seconds*, Horoshi Teshigahara's film *The Face of Another* (1966), based on the novel by Kobo Abe, examines the psychological repercussions that occur after a chemist, disfigured by an industrial accident and alienated from his wife and family, undergoes a face transplant procedure. In Georges Franju's horrifying film *Eyes Without a Face*, also from 1966, a sociopathic plastic surgeon and his female accomplice, Louise, abduct young women in order to procure a donor face for his disfigured daughter, Christiane. Exhausted from the procedures, Christiane ultimately stabs Louise in the neck and releases her father's pack of rabid dogs, who maul him to death while disfiguring his face beyond recognition.

Such films connect the horror that attends the surgical loss or acquisition of a face to the problem of consent and to the consequent death of the subject. The most recent iteration of these is Jordan Peele's *Get Out* (2017), a racialized riff on the theme of total bodily overhaul in *Seconds*.[16] Rather than an unnamed company, affluent white sponsors practice what Zadie Smith calls a "new kind of cannibalism"; they want not only to inhabit black bodies but also to claim their experience, their vision, their eyes, their particularly black ways of forming things.[17] The goal for such "reborns," then, is not the consumption of experiences designed to make them equal to their new faces, as with Arthur Hamilton in *Seconds*, but, more radically, to go far inside lived experience in the most intimate physiological ways.[18] For Smith, the film's many close-ups of "suffering black faces" expose the lie of this seamless transition.[19] As if forcibly sedated, these phantom faces are rather like heavily Botoxed faces, their capacity for expression damaged. Having lost their formal qualities, only their agonized eyes, working alone with their tears, speak for what's behind the face, desperately begging to "get out." What part of the person, though, is there left to "get out?" For the art critic E. H. Gombrich, whose ideas permeate this book, masks allow us to see what is in a face—through a mode of criticism in which likeness is "caught" and meaning subsequently articulated.[20] What do we "catch" in these faces, which resist formalization? Unlike the blackfaced caricatures of Oscar Wilde, in *Get Out* the subject's blackness does not work to formalize a clear idea of the person inside. Rather than black skin, the eyes are part of an intractable bodily texture that maintains itself against racial synthesis, or the white liberal fantasy that we can all live in another person's skin. But it's not enough to have a new skin. Chris's eyes—and his particular mode of seeing and formalizing the world—are most desired.

This idea of the skin as a pliant surface material that can be seamlessly processed into new persons links *Get Out*'s commentary on racial identity to other contemporary films that dabble in the same speculative tradition. Midway through Pedro Almodóvar's 2011 film *The Skin I Live In* (*La piel que habito*), we realize that plastic surgeon Robert Ledgard, played by a menacing Antonio Banderas, has abducted his daughter's rapist, Vicente, whom he has surgically transformed into a replica of his deceased wife, Gal. Gal previously suffered massive burns all over her body, sustained in a car accident that occurred while she was running away from Ledgard with his estranged half-brother, Veca. After viewing her damaged face in the mirror, Gal jumps out of a window, a suicidal act that, Ledgard believes, precipitates Norma's subsequent one.[21] In the film's present, Veca breaks into the house and rapes Vera, believing them to be Gal. Vera, traumatized, submits to the surgeon's care, and they become lovers. Is Vera still Vicente, Norma's rapist, or are they someone new? As viewers, we are drawn to the alabaster opacity of Vera's new face, the surgeon's supreme accomplishment, broadcast on various screens throughout the house; it's the source and conduit of our fascination with the nature of the person inside. Vera's sense of personal violation does not arise as much from the change in their face as it does from the change in their genitals. Indeed, there is evidence in the film that the sex change, performed by Ledgard, doesn't exactly work, at least, the new vagina doesn't quite function as it should, and this is the part of their new body that Vera rejects. It's the pain of their new vagina, along with a newspaper photograph that establishes Vicente as a missing person, that leads Vera to murder the doctor and to reclaim their identity as Vicente. Like *Seconds* and *Get Out*, the film explores the secret that withstands the nonconsensual processing of persons into material, artificial flesh or superskin, evacuated of interiority.

The film has been criticized as superficial, and its ending is ethically ambivalent.[22] It is a fantastic recalibration of the plot of *Seconds* that proceeds as if Tony Wilson/Arthur Hamilton were a transformed rapist who killed his captors and, without problem, returned to his earlier life in a new body. *Seconds*, *Get Out*, and *The Skin I Live In* each open avenues for thinking about the question of transition, as well as our reading of images—in particular faces. How do we read the alien faces that, in one way or the other, block the familiar scripts that form them? Throughout this book, I have clung to a rather simple argument that faces stand in for the act of reading in a variety of literary and visual texts spanning the twentieth century. I have also posed the question of how a face might be processed or perceived when evacuated in some way of the content it is presumed to represent. For example, in chapter one, I showed how, in the case of caricatures of Oscar Wilde, personality operates as a script that allows us to read modern expression. Forging likeness and difference while privileging more mobile forms of viewing, caricature problematizes any singular account of a work's (or subject's) surface, engaging the deforming vision of the modern (and self-conscious) viewer. However, as I demonstrate in chapter two, on Dreiser's *Sister Carrie*, this surface, exemplified by the urban environment, may ultimately prove too fragmented or dispersed, producing an urban prosopagnosia, or face blindness, in which expression does not cohere and faces do not form. Expression in this context does not "devour" the real face, but rather is rerouted into a sphere of serialized existence that disables the novel's realist project of accurately picturing the urban environment.[23] Conrad's *The Secret Agent*, I have argued, dwells on a similar problem of legibility that is symbolized in the absence of Stevie's blasted face and the blank face of his sister Winnie. But as I suggest in chapter four, however poorly they conform to the sort of "facial integrity" or legibility Mina Loy elaborates in her pamphlet *Auto-Facial-Construction*, modernist representations of faces, as in Gaudier-Brzeska's stone portrait *The Hieratic Head of Ezra Pound* or Henry Tonks's medical portraits of facially injured World War I soldiers, do contain within them a deep structure or form that in fact bears "witness" to even the most devastating experiences.[24] As I note in chapter five, in the case of W. H. Auden's aging face and Rock Hudson's seemingly "changeless" face, this sort of remote or damaged face complicates the task of the observer, allegorizing what it is about a person that cannot be concretely regulated, registered, or read, but which solicits that reading nonetheless.[25]

In the modernist texts I have examined, the explicit thematics of faces and facing are linked to the practices of reading and writing and, more generally, the work of aesthetic expression, which is often understood as, following Erving Goffman, "face-work" that abstracts the self or subject.[26] Consequently, as is evident in Matthew O'Connor's tirade against facing in *Nightwood*, what we see in modernism is an effort to reorient vision, and accordingly expression, away from the ontological toward the physiological. At the not quite beginning of the twenty first century, how does such a physiological conception of the person as a surface that may or may not reflect meaningful content or "being" change the way we read a face? While *The Skin I Live In* makes explicit various ethical questions surrounding Ledgard's experimentation on humans in his quest for the most resilient skin, the film, true to its style, lingers on the surface of things. François Delaporte has offered fascinating inquiries into the ethics of these questions in his recent book *Figures of Medicine*, where he emphasizes the right of those with "severe disfigurement" to "normalize their lives" as a way of "saving a life."[27] The ethical issues surrounding the repair of disfigurement are extensive and deep, and I touch on only a few of them here, but most significantly they involve the agency of the facially disfigured and the experimental nature of facial transplant surgery, which has no history of routine procedures.

Delaporte describes how media depictions of Isabelle Dinoire's 2005 face transplant used images of the mutilated face to intensify a division between the normal and the pathological; the photos thus staged surgery as a necessary act of liberation without addressing the problem of what it is like to live with a "dead man's face"—the complications for which there are no psychological precedents or resources.[28] He thus asks whether such a particular "problem of identity" should be "approached solely via the detour of one's self image," when identity "belongs to the imaginary" and is "also the repre-

Epilogue

sentation of a being one wants to remember."[29] Delaporte's question about the relationship between self-image and the "imaginary" face not only recognizes the problem of wearing a face that is not one's own but also implicitly corroborates biopolitical arguments that see the "dismantl[ing]" of "the face and facializations" as the only means of avoiding our inevitable instrumentalization at the hands of powerful biometric systems and regimes.[30] For Deleuze and Guattari, the face represents the "inhuman in human beings"— and this inhumanity is perhaps the nerve that Almodóvar's film touches most intimately, where the inhuman artificial superskin is the medium that literalizes the inhumanity involved in the construction, viewing, and processing of faces.[31]

But what is a world without faces? As I argue of Harold Gillies's pioneering research and Tonks's evocative portraits, we cannot simply cast facial reconstruction as a normative ideal that develops against an authentically war-damaged face, nor should we see the pair's work as merely instrumental. Given this argument, I likely do not spend enough time in this book addressing arguments that see in the production and reading of faces an algorithmic reduction of humanity spurred on by instrumental reason, which represents one potential outcome of the increased technological mobilization of the human face.[32] In the introduction, I briefly argue that technological advancements such as facial recognition technology, whose goal is automatic recognition and identification, were designed to eradicate reading altogether—insofar as reading entails making subjective and potentially fallible judgments and inferences. I have suggested that such technologies— where knowledge is produced in a swipe of a chip or a secret scan of the face—are the mutant offspring of another, earlier fantasy, that of the trained facial observer, capable of deciphering human intention with inhuman speed. Beyond the obvious repercussions for our privacy and autonomy, this idealization of immediacy and objectivity obscures another world of apprehension characterized, I've argued, by delay, distortion, mystery, and attachment.

As a reparative antidote to this vision of modernity, I would like to suggest instead that there is no poetry without faces and, further, that a purely surface account of a text discounts what Allen Grossman calls both the "power of imaging" and poetry more generally.[33] Poetry, following Grossman, occurs at the moment that "experience ceases to be intelligible"—where language retreats from *"generality"* and the image "demand[s] a text," or a reading.[34] The "capacity to value persons" occurs through this poetic "imaging," or the giving of faces. "My purpose," writes Grossman, "is to look into the face of Laocoön once again, where the face of blind Homer can be seen (and the faces it sees seen) and some answer to the question of what poetry knows rearticulated."[35] Reading, and consequently the "valuing of persons," is seeing a face within a face, and seeing what a blind person sees.[36] This understanding of poetry as the construction and reading of faces entails an alternate form of visual and sensual engagement with what is not immediately "intelligible" or apprehensible on the surface of things. It is part of the theoretical trajectory I construct in this book—beginning with Georg Simmel and Charles Baudelaire and extending through E. H. Gombrich, Paul de Man, and J. Hillis Miller to Michael Taussig and Eve Sedgwick. Extrapolating from this line of thought, there would be no art without faces, and the building of faces also demands our reading of them. However formed from our experiences, art retreats from them into an unknown that asks for our reading. In *The Skin I Live In*, Vera is the surgeon's finest work, to some degree an artificial being. At the end of the film, tears emanate from a person with a phantom face who wears the face of another. The film leaves us, the audience, with the question of how we are to "image," to use Grossman's terms, this face, for which we may or may not feel empathy.

How do we, for example, read Vera/Vicente's tears, or, for that matter, the tears that fall from faces in *Get Out*, which seem to be intentionally expressive, meaningful, but not the product of a natural, unmodified face? As an "affective facial respons[e]" they do not seem "innate" or "involuntary," as described in Silvan Tomkins's important tome *Affect, Imagery, Consciousness*, which emphasizes the automaticity of learned facial behaviors.[37] The face, for Tomkins, expresses affect by processing what he calls "feedback" from other faces; "memory images" retained from years of "experience in interaction" create a form of "interfacial awareness" that guides our interpretation of our affects.[38] This face-work all occurs so rapidly that it is basically imperceptible. At the same time, there is no purely involuntary affect outside of our perception of it. Our affects are one thing; our perceptions of our affects, which involve our reading and processing of them, are another. Through face-to-face interaction, according to Tomkins, we "lear[n] the language of the face" and develop an ability to process other faces and affects much like a scanner—automatically and without reflection.[39]

This is why Tomkins characterizes such actions as "involuntary" and "innate," though in my mind these words do not characterize a relation that is "learn[ed]" from "experience." Tomkins's work rather presupposes a kind of universal automaticity that cannot possibly characterize all facial responses.

He admits to as much, but he either does not discuss alternate models of facial affectivity or characterizes deviations from the norm as an impairment. What continues to interest me in Tomkins's theory, however, is his understanding of facial affectivity as a mutually reciprocal act of synthesis or formalization that coheres with the models of faciality I discuss in this book, by Gombrich and Simmel in particular. Gombrich's account of reading, as I have illustrated, demonstrates how this tension between the automaticity and deliberation of reading may actually cohere. In reading a face, or an object for that matter, we supply it with our projections, "mobilized" by the author but formed through our actual experiences with other faces.[40] Reading is automatic, based on fixed response and the sense of "constancy" we have learned from our familiarity with specific faces. At the same time, reading is deliberate; while we see such "dominant" or "fixed" expression in the face's form, the structural dimensionality of the face renders it "living" with "ambiguities," a characteristic Gombrich also relates to the "definition" of a particular face, or its unique "variables."[41] This is the moment where a reader, adhering to the physiognomic forms that automatically direct their readings, may possibly go wrong. With visual art, "ambiguities" allow a viewer to become a critic, assisting them, as Gombrich puts it, in producing a "valid articulation" of the "mystery of ordered form."[42]

For Gombrich, criticism requires something like "symptomatic reading"; it involves making guesses and forming hypotheses, the same sorts of inferences required for us to read the artificial veneer of Vera's face as it conceals, I have argued, an unseen disfigurement.[43] The reverence for what can be immediately ascertained from a manageable surface that yields easily to our descriptions is inherently normative, invalidating any seemingly inaccurate mode of perception, or "reading." With the idea of "feedback" and its rapid processing in facial affective responses, Tomkins elaborates a model of "immediate reading" and response to other faces.[44] While Tomkins briefly discusses how some forms of individual impairment, usually resulting from an atypical history of socialization or family life, might affect this "interfacial awareness," his account of how we learn the "language of the face" leaves out a host of people affected by what Jonathan Cole has termed "various losses of the face."[45] Cole's *About Face* narrates the experiences of people with "facial problems," which include difficulties with facial expression resulting from strokes or blindness or from more rare conditions such as Bell's palsy, Parkinson's disease, or Moebius syndrome.[46]

For Cole, the "facial problem" is a very peculiar type of problem. It is not enough to simply reverse or challenge these norms since our faces connect us to a world of socialization, our experiences of intimacy and well-being. In the example of Moebius syndrome, not only does the lack of expression and facial musculature that typifies the condition isolate people from social interaction, but it also leads to the possible difficulty of "calibrating a mental state" or, further, of assessing their own feelings and their expressions.[47] Ultimately, when a person cannot express emotions on their face, Cole argues, they may not be able to experience them at all. This produces a different kind of selfhood, defined by the problem of the face that doesn't represent what a person feels and the absence of "the most basic human affective interactions."[48] For Cole, the solution to such problems would not be to "dismantle" the face or, like *Nightwood*'s Matthew O'Connor, to idealize a world that is not "countenanced" or un-faced.[49] The answer instead consists in the therapeutic relation, in which the listener is also the reader of the story of the subject's problem. Through this relation, face can to some extent be restored through the verbal articulation of feelings and through the action of listening. This interaction is both communicative and, in many cases but not always, visually constitutive. It is marked, as is any therapeutic relationship, and as in Tonks's relation to the subjects of his drawings, by a "fantasy of repair," to return to Suzannah Biernoff and her analysis of facial injury in World War I, and it is a relationship, to return to Paul de Man's account of prosopopoeia, that "deprives and disfigures to the precise extent that it restores."[50] As I have suggested, prosopopoeia, a visual model of reading with disfigurement at its core, alters a subject's mimetic relation to themselves, their imagined self-identification, making the face known while preserving its essential strangeness. As a visual construct, it privileges incompletion over completion, deliberation over resolution, ambiguity over definition. And as an act of construction and as a figure for reading, it lingers, often insecurely, on what we cannot apprehend.

Notes

Introduction. What's in a Face?

1. For an in-depth analysis of the "Instagram Face," see Jia Tolentino, "The Age of Instagram Face," *New Yorker*, December 12, 2019, https://www.newyorker.com/culture/decade-in-review/the-age-of-instagram-face.

2. The term comes from Thomas Macho, "Vision und Visage: Überlegungen zur Faszinationsgeschichte der Medien," in *Inszenierte Imagination: Beiträge zu einer historischen Anthropolgie der Medien*, ed. Wolfgang Müler-Funk and Han-Ulrich Rec (Vienna: Springer, 1996), 87, and refers to a society oriented around the consumption of faces, in which mass media has divested the body from the face.

3. Georg Simmel, "The Aesthetic Significance of the Face," in *Georg Simmel 1858-1918: A Collection of Essays with Translations and a Bibliography*, ed. Kurt H. Wolf (Columbus: Ohio State University Press, 1959), 281. For more on this essay, see also Margaret Werth, "Modernity and the Face," *Intermédialités: Histoire et Théorie des Arts, des Lettres et des Techniques / Intermediality: History and Theory of the Arts, Literature, and Technologies*, no. 8 (2006): 83-102, who argues that 1900 marked a turning point in the way the face "figure[ed] identity and aesthetic value or register[ed] individual and social experience" (83).

4. Simmel, "Aesthetic Significance of the Face," 277.

5. I reference here Stephen Best and Sharon Marcus, "Surface Reading: An Introduction," *Representations* 108, no. 1 (Fall 2009): 1-21.

6. Allen Grossman, "The Passion of Laocoön: Warfare of the Religious against the Poetic Institution," in *True-Love: Essays on Poetry and Valuing* (Chicago: University of Chicago Press, 2009), 77.

7. Grossman, "Passion of Laocoön," 77.

8. See E. H. Gombrich, "Action and Expression in Western Art," in *The Image and the Eye: Further Studies in the Psychology of Pictorial Representation* (London: Phaidon, 1982), 100.

9. Gilles Deleuze, *Cinema 1: The Movement-Image*, trans. Hugh Tomlinson and Barbara Habberjam (Minneapolis: University of Minnesota Press, 1986), 88.

10. Gombrich, "Action and Expression," 100.

11. Simmel, "Aesthetic Significance of the Face," 276.

12. Simmel, "Aesthetic Significance of the Face," 276.

13. William Empson, *The Face of the Buddha*, ed. Rupert Arrowsmith (Oxford: Oxford University Press, 2016), 84.

14. Empson, *Face of the Buddha*, 84, 67.

15. Gombrich, "Action and Expression," 100.

16. Jonathan Crary, *Techniques of the Observer: On Vision and Modernity in the Nineteenth Century* (Cambridge, MA: MIT Press, 2022), 16.

17. See her brilliant study of the "close-up" in cinema in Mary Ann Doane, *Bigger Than Life: The Close-Up and Scale in the Cinema* (Durham, NC: Duke University Press, 2022), 121.

18. Doane, *Bigger Than Life*, 121.

19. Erving Goffman, "On Face-Work," in *Interaction Ritual: Essays on Face-to-Face Behavior* (New York: Pantheon, 1967), 5.

20. Goffman, "On Face-Work," 5-6.

21. See Lois Tyson's account of self-abstraction and "waste" in "Beyond Morality: Lily Bart, Lawrence Selden and the Aesthetic Commodity in 'The House of Mirth,'" *Edith Wharton Review* 9, no. 2 (1992): 4.

22. Goffman, "On Face-Work," 5. See also Warren Susman, "'Personality' and the Making of Twentieth-Century Culture," in *New Directions in American Intellectual History*, ed. John Higham and Paul K. Conkin (Baltimore: Johns Hopkins University Press, 1979), 218.

23. Goffman, "On Face-Work," 5-6.

24. Simmel, "Aesthetic Significance of the Face," 281. For Loy's *Auto-Facial-Construction* (1919), see *The Lost Lunar Baedecker: Poems of Mina Loy*, ed. Roger L. Conover (New York: Farrar, Strauss & Giroux, 1997), 165.

25. Sara K. Schneider, "Body Design, Variable Realisms: The Case of Female Fashion Mannequins," *Design Issues* 13, no. 3 (Autumn 1997): 6, 8.

26. Schneider, "Body Design, Variable Realisms," 5, 7.

27. For a history of the Myers-Briggs personality type indicator and personality tests in general, see Merve Emre, *The Personality Brokers: The Strange History of Myers-Briggs and the Birth of Personality Testing* (New York: Doubleday, 2018).

28. For this terminology, see Scott Herring's *Aging Moderns: Art, Literature, and the Experiment of Later Life* (New York: Columbia University Press, 2022), 5, which asks how "embodiments" of old age might "supplement our understandings of modernism's pacings alongside its revised time lines" (11). I also have in mind three other recent studies focused on aesthetics: Nico Israel, *Spirals: The Whirled Image in Twentieth-Century Literature and Art* (New York: Columbia University Press, 2017);

Sam Rose, *Art and Form: From Roger Fry to Global Modernism* (University Park: Pennsylvania State University Press, 2019); and Alys Moody, *The Art of Hunger: Aesthetic Autonomy and the Afterlives of Modernism* (Oxford: Oxford University Press, 2018). For revisions of "impersonality," see Christina Walter, *Optical Impersonality: Science, Images and Literary Modernism* (Baltimore: Johns Hopkins University Press, 2014); and Rochelle Rives, *Modernist Impersonalities: Affect, Authority, and the Subject* (New York: Palgrave, 2012).

29. See Hans Belting, *Face and Mask: A Double History* (Princeton, NJ: Princeton University Press, 2017), 19. Classic accounts of modernism such as Maud Ellmann's *The Poetics of Impersonality: T. S. Eliot and Ezra Pound* (Cambridge, MA: Harvard University Press, 1987) and Hugh Kenner's *The Pound Era* (Berkeley: University of California Press, 1973) equated the mask with the idea of poetic personae and thus centralized its relationship to poetic voice. For recent works on the global and transnational aspects of masking, see Carrie J. Preston, *Learning to Kneel: Noh, Modernism, and Journeys in Teaching* (New York: Columbia University Press, 2016); Andrew Reynolds and Bonnie Roos, *Behind the Masks of Modernism: Global and Transnational Perspectives* (Gainesville: University Press of Florida, 2016); and Tim Keane's review of the Japan Society's 2017 exhibit *Simon Starling: At Twilight (After W. B. Yeats' Noh Reincarnation)*, "The Irish for Noh: The Masks of William Butler Yeats," *Hyperallergic*, January 2017, https://hyperallergic.com/349703/the-irish-for-noh-the-masks-of-william-butler-yeats/.

30. See Robert F. Storey, *Pierrot: A Critical History of the Mask* (Princeton, NJ: Princeton University Press, 1978), 30–31; italics in the original.

31. Crary, *Techniques of the Observer*, 16. See Sarah Blackwood's account of Henry James's proto-modernist portrait fiction in *The Portrait's Subject: Inventing Inner Life in the Nineteenth-Century United States* (Chapel Hill: University of North Carolina Press, 2019), 108, 109. My thoughts here are also clearly indebted to Michael Fried's *Realism, Writing, Figuration: On Thomas Eakins and Stephen Crane* (Chicago: University of Chicago Press, 1987).

32. Djuna Barnes, *Nightwood* (New York: New Directions, 2006), 87 (hereafter cited in text as *NW*).

33. Vincent Sherry notes in *Modernism and the Reinvention of Decadence* (Cambridge: Cambridge University Press, 2015) that "petropus," as it appears in *Nightwood*, is not actually a word, but rather "a piece of language facticity that captures not only the utter dubiety of O'Connor's utterances" but also "something of the petrified and extinct creature of the speech it typifies" (281–82).

34. Sherry, *Modernism*, 282.

35. Crary, *Techniques of the Observer*, 16.

36. Belting, *Face and Mask*, 105, 142.

37. Belting, *Face and Mask*, 153.

38. Belting, *Face and Mask*, 153; Deleuze, *Cinema 1*, 88.

39. Deleuze, *Cinema 1*, 88. For more on Le Brun and the passions, see Stephanie Ross, "Painting the Passions: Charles LeBrun's *Conference Sur L'Expression*," *Journal of the History of Ideas* 45, no. 1 (January-March 1984): 25-47. See also René Descartes, *The Passions of the Soul*, trans. Stephen Voss (Indianapolis: Hackett, 1989); and Charles Le Brun, *A Method to Learn to Design the Passions, Proposed in a Conference on Their General and Particular Expression. Written in French, and Illustrated With a Great Many Figures Excellently Designed* (1734), trans. John Williams (n.p.: Gale Ecco, 2018).

40. Lucy Hartley, *Physiognomy and the Meaning of Expression in Nineteenth-Century Culture* (Cambridge: Cambridge University Press, 2001), 17.

41. See Walter Benjamin, "Little History of Photography," in *Selected Writings: Volume 2, Part 2, 1931-1934*, ed. Michael W. Jennings, Howard Eiland, and Gary Smith, trans. Rodney Livingstone (Cambridge, MA: Harvard University Press, 1999), 507, 510.

42. See François Delaporte, *Anatomy of the Passions*, trans. Susan Emanuel (Stanford, CA: Stanford University Press, 2008), 5. See also Guillaume-Benjamin-Amand Duchenne de Boulogne, *The Mechanism of Human Facial Expression*, ed. and trans. R. Andrew Cuthbertson (1862; repr., Cambridge: Cambridge University Press, 1990). For a compelling study of photography and expression, see Phillip Prodger, *Darwin's Camera: Art and Photography in the Theory of Evolution* (Oxford: Oxford University Press, 2009).

43. Ekman began writing academic articles about decoding facial expression as early as the 1960s, but his work was popularized after the terrorist attacks on New York in 2001; he appeared as a scientific advisor on the Fox TV show *Lie to Me*, which ran from 2009 to 2011. Popular books include Paul Ekman, *Emotions Revealed: Recognizing Faces and Feelings to Improve Communication and Emotional Life* (New York: Harper, 2003); and Paul Ekman, *Telling Lies: Clues to Deceit in the Marketplace, Politics, and Marriage* (New York: Norton, 2009).

44. See Ruth Leys's "How Did Fear Become a Scientific Object and What Kind of Object Is It?," *Representations* 110, no. 1 (Spring 2010): 66-104, as well as her more expansive survey of empirical research on the face and its expressions in *The Ascent of Affect: Genealogy and Critique* (Chicago: University of Chicago Press, 2017).

45. George Orwell, *1984* (New York: Signet, 1981), 54.

46. Orwell, *1984*, 54.

47. See Doane, *Bigger Than Life*, 100, where she notes the eighteenth-century phrenological projects of Carl Gustav Carus and Petrus Campers, which analyzed skulls to classify racial types. Stephen Jay Gould offers a radical critique of these practices in *The Mismeasure of Man* (New York: Norton, 1996).

48. Orwell, *1984*, 14.

49. Orwell, *1984*, 14.

50. Ellen Samuels, *Fantasies of Identification: Disability, Gender, Race* (New York: New York University Press, 2014), 2.

51. Susan Schweik, *The Ugly Laws: Disability in Public* (New York: New York University Press, 2009), 3, 11.

52. See Sander Gilman, *Making the Body Beautiful: A Cultural History of Aesthetic Surgery* (Princeton, NJ: Princeton University Press, 2000).

53. Amade M'charek, "Tentacular Faces: Race and the Return of the Phenotype in Forensic Identification," *American Anthropologist* 122, no. 2 (June 2020): 377.

54. M'charek, "Tentacular Faces," 372.

55. M'charek, "Tentacular Faces," 372; italics in the original.

56. Schweik, *Ugly Laws*, 3.

57. Works in modernist disability studies such as Rebecca Sanchez's *Deafening Modernism: Embodied Language and Visual Poetics in American Literature* (New York: New York University Press, 2015), Michael Davidson's *Invalid Modernism: Disability and the Missing Body of the Aesthetic* (Oxford: Oxford University Press, 2019), and Maren Tova Linett's *Bodies of Modernism: Physical Disability in Transatlantic Modernist Literature* (Ann Arbor: University of Michigan Press, 2017) similarly address the relations among the nonnormative body, form, and modern technologies of vision. For reflection on the potential of medical humanities to intervene in "ontological questions" that were previously left to the "life sciences" and "biomedicine," see William Viney, Felicity Callard, and Angela Woods, eds., "Critical Medical Humanities: Embracing Entanglement, Taking Risks," *Critical Medical Humanities* 141, no. 1 (2015): 3. For a more comprehensive view of the field, including its relationship to disability studies, see Anne Whitehead and Angela Woods, eds., *Edinburgh Companion to the Critical Medical Humanities* (Edinburgh: Edinburgh University Press, 2022); and Diane Price Herndl, "Disease versus Disability: The Medical Humanities and Disability Studies," *PMLA* 120, no. 2 (2005): 593-98.

58. See Georges Canguilhem, *The Normal and the Pathological*, trans. Carolyn Fawcett (New York: Zone Books, 1991).

59. Namwali Serpell reflects on a range of faces that include the elephant man's, Joseph Merrick's, Hannah Crafts's, and animal faces in Werner Herzog's *Grizzly Man*. On emojis, see Namwali Serpell, *Stranger Faces* (Oakland, CA: Transit Books, 2020), 11, 18.

60. Grossman, "Passion of Laocoön," 87.

61. I quote from Sianne Ngai's analysis of the happy face in "Visceral Abstractions," *GLQ: A Journal of Lesbian and Gay Studies* 21, no. 1 (January 2015): 36.

62. Paul de Man, *The Rhetoric of Romanticism* (Cambridge, MA: Harvard University Press, 1984), 76.

63. Emmanuel Levinas, *Totality and Infinity: An Essay on Exteriority*, trans. Alphonso Lingis (Pittsburgh: Duquesne University Press, 1969), 47.

64. Goffman, "On Face-Work," 5; Jenny Edkins writes extensively about the

face's instrumentalization in *Face Politics* (New York: Routledge, 2015), claiming that a "politics that makes the face is a politics that produces the person as object" (7).

65. Deleuze, *Cinema 1*, 88.

66. On Clearview AI and its facial recognition app, see Kashmir Hill, "The Secretive Company That Might End Privacy as We Know It," *New York Times*, January 17, 2020, https://www.nytimes.com/2020/01/18/technology/clearview-privacy-facial-recognition.html.

67. See Drew Harwell, "ACLU Sues FBI, DOJ over Facial-Recognition Technology, Criticizing 'Unprecedented' Surveillance and Secrecy," *Washington Post*, September 7, 2019, https://www.washingtonpost.com/technology/2019/10/31/aclu-sues-fbi-doj-over-facial-recognition-technology-criticizing-unprecedented-surveillance-secrecy/.

68. See Paul Mozur, "China Uses DNA to Map Faces with Help from the West," *New York Times*, December 3, 2019, https://www.nytimes.com/2019/12/03/business/china-dna-uighurs-xinjiang.html.

69. Quoted in Daniel M. Gross, "Defending the Humanities with Charles Darwin's *The Expression of the Emotions in Man and Animals* (1872)," *Critical Inquiry* 37, no. 1 (Autumn 2010): 48; italics in the original.

70. E. H. Gombrich, "The Mask and the Face: The Perception of Physiognomic Likeness in Life and in Art," in *The Image and the Eye: Further Studies in the Psychology of Pictorial Representation* (New York: Phaidon, 1994), 135.

71. For more on Gombrich's collaboration with Viennese psychoanalyst and curator Ernst Kris, see Louis Rose, *Psychology, Art, and Antifascism: Ernst Kris, E. H. Gombrich, and the Politics of Caricature* (New Haven, CT: Yale University Press, 2016).

72. See Theodor Adorno and Max Horkheimer, "The Culture Industry: Enlightenment as Mass Deception" (1947), in *The Dialectic of Enlightenment*, ed. Gunzelin Schmid Noerr, trans. Edmund Jephcott (Stanford, CA: Stanford University Press, 2002), 112. See Ezra Pound, *ABC of Reading* (1934; repr., New York: New Directions, 1960), for his approach to reading as related to what everyone already "KNOWS" (22).

73. Louis Rose, "Interpreting Propaganda: Successors to Warburg and Freud in Wartime," *American Imago* 60, no. 1 (2003): 124.

74. Rose, "Interpreting Propaganda," 124.

75. E. H. Gombrich, "On Physiognomic Perception," in *Meditations on a Hobby Horse and Other Essays on the Theory of Art* (London: Phaidon, 1985), 47.

76. Gombrich, "Mask and the Face," 106.

77. Gombrich, "Mask and the Face," 106.

78. Gombrich, "Mask and the Face," 113.

79. Gombrich, "Mask and the Face," 113.

80. Gombrich, "Mask and the Face," 116.

81. Roland Barthes, *Mythologies*, trans. Richard Howard and Annette Lavers (New York: Hill & Wang, 2013), 73.
82. Barthes, *Mythologies*, 73.
83. Gombrich, "Mask and the Face," 117.
84. Gombrich, "Mask and the Face," 117.
85. Gombrich, "Mask and the Face," 117.
86. For the description of Hepburn's face, see Barthes, *Mythologies*, 74.
87. Gombrich, "On Physiognomic Perception," 45.
88. Gombrich, "Mask and the Face," 126.
89. Gombrich, "Mask and the Face," 124.
90. Gombrich, "On Physiognomic Perception," 55.
91. Gombrich, "On Physiognomic Perception," 55.
92. Gombrich, "On Physiognomic Perception," 55.
93. Gombrich, "Mask and the Face," 124.
94. David Kurnick, "A Few Lies: Queer Theory and Our Method Melodramas," *ELH* 87, no. 2 (Summer 2020): 350.
95. See Best and Marcus, "Surface Reading," 3. Fredric Jameson's *The Political Unconscious: Narrative as a Socially Symbolic Act* (Ithaca, NY: Cornell University Press, 1981) is credited as the source text for symptomatic reading. Most recently, John Guillory has argued in *Professing Criticism: Essays on the Organization of Literary Study* (Chicago: University of Chicago Press, 2022) that "surface reading" failed to "catch on" because the "refusal to interpret" does not actually have any "impact in the public sphere" (88, 86). For more on post-critical reading practices, see also Rita Felski, *The Uses of Literature* (New York: Blackwell, 2008); Rita Felski, *The Limits of Critique* (Chicago: University of Chicago Press, 2015); Franco Moretti, *Distant Reading* (New York: Verso, 2013); and Franco Moretti, *Graphs, Maps, Trees: Abstract Models for Literary History* (London: Verso, 2005).
96. Best and Marcus, "Surface Reading," 3.
97. Best and Marcus, "Surface Reading," 3.
98. See Ellen Rooney, "Live Free or Describe: The Reading Effect and the Persistence of Form," *Differences* 21, no. 3 (2010): 116. See also Anahid Nersessian and Jonathan Kramnick, *Critical Inquiry* 43 (Spring 2017): 650-69, who argue that the ideology of "surface reading" grants description power to forge connections between our own discipline and the natural and social sciences, ultimately diminishing our own methods of analysis and the "kind[s] of questions" and "kinds of explanations" they provide (651). For more on the history of "close reading," see Jane Gallop, "The Ethics of Reading: Close Encounters," *Journal of Curriculum Theorizing* 16, no. 3 (Fall 2000): 11-17; Rachel Sagner Buurma and Laura Heffernan, *The Teaching Archive* (Chicago: University of Chicago Press, 2020); and Heather Love, "Close but Not Deep: Literary Ethics and the Descriptive Turn," *New Literary History* 41, no. 2 (Spring 2010): 371-91. For a defense of aesthetic "judgment,"

which includes close reading, see Michael Clune, *A Defense of Judgment* (Chicago: University of Chicago Press, 2021), as well as Joseph North's *Literary Criticism: A Concise Political History* (Cambridge, MA: Harvard University Press, 2017), which elevates the political potential of "critical" work over "scholarly" historicism (2).

99. I invoke Michael Fried's description of the act of reading as a "visible marking over an existing writing" in his essay "Almayer's Face: On 'Impressionism' in Conrad, Crane, and Norris," *Critical Inquiry* 17, no. 1 (Autumn 1990): 211.

100. Conrad's well-known formulation of impressionism appears in his 1914 preface to *The Nigger of the "Narcissus"* (New York: Penguin, 1987), xlix.

101. Rooney, "Live Free or Describe," 116. I also quote one of my students, who claimed that they used a "paraphrase tool" not to plagiarize web content but to "enhance" their writing. See also Stephen Marche, "The College Essay Is Dead: Nobody Is Prepared for How AI Will Transform Academia," *Atlantic*, December 6, 2022, https://www.theatlantic.com/technology/archive/2022/12/chatgpt-ai-writing-college-student-essays/672371/.

102. Sam Rose, "The Fear of Aesthetics in Art and Literary Theory," *New Literary History* 48, no. 2 (Spring 2017): 226.

103. Anna Kornbluh, *The Order of Forms: Realism, Formalism, and Social Space* (Chicago: University of Chicago Press, 2019), 156. For other works on form, see Caroline Levine's *Forms* (Princeton, NJ: Princeton University Press, 2015), as well as Marjorie Levinson's "What Is New Formalism?," *PMLA* 122 (Winter 2007): 558-69, and Sandra MacPherson's "A Little Formalism," *English Literary History* 82, no. 2 (Winter 2015): 385-405.

104. Regarding "paranoid" reading, Merve Emre describes Eve Sedgwick as "one of the more flagrantly misread theorists of reading" in *Paraliterary: The Making of Bad Readers in Postwar America* (Chicago: University of Chicago Press, 2017), 222. For more on "paranoid" reading, see Eve Kosofsky Sedgwick, *Touching Feeling: Affect, Pedagogy, Performativity* (Durham, NC: Duke University Press, 2003).

105. Daniel Gross, "Defending the Humanities," 48; italics in the original.

106. Ruth Leys, "The Turn to Affect: A Critique," *Critical Inquiry* 37, no. 3 (Spring 2011): 449.

107. Leys, "Turn to Affect," 449.

108. See Charles Baudelaire, "On the Essence of Laughter," in *"The Painter of Modern Life" and Other Essays*, ed. and trans. Jonathan Mayne (London: Phaidon, 1995), 157.

109. Gombrich, "Mask and the Face," 124.

110. For Kurnick's take on "surface" and "symptomatic" reading, see Kurnick, "Few Lies," 350. Best and Marcus ("Surface Reading," 3) fault Eve Kosofsky Sedgwick's *The Epistemology of the Closet* (Berkeley: University of California Press, 1991) for a "queer symptomatic reading" that sees the "closet" as "surface signs of the deep truth of a homosexuality that cannot be overtly depicted."

111. Deleuze, *Cinema 1*, 88.
112. Georg Lukács, "The Ideology of Modernism," in *Realism in Our Time*, trans. John and Necke Mander (New York: Harper, 1971), 17-46.
113. For this terminology, see Tyson, "Beyond Morality," 3.
114. Joseph Conrad, *The Secret Agent* (New York: Modern Library, 1993), 58.
115. Jesse Matz, *Literary Impressionism and Modernist Aesthetics* (Cambridge: Cambridge University Press 2001), 142.
116. The language here comes from Conrad's "Author's Note," added in 1920 to *The Secret Agent*, ed. Martin Seymour-Smith (New York: Penguin, 1984), 39, which is different from the aforementioned edition.
117. Levinas, *Totality and Infinity*, 292.
118. Crary, *Techniques of the Observer*, 16.
119. In "Wanting Paul de Man: A Critique of the 'Logic' of New Historicism in American Studies," *Texas Studies in Literature and Language* 35, no. 2 (Summer 1993): 251-77, Tim Dean observes that while the negative attitude toward deconstruction began with the New Historicism's mischaracterization of it in the wake of the revelation of de Man's wartime journalism, the more specific problem for the historicists was the perceived failure of deconstruction to adequately "efface the boundary between literary and non-literary" (272). See also Best and Marcus, "Surface Reading," 2, for their assessment of deconstruction as a "demystifying protocol" that is "superfluous" to an era that no longer needs it.
120. Suzannah Biernoff, *Portraits of Violence: War and the Aesthetics of Disfigurement* (Ann Arbor: University of Michigan Press, 2017), 167.
121. Ezra Pound, *A Memoir of Gaudier-Brzeska* (New York: New Directions, 1970), 49; Belting, *Face and Mask*, 153.
122. Rooney, "Live Free or Describe," 116.
123. Grossman, "Passion of Laocoön," 87, 86.
124. Grossman, "Passion of Laocoön," 75.
125. Grossman, "Passion of Laocoön," 77.
126. W. H. Auden, "Old People's Home" (1970), in *Collected Poems*, ed. Edward Mendelson (New York: Modern Library, 1976), 861.
127. Grossman, "Passion of Laocoön," 77.
128. Michael Taussig, *Defacement: Public Secrecy and the Labor of the Negative* (Stanford, CA: Stanford University Press, 1999), 43, 3.
129. See Gilles Deleuze and Félix Guattari, "Year Zero: Faciality," in *A Thousand Plateaus*, trans. Brian Massumi (Minneapolis: University of Minnesota Press, 1987), 171.
130. See Jonathan Cole, *About Face* (Cambridge, MA: MIT Press, 1999), 5, for this terminology.
131. Deleuze and Guattari, *Thousand Plateaus*, 171.
132. Grossman, "Passion of Laocoön," 77, 75.

Chapter 1. Facing Wilde; or, Emotion's Image

1. Guillaume-Benjamin-Amand Duchenne de Boulogne, *The Mechanism of Human Facial Expression*, ed. and trans. R. Andrew Cuthbertson (1862; repr., Cambridge: Cambridge University Press, 1990), 28.

2. Duchenne, *Mechanism*, 28.

3. See Silvan Tomkins, *Affect, Imagery, Consciousness* (New York: Springer, 2008), 114, for his identification of the face as the "primary site" of affect, in contrast to the secondary "bodily" behavior to which affect can be related.

4. Arthur Symons, "Sex and Aversion," in *The Memoirs of Arthur Symons*, ed. Karl Beckson (University Park: Pennsylvania State University Press, 1977), 129.

5. In *Effeminate England: Homoerotic Writing after 1885* (New York: Columbia University Press, 1995), Joseph Bristow describes this passage as a "single paragraph of contemptuous loathing" that "shows how troublingly Wilde had come to represent all that was sexually other to the so-called normal virile man" (17).

6. See Robert Harborough Sherard, *The Life of Oscar Wilde* (New York: Mitchell, 1906), 2; and Frank Harris, *Oscar Wilde: His Life and Confessions* (New York: printed by the author, 1916), 92.

7. Symons, "Sex and Aversion," 139.

8. Symons, "Sex and Aversion," 139.

9. Symons, "Sex and Aversion," 139.

10. See Symons, "Sex and Aversion," 139; Bristow, *Effeminate England*, 18. For an excellent analysis of the concepts of degeneration and decadence in relation to the trials, see Michael Foldy, *The Trials of Oscar Wilde: Deviance, Morality, and Late-Victorian Society* (New Haven, CT: Yale University Press, 1997).

11. See Warren Susman, *"Personality" and the Making of Twentieth-Century Culture* (self-pub., 1984), mediastudies.press, 218.

12. Louis Berman, MD, *The Glands Regulating Personality: A Study of the Glands of Internal Secretion in Relation to the Types of Human Nature* (New York: Macmillan, 1922), 121, 250.

13. Berman, *Glands Regulating Personality*, 251; italics in the original.

14. Berman, *Glands Regulating Personality*, 251; italics in the original.

15. Berman, *Glands Regulating Personality*, 251.

16. Berman, *Glands Regulating Personality*, 251.

17. Berman, *Glands Regulating Personality*, 121.

18. See Gordon Allport, review of *The Glands Regulating Personality*, by Louis Berman, *Journal of Abnormal Psychology and Social Psychology* 17, no. 2 (1922): 222.

19. Allport, review of *The Glands Regulating Personality*, 22.

20. François Delaporte, *Anatomy of the Passions*, trans. Susan Emanuel (Stanford, CA: Stanford University Press, 2008), 28.

21. Delaporte, *Anatomy of the Passions*, 28.

22. Delaporte, *Anatomy of the Passions*, 6.
23. Duchenne, *Mechanism*, 28.
24. Delaporte, *Anatomy of the Passions*, 91.
25. Berman, *Glands Regulating Personality*, 202.
26. Berman, *Glands Regulating Personality*, 203.
27. Berman, *Glands Regulating Personality*, 203.
28. Berman, *Glands Regulating Personality*, 121.
29. Bristow, *Effeminate England*, 5. For classic studies that address the significance of the trials, see Alan Sinfield, *The Wilde Century: Effeminacy, Oscar Wilde, and the Queer Moment* (New York: Columbia University Press, 1994); Ed Cohen, *Talk on the Wilde Side* (New York: Routledge, 1993); and Linda Dowling, *Hellenism and Homosexuality in Victorian Oxford* (Ithaca, NY: Cornell University Press, 1994).
30. Cohen, *Talk*, 2, 131.
31. Quoted in Cohen, *Talk*, 127.
32. Cohen, *Talk*, 127.
33. Cohen, *Talk*, 129.
34. Cohen, *Talk*, 206, 209.
35. Cohen, *Talk*, 138.
36. I am again following Warren Susman by distinguishing "personality" from "character"—which was predicated on a nineteenth-century idea that emphasized moral self-mastery and a subject's intentional relationship to their inner state of being. See Susman, *"Personality,"* 218.
37. Brian Massumi argues in *Parables of the Virtual: Movement, Affect, Sensation* (Durham, NC: Duke University Press, 2002) that affect is "intensity," an *"autonomic"* reaction to the image (27, 28; italics in the original). For a useful distinction between affect and emotion as the terms have been employed in the work of Connolly, Massumi, and others, see also Constantina Papoulias and Felicity Callard, "Biology's Gift: Interrogating the Turn to Affect," in *Body and Society* 16, no. 1 (2010): 29-56.
38. Ruth Leys, "The Turn to Affect: A Critique," *Critical Inquiry* 37, no. 3 (2011): 438, 450. The article is included in her book *The Ascent of Affect: Genealogy and Critique* (Chicago: University of Chicago Press, 2017), which surveys ideas related to affect and the emotions in works by Silvan Tomkins, Paul Ekman, and Alan J. Fridlund, among others.
39. Daniel M. Gross, *The Secret History of Emotion: From Aristotle's Rhetoric to Modern Brain Science* (Chicago: University of Chicago Press, 2007), 31.
40. Gross, *Secret History of Emotion*, 38.
41. Gross, *Secret History of Emotion*, 32.
42. Gross, *Secret History of Emotion*, 50.
43. Ruth Leys, "Turn to Affect," 465.
44. The description here is from Adam Frank and Elizabeth A. Wilson's "Like-Minded," their response to Leys's reading of Tomkins work and his concept of

"facial affectivity" in *Critical Inquiry* 38, no. 4 (Summer 2012): 876. The pair faults Leys with overexaggerating Tomkins's influence on affect theory more generally to serve her own rhetorical needs, arguing that there has been in actuality very little close critical engagement with Tomkins's theories of facial affectivity, script theory, or work on personality in major humanistic studies of affect and the emotions.

45. See Eve Kosofsky Sedgwick, *Touching Feeling: Affect, Pedagogy, Performativity* (Durham, NC: Duke University Press, 2003), 108.

46. Frank and Wilson, "Like-Minded," 867.

47. For more on the question of what expression is or means, via the example of Ludwig Wittgenstein's attention to the "face itself and the so-called 'face' of the work of art," see Bernard Rhie, "Wittgenstein on the Face of a Work of Art," *Nonsite.org*, no. 3 (October 2014), https://nonsite.org/wittgenstein-on-the-face-of-a-work-of-art/.

48. Delaporte, *Anatomy of the Passions*, 70.

49. Delaporte, *Anatomy of the Passions*, 71, 72.

50. E. H. Gombrich, "On Physiognomic Perception," in *Meditations on a Hobby Horse and Other Essays on the Theory of Art* (London: Phaidon, 1985), 47.

51. Tomkins, *Affect, Imagery, Consciousness*, 114.

52. Berman, *Glands Regulating Personality*, 254, 253.

53. For the quotation and accompanying narrative, see Richard Ellmann, *Oscar Wilde* (New York: Vintage, 1984), 397.

54. Gross, *Secret History of Emotion*, 5.

55. See Wyndham Lewis, "The Physiological Norm and the 'Vicious,'" in *The Art of Being Ruled* (Santa Rosa, CA: Black Sparrow, 1989), 210.

56. Lewis, "Physiological Norm," 209.

57. Lewis, "Physiological Norm," 210.

58. Lewis, "Physiological Norm," 211.

59. Lewis, "Physiological Norm," 212; italics in the original.

60. Lewis, "Physiological Norm," 211, 212; italics in the original.

61. Lewis, "Physiological Norm," 211.

62. Lewis, "Physiological Norm," 209.

63. Lewis, "Physiological Norm," 212.

64. Lewis, "Physiological Norm," 212.

65. Lewis, "Physiological Norm," 212.

66. Lewis, "Physiological Norm," 209.

67. Delaporte, *Anatomy of the Passions*, 70, 71; Symons, "Sex and Aversion," 139.

68. See Edgar C. Beall, MD, *The Life Sexual: A Study of the Philosophy, Physiology, Science, Art, and Hygiene of Love* (New York: Vim, 1905), 173.

69. Beall, *Life Sexual*, 173.

70. Beall, *Life Sexual*, 171.

71. Berman, *Glands Regulating Personality*, 113.
72. Berman, *Glands Regulating Personality*, 113.
73. Berman, *Glands Regulating Personality*, 113.
74. See Georges Canguilhem, *The Normal and the Pathological*, trans. Carolyn Fawcett (New York: Zone Books, 1991). See also Perry Curtis's *Apes and Angels: The Irishman in Victorian Caricature* (Washington, DC: Smithsonian Institution, 1971) for an analysis of how such physiognomic theories informed caricature as a technique.
75. In *Who Was That Man? A Present for Mr. Oscar Wilde* (London: Serpent's Tail, 1988), Neil Bartlett argues that while homosexuality was clearly "visible" in Victorian London, the critical discourse that developed before and after the trials has contributed to a "fiction of our invisibility" before that date (128).
76. Foldy, *Trials of Oscar Wilde*, 50.
77. Foldy, *Trials of Oscar Wilde*, 70.
78. See Regina Gagnier, *Idylls of the Market Place: Oscar Wilde and the Victorian Public* (Stanford, CA: Stanford University Press, 1986). For the quotations, see Heather Marcovitch, *The Art of the Pose: Oscar Wilde's Performance Theory* (New York: Lange, 2010), 54; and Curtis Marez, "The Other Addict: Reflections on Colonialism and Oscar Wilde's Opium Smoke Screen," *ELH* 64, no. 1 (Spring 1997): 257–87.
79. Bristow, *Effeminate England*, 18. Jonathan Goldman, in *Modernism Is the Literature of Celebrity* (Austin: University of Texas Press, 2011), has noted that similar caricatures "invoke Wilde with just a few features of physiognomy and dress" while "expand[ing] the circulation of Wilde's image . . . increasing its recognizability" (28, 31).
80. See Mary Warner Blanchard's *Oscar Wilde's America: Counterculture in the Gilded Age* (New Haven, CT: Yale University Press, 1998), which details the rise of aestheticism in America in relation to cultural fears about manhood and idleness.
81. For an analysis of the *Darktown Comics* series in relation to the overall framework of post-Reconstruction history, see Rayford W. Logan, *The Betrayal of the Negro: From Rutherford B. Hayes to Woodrow Wilson* (Chicago: Da Capo, 1965), 164.
82. Blanchard, *Oscar Wilde's America*, 214.
83. See the 1882 pamphlet, illustrated by Chas. Kendrick and published anonymously, *Ye Soul in Agonies in Ye Life of Oscar Wilde* (New York: n.p., 1882), 21, Wildeana Collection, William Andrews Clark Memorial Library, University of California, Los Angeles, which comically details the coming of age of Oscar Wilde, from infancy to his appearance in America. The pamphlet, as well as "The Aesthetic Craze," overtly mocks many of the ideas about the instructiveness of art that, according to Douglas Mao in *Fateful Beauty: Aesthetic Environments, Juvenile Development and Literature, 1860–1960* (Princeton, NJ: Princeton University Press, 2010), guided Wilde's 1882 visit to North America.

84. In *Stranger Faces* (Oakland, CA: Transit Books, 2020), Namwali Serpell makes a similar claim about Hannah Craft's two faces, arguing that "to live is to have a face—or rather two faces, the physical form always haunted by the possibility of expression" (62). In the case of Craft, Serpell examines how her "biracial face paints a white portrait" (62).

85. For classic accounts of the development of blackface minstrelsy before and after the American Civil War, see Dale Cockrell, *Demons of Disorder: Early Blackface Minstrels and Their World* (Cambridge: Cambridge University Press, 1997); and Eric Lott, *Love and Theft: Blackface Minstrelsy and the American Working Class* (Oxford: Oxford University Press, 1993).

86. Amade M'charek, "Tentacular Faces: Race and the Return of the Phenotype in Forensic Identification," *American Anthropologist* 122, no. 2 (June 2020): 369, 370.

87. Delaporte, *Anatomy of the Passions*, 70.

88. Delaporte, *Anatomy of the Passions*, 5.

89. Delaporte, *Anatomy of the Passions*, 71.

90. For this description, see the July 1883 edition of the British political magazine *Truth* and the analysis that follows: "People wanted to see the man, not to hear him talk, and the apostle of sweetness and light was well advised to parade his knee breaches and sea green neckties, for no one would have paid his money had he lectured in the ordinary attire of an English gentlemen"; *Truth*, July 1883, Wildeana Collection, William Andrews Clark Memorial Library, University of California, Los Angeles.

91. See "Oscar Wilde in America," a review of Wilde's lecture in the *Houston Daily Post*, June 23, 1882, Wildeana Collection, William Andrews Clark Memorial Library, University of California, Los Angeles.

92. Lewis, "Physiological Norm," 217.

93. Max Beerbohm, "The Spirit of Caricature," *Pall Mall Magazine* 22, no. 93 (1901): 123.

94. Beerbohm, "Spirit of Caricature," 124.

95. Beerbohm, "Spirit of Caricature," 124.

96. Beerbohm, "Spirit of Caricature," 123.

97. For the quotation, see Charles Baudelaire, "On the Essence of Laughter," in *"The Painter of Modern Life" and Other Essays*, ed. and trans. Jonathan Mayne (London: Phaidon, 1995), 159; italics in the original (hereafter cited in text as "OEL").

98. Jacques-Henri Bernardin de Saint-Pierre's popular Enlightenment-era novel, *Paul et Virginie* (New York: Hachette Livre, 2018), first published in 1787 on the eve of the French Revolution, critiques the social divisions of eighteenth-century French society.

99. Beerbohm, "Spirit of Caricature," 123.

100. Regarding the question whether laughter is "permissible," one is reminded

of Sigmund Freud's contention in *The Joke and Its Relation to the Unconscious*, trans. Joyce Crick (New York: Penguin, 2003), that laughter is an expression of inhibition related to feelings that are, in fact, forbidden.

101. See Maurice Merleau-Ponty, *Phenomenology of Perception*, trans. Colin Smith (London: Routledge, 1962), 198, for an explanation of phenomenology as it reorients Cartesian models of identity.

102. Leys, "Turn to Affect," 449.

103. Brian Massumi, "Sensing the Virtual: Building the Insensible," in *Hypersurface Architecture*, ed. Stephen Perrella (New York: Wiley, 1998), 16, 17.

104. See also Massumi, *Parables for the Virtual*, 244.

105. See E. H. Gombrich and Ernst Kris, "The Principles of Caricature," Gombrich Archive, University of Birmingham, 2005, https://gombricharchive.files.wordpress.com/2011/05/showdoc85.pdf; originally published in *British Journal of Medical Psychology* 17 (1938): 319–42.

106. Gombrich and Kris, "Principles of Caricature."

107. Gombrich and Kris, "Principles of Caricature."

108. Gombrich and Kris, "Principles of Caricature." For Freud's explanation of the "primary process," which exists more generally in contrast to the "secondary processes" of "normal waking life," see Sigmund Freud, *Beyond the Pleasure Principle*, ed. James Strachey (New York: Norton, 1990), 41.

109. Gombrich and Kris, "Principles of Caricature."

110. Oscar Wilde, *The Picture of Dorian Gray* (New York: Penguin, 2000), 3 (hereafter cited in text as *PDG*). I must also note here "The Portrait of Mr. W.H.," in which Wilde's theory of art as forgery could be seen as exploring the readerly "facing" of Shakespeare's sonnets in a sort of prosopopoeia constructed by the reader, not the poet; Oscar Wilde, *The Portrait of Mr. W.H.* (Bridlington, UK: Moorside, 2013).

111. Tomkins, *Affect, Imagery, Consciousness*, 119.

112. See Elisha Cohn, "'One single ivory cell': Oscar Wilde and the Brain," *Journal of Victorian Culture* 17, no. 2 (June 2012): 192, 191. Regarding biological determinism, Douglas Mao (*Fateful Beauty*, 83) also examines the complexity of Wilde's interest in the "material basis of mind" and his "critique of materialism." Mao notes a number of accounts, such as Phillip Smith and Michael Helfand's *Oscar Wilde's Oxford Notebooks: A Portrait of Mind in the Making* (Oxford: Oxford University Press, 1989), that too resolutely see in *The Picture of Dorian Gray* an opposition to a soul-crushing materialist science, arguing instead that "what matters is a physiological process occurring at so molecular a level that it cannot be observed" (85).

113. Sedgwick, *Touching Feeling*, 108.

114. Sedgwick, *Touching Feeling*, 108.

Chapter 2. Realist Prosopagnosia; or, Face Blindness in Theodore Dreiser's *Sister Carrie*

1. Theodore Dreiser, *Sister Carrie*, Norton Critical Editions, 3rd ed., ed. Donald Pizer, (Norton: New York, 2005), 325 (hereafter cited in text as *SC*).

2. Jonathan Crary, *Techniques of the Observer: On Vision and Modernity in the Nineteenth Century* (Cambridge, MA: MIT Press, 2022), 20.

3. Crary, *Techniques of the Observer*, 20.

4. For more on Duchenne, see François Delaporte, *Anatomy of the Passions*, trans. Susan Emanuel (Stanford, CA: Stanford University Press, 2008). For Duchenne's photographs, see Guillaume-Benjamin de Boulogne, *The Mechanism of Human Facial Expression*, ed. and trans. R. Andrew Cuthbertson (1862; repr., Cambridge: Cambridge University Press, 1990).

5. Richard Grant White, "A Morning at Sarony's," *Galaxy: An Illustrated Magazine of Entertaining Reading* 9 (March 1870): 409.

6. White, "Morning at Sarony's," 409.

7. White, "Morning at Sarony's," 411.

8. White, "Morning at Sarony's," 411.

9. White, "Morning at Sarony's," 411.

10. See E. H. Gombrich's definition of criticism in "The Mask and the Face: The Perception of Physiognomic Likeness in Life and in Art," in *The Image and the Eye: Further Studies in the Psychology of Pictorial Representation* (New York: Phaidon, 1994), 124.

11. Stuart Burrows, *Familiar Strangeness: American Fiction and the Language of Photography 1839-1945* (Athens: University of Georgia Press, 2008), 5.

12. Burrows, *Familiar Strangeness*, 5.

13. See Alix Beeston, *In and Out of Sight: Modernist Writing and the Photographic Unseen* (Oxford: Oxford University Press, 2018), 5.

14. Douglas Mao, *Fateful Beauty: Aesthetic Environments, Juvenile Development and Literature, 1860-1960* (Princeton, NJ: Princeton University Press, 2010), 171.

15. Amy Kaplan, *The Social Construction of American Realism* (Chicago: University of Chicago Press, 1992), 142.

16. Kaplan, *Social Construction of American Realism*, 144.

17. For the quotation, see Otis Notman, "Talk with Four Novelists," *New York Saturday Review of Books*, June 15, 1907, 393.

18. Notman, "Talk with Four Novelists," 471.

19. See Lionel Trilling, "Reality in America," in *The Liberal Imagination* (New York: New York Review Books Classics, 2008), pt. 2, 20, 13; the essay originally appeared in 1946 in the *Nation*.

20. Trilling, "Reality in America," 14.

21. Trilling, "Reality in America," 14.

22. See Paul Lauter, "Caste, Class, and Character," in *Feminisms Redux: An Anthology of Literary Theory and Criticism*, ed. Robyn Warhol-Down and Diane Price Herndl (New Brunswick, NJ: Rutgers University Press, 2009), 70-91, which credits Trilling with politicizing matters of critical opinion by converting "the question of the canon into a question of political judgment" (81).

23. Trilling, "Reality in America," 20.

24. This description appears in Christophe Den Tandt, *The Urban Sublime in American Literary Naturalism* (Urbana: University of Illinois Press, 1998), 25.

25. Den Tandt, *Urban Sublime*, 25.

26. Georg Lukács, "Narrate or Describe?," in *Writer and Critic and Other Essays*, ed. and trans. Arthur Kahn (London: Merlin, 1970), 130.

27. Lukács, "Narrate or Describe?," 131, 130, 134.

28. Lukács, "Narrate or Describe?," 146.

29. Georg Lukács, *The Historical Novel*, trans. Hannah and Stanley Mitchell (London: Merlin, 1989), 138.

30. Lukács, "Narrate or Describe?," 128, 127.

31. Lukács, "Narrate or Describe?," 130.

32. See Cannon Schmitt, "Interpret or Describe?," *Representations* 135, no. 1 (Summer 2016): 102, for a useful reading of Lukács's "Narrate or Describe?" as a "model for how we might consider the relationship between description and interpretation" when these terms have been increasingly polarized as distinct critical practices.

33. Lukács, "Narrate or Describe?," 129.

34. See George Lukács, "The Ideology of Modernism," in *Realism in Our Time*, trans. John and Necke Mander (New York: Harper, 1971), 23.

35. Lukács, "Ideology of Modernism," 25.

36. Lukács, "Ideology of Modernism," 25.

37. Lukács, "Ideology of Modernism," 26.

38. Lukács, "Ideology of Modernism," 26.

39. See T. S. Eliot, "Tradition and the Individual Talent," in *Selected Prose of T. S. Eliot*, ed. Frank Kermode (New York: Harcourt, 1975), 43, for Eliot's articulation of impersonality as a dialectical phenomenon, in which "only those who have personality and emotions know what it means to want to escape from these things."

40. Lukács, "Ideology of Modernism," 26.

41. Sarah Blackwood, *The Portrait's Subject: Inventing Inner Life in the Nineteenth-Century United States* (Chapel Hill: University of North Carolina Press, 2019), 108.

42. Blackwood, *Portrait's Subject*, 110.

43. E. H. Gombrich, "On Physiognomic Perception," in *Meditations on a Hobby Horse and Other Essays on the Theory of Art* (London: Phaidon, 1985), 45.

44. Gombrich, "On Physiognomic Perception," 47.

45. Gombrich, "On Physiognomic Perception," 55.

46. Gombrich, "On Physiognomic Perception," 54.
47. Gombrich, "On Physiognomic Perception," 55.
48. Den Tandt, *Urban Sublime*, 24.
49. Den Tandt, *Urban Sublime*, 35.
50. Walter Benn Michaels, *The Gold Standard and the Logic of Naturalism* (Berkeley: University of California Press, 1988), 57. For more on naturalism and consumption, see Rachel Bowlby, *Just Looking: Consumer Culture in Dreiser, Gissing and Zola* (New York: Routledge, 2009).
51. Michaels, *Gold Standard*, 57.
52. Michaels, *Gold Standard*, 27; italics in the original.
53. Michaels, *Gold Standard*, 21. I discuss Erving Goffman's "On Face-Work" more specifically in the introduction to this book. "Face-work" involves the work a person does not only to avoid a loss of face but also to protect the faces of others.
54. Edith Wharton, *The House of Mirth*, ed. Janet Beer and Elizabeth Nolan (Peterborough, ON: Broadview, 2005), 39 (hereafter cited in text as *HM*).
55. Lois Tyson, "Beyond Morality: Lily Bart, Lawrence Selden and the Aesthetic Commodity in *The House of Mirth*," *Edith Wharton Review* 9, no. 2 (Fall 1992): 3.
56. Tyson, "Beyond Morality," 4.
57. Tyson, "Beyond Morality," 4.
58. Tyson, "Beyond Morality," 3.
59. Blackwood, *Portrait's Subject*, 1.
60. Blackwood, *Portrait's Subject*, 1; Tyson, "Beyond Morality," 4.
61. *Under the Gaslight* was immensely popular in American cities because its story of two young women of different social classes whose identities were confused at birth appealed to members of all social classes. For more on the play and its role in the women's suffrage movement, see Amy Hughes, *Spectacles of Reform: Theater and Activism in Nineteenth-Century America* (Ann Arbor: University of Michigan Press, 2012).
62. Philip Fisher, *Hard Facts: Setting and Form in the American Novel* (New York: Oxford University Press, 1985), 165.
63. Fisher, *Hard Facts*, 165.
64. Fisher, *Hard Facts*, 165.
65. Warren Susman, *"Personality" and the Making of Twentieth-Century Culture* (self-pub., 1984), mediastudies.press, 212.
66. Susman, *"Personality,"* 214.
67. See Stephen Best and Sharon Marcus, "Surface Reading: An Introduction," *Representations* 108, no. 1 (Fall 2009): 2.
68. Janet Lyon, "Sociability in the Metropole: Modernism's Bohemian Salons," *English Literary History* 76, no. 3 (Fall 2009): 689.
69. Fisher, *Hard Facts*, 176.

70. I return here to Ellen Rooney, "Live Free or Describe: The Reading Effect and the Persistence of Form," *Differences* 21, no. 3 (2010): 116, and her contention that the ideology of "surface reading" as a fantasy of "immediate reading" disregards literature's "formal activities."

71. Michael Fried, *Realism, Writing, Disfiguration: On Thomas Eakins and Stephen Crane* (Chicago: University of Chicago Press, 1987), 147, 121.

72. Fried, *Realism, Writing, Disfiguration*, 114.

73. See Joseph Conrad's 1914 preface to *The Nigger of the "Narcissus"* (New York: Penguin, 1987), where Conrad elaborates his creative "task": "by the power of the written word, to make you hear, to make you feel—it is, before all, to make you *see*" (xlix).

74. Michaels, *Gold Standard*, 21.

75. Georg Simmel, "Sociology of the Senses: Visual Interaction," in *Introduction to the Science of Sociology*, ed. Robert E. Park and Ernest W. Burgess (Chicago: University of Chicago Press, 1921), 356-60.

76. Simmel, "Sociology of the Senses," 358.

77. Simmel, "Sociology of the Senses," 359.

78. Simmel, "Sociology of the Senses," 356.

79. Simmel, "Sociology of the Senses," 358.

80. Simmel, "Sociology of the Senses," 359.

81. Simmel, "Sociology of the Senses," 359.

82. Simmel, "Sociology of the Senses," 360.

83. Simmel, "Sociology of the Senses," 358.

84. Charles Baudelaire, "The Painter of Modern Life," in *"The Painter of Modern Life" and Other Essays*, ed. and trans. Jonathan Mayne (London: Phaidon, 1995), 2.

85. Baudelaire, "Painter of Modern Life," 11; italics in the original.

86. Baudelaire, "Painter of Modern Life," 11.

87. Baudelaire, "Painter of Modern Life," 11.

88. Baudelaire, "Painter of Modern Life," 11.

89. Ben Highmore, *Cityscapes: Cultural Readings in the Material and Symbolic City* (New York: Palgrave Macmillan, 2005), 6.

90. Highmore, *Cityscapes*, 26.

91. Highmore, *Cityscapes*, 31; italics in the original.

92. Highmore, *Cityscapes*, 27, 29.

93. Edgar Allan Poe, "The Man of the Crowd," in *The Complete Stories and Poems of Edgar Allan Poe* (New York: Doubleday, 1984), 216 (hereafter cited in text as "MC").

94. Delaporte (*Anatomy of the Passions*, 70) argues, following Duchenne, that expressions must be "situated within a field of expressivity" if they are to be understood as more than a "muscular contraction" of the face.

95. Fried, *Realism, Writing, Disfiguration*, 100.
96. Fried, *Realism, Writing, Disfiguration*, 100.
97. Fried, *Realism, Writing, Disfiguration*, 108.
98. Stephen Crane, "When Man Falls, a Crowd Gathers," in *Stephen Crane: Prose and Poetry* (New York: Library of America, 1984), 600 (hereafter cited in text as "WMF").
99. Rebecca Zurier, *Picturing the City: Urban Vision and the Ashcan School* (Berkeley: University of California Press, 2006), 53.
100. Zurier, *Picturing the City*, 39.
101. Originally published in 1915, Theodore Dreiser's *The "Genius"* (Oxford: Oxford World's Classics, 2016), although semiautobiographical, was based loosely on the life of Everitt Shin and detailed a painter's struggles with his sexual passions.
102. Zurier, *Picturing the City*, 26.
103. See Oliver Sachs, *The Mind's Eye* (New York: Knopf, 2010), which details his own struggle with the inability to recognize other faces.
104. Blackwood, *Portrait's Subject*, 110.
105. Jean Rhys, *Voyage in the Dark* (New York: Norton, 1982), 8, 9 (hereafter cited in text as VD). For an examination of Rhys's use of "Zolaesque motifs" in *After Leaving Mr. Mackenzie* (1931), see Betsy Berry, "'Between Dog and Whiff': Jean Rhys' Version of Naturalism in *After Leaving Mr. Mackenzie*," *Studies in the Novel* 27, no. 4 (Winter 1995): 544.
106. In chap. one, I discuss Silvan Tomkins's concept of "facial awareness" as it involves one's coming to understand what it "feels like" to have certain expressions and affective reactions. See Silvan Tomkins, *Affect, Imagery, Consciousness* (New York: Springer, 2008), 119.
107. Blackwood, *Portrait's Subject*, 110.
108. Tyson, "Beyond Morality," 4.
109. See Rae Beth Gordon, *Why the French Love Jerry Lewis* (Stanford, CA: Stanford University Press, 2001), 17.
110. Peter Brooks, *The Melodramatic Imagination: Balzac, Henry James, Melodrama, and the Mode of Excess* (New Haven, CT: Yale University Press, 1976), 47, 62, 59.
111. Brooks, *Melodramatic Imagination*, 62.
112. Brooks, *Melodramatic Imagination*, 63.
113. Brooks, *Melodramatic Imagination*, 65, 64.
114. See Judith Wechsler's classic study of Parisian caricature, *A Human Comedy: Physiognomy and Caricature in 19th Century Paris* (Chicago: University of Chicago Press, 1982), 42.
115. Wechsler, *Human Comedy*, 42.
116. Charles Baudelaire, "Some French Caricaturists," in *"The Painter of Modern Life" and Other Essays*, ed. and trans. Jonathan Mayne (London: Phaidon, 1995), 185.

117. Baudelaire, "Some French Caricaturists," 185.

118. Robert Storey, *Pierrot: A Critical History of a Mask* (Princeton, NJ: Princeton University Press, 1978), 73.

119. Storey, *Pierrot*, 73.

120. Gombrich, "On Physiognomic Perception," 45.

Chapter 3. Nothing "Conclusive": Optics as Ethics in Joseph Conrad's *The Secret Agent*

1. Paul Ekman and Wallace V. Friesen, "Nonverbal Leakage and Clues to Deception," *Psychiatry: Journal for the Study of Interpersonal Processes* 32, no. 1 (February 1969): 98-99.

2. See Sigmund Freud, *Dora: An Analysis of a Case of Hysteria* (New York: Collier, 1963), 96.

3. Joseph Conrad, *The Secret Agent* (New York: Modern Library, 1993), 52 (hereafter cited in text as *SA*).

4. See Brian Schaffer, "'The Commerce of Shady Wares': Politics and Pornography in Conrad's *The Secret Agent*," *ELH* 62, no. 2 (1995): 443; Matthew Oliver, "Conrad's Grotesque Public: Pornography and the Politics of Reading in *The Secret Agent*," *Twentieth-Century Literature* 55, no. 2 (Summer 2009): 209; and Rishona Zimring, "Conrad's Pornography Shop," *Modern Fiction Studies* 43, no. 2 (Summer 1997): 320.

5. See Stephen Arata, *Fictions of Loss in the Victorian Fin de Siècle: Identity and Empire* (Cambridge: Cambridge University Press, 2009), 4.

6. Arata, *Fictions of Loss*, 4.

7. Freud, *Dora*, 96.

8. Ruth Leys, "How Did Fear Become a Scientific Object and What Kind of Object Is It?," *Representations* 110, no. 1 (Spring 2010): 66. Ekman's recent popularity has been confirmed by his appearances as a scientific advisor on the Fox TV show *Lie to Me*, a fictional drama about a scientist (based on Ekman but played by Tim Roth) who is an expert at detecting micro-expressions and his consulting agency. Officially charged with advising the Transportation Security Administration's SPOT program (Screening Passengers by Observational Techniques), Ekman credits himself with the ability to spot suspicious persons from a distance; see Paul Ekman, "How to Spot a Terrorist on the Fly," *Washington Post*, October 29, 2006, http://www.washingtonpost.com/wp-dyn/content/article/2006/10/27/AR2006102701478.html. See also Daniel Gross's critique of Ekman's application of the word "basic" to describe all emotions in "Defending the Humanities with Charles Darwin's *The Expression of the Emotions in Man and Animals* (1872)," *Critical Inquiry* 37, no. 1 (Autumn 2010): 43.

9. Leys, "How Did Fear," 89.

10. See Joseph Conrad, "Author's Note" (1920), in *The Secret Agent*, ed. Martin Seymour-Smith (New York: Penguin, 1984), 39.

11. Stephen Kern, *The Culture of Time and Space, 1880–1920* (Cambridge, MA: Harvard University Press, 2003), 16.

12. Kern, *Culture of Time and Space*, 16.

13. Kern, *Culture of Time and Space*, 12.

14. Kern, *Culture of Time and Space*; Conrad, "Author's Note," 39.

15. Conrad, "Author's Note," 39.

16. Randall Stevenson, "Greenwich Meanings: Clocks and Things in Modernist and Postmodernist Fiction," *Yearbook of English Studies* 30 (2000): 130.

17. I reference again Gombrich's description of criticism in "The Mask and the Face," where "likeness has to be caught rather than constructed"; E. H. Gombrich, "The Mask and the Face: The Perception of Physiognomic Likeness in Life and in Art," in *The Image and the Eye: Further Studies in the Psychology of Pictorial Representation* (New York: Phaidon, 1994), 124.

18. Cesare Lombroso, "The Physiognomy of the Anarchists," *Monist* 1, no. 3 (April 1891): 340, 339.

19. Lombroso, "Physiognomy of the Anarchists," 339, 340.

20. Carlo Ginzburg, "Clues: Roots of an Evidential Paradigm," in *Clues, Myths, and the Historical Method*, trans. John and Anne C. Tedeschi (Baltimore: Johns Hopkins University Press), 104.

21. Ginzburg, "Clues," 119.

22. Ginzburg, "Clues," 120.

23. Tom Gunning, "Tracing the Individual Body: Photography, Detectives and Early Cinema," in *Cinema and the Invention of Modern Life*, ed. Leo Charney and Vanessa R. Schwartz (Berkeley: University of California Press, 1995), 21, 23.

24. Gunning, "Tracing the Individual Body," 23.

25. Ginzburg, "Clues," 120.

26. Ginzburg, "Clues," 120.

27. Ginzburg, "Clues," 120.

28. Ellen Samuels, *Fantasies of Identification: Disability, Gender, Race* (New York: New York University Press, 2014), 122, 98.

29. For the original, see Francis Galton, *Finger Prints: The Classic 1892 Treatise* (Mineola, NY: Dover, 2012); quoted in Samuels, *Fantasies of Identification*, 111.

30. Quoted in Samuels, *Fantasies of Identification*, 112.

31. Samuels, *Fantasies of Identification*, 112.

32. Ginzburg, "Clues," 120.

33. Samuels, *Fantasies of Identification*, 2.

34. For more on the secret agency and the subject of content, see Alex Segal, "Deconstruction, Radical Secrecy, and *The Secret Agent*," *Modern Fiction Studies* 54,

no. 2 (Summer 2008): 189-208; and Christian Haines, "Life in Crisis: The Biopolitical Ambivalence of Joseph Conrad's *The Secret Agent*," *Criticism* 54, no. 1 (Winter 2012): 85-115.

35. For original reference, see Alphonse Bertillon, *Identification Anthropométrique: Instructions signaletiques* (Melun: Paris, 1893), lxxxiii; quoted in Josh Ellenbogen, *Reasoned and Unreasoned Images: The Photography of Bertillon, Galton, and Marey* (University Park: Pennsylvania State University Press, 2012), 30.

36. Ellenbogen, *Reasoned and Unreasoned Images*, 27.

37. Ellenbogen, *Reasoned and Unreasoned Images*, 46.

38. Ellenbogen, *Reasoned and Unreasoned Images*, 46.

39. Jason Coats, "Unreliable Heterodiegesis and Scientific Racism in Conrad's *Secret Agent*," *Modernism/Modernity* 20, no. 4 (November 2013): 646. See also Max Nordau's *Degeneration* (1895; repr., Lincoln: University of Nebraska Press, 1993), which succeeded in linking the world of art to the pathologized, sick body of the degenerate artist.

40. Coats, "Unreliable Heterodiegesis," 662.

41. Coats, "Unreliable Heterodiegesis," 660.

42. Gunning, "Tracing the Individual Body," 32.

43. Arata, *Fictions of Loss*, 4.

44. As Michaela Bronstein has observed in her short essay on Ford Madox Ford's *Joseph Conrad: A Personal Remembrance* (1924), Conrad's identity as an "impressionist" writer survives largely because of Ford's claiming of him as such. See Michaela Bronstein, "Joseph Conrad: A Personal Remembrance" (2010), in *Modernism Lab Essays*, ed. Pericles Lewis, https://campuspress.yale.edu/modernismlab/joseph-conrad-a-personal-remembrance/.

45. Coats, "Unreliable Heterodiegesis," 662.

46. Quoted in Ellenbogen, *Reasoned and Unreasoned Images*, 41.

47. Gombrich, "Mask and the Face," 135.

48. See what is now understood as the foundational document in the formation of literary impressionism, Joseph Conrad's 1914 preface to *The Nigger of the "Narcissus"* (New York: Penguin, 1987), xlix.

49. Jesse Matz, *Literary Impressionism and Modernist Aesthetics* (Cambridge: Cambridge University Press, 2001), 142. See also Tamar Katz, *Impressionist Subjects: Gender, Interiority and Modernist Fiction in England* (Urbana: University of Illinois Press, 2000).

50. Matz, *Literary Impressionism*, 43, 11.

51. Matz, *Literary Impressionism*, 43.

52. For his analysis of Conrad's earlier novel *Almayer's Folly*, see Michael Fried, "Almayer's Face: On 'Impressionism' in Conrad, Crane, and Norris," *Critical Inquiry* 17, no. 1 (Autumn 1990): 212.

53. Fried, "Almayer's Face," 213.

54. See Sarah Cole, "Dynamite Violence and Literary Culture," *Modernism/Modernity* 16, no. 2 (April 2009): 319.

55. Matz, *Literary Impressionism*, 142.

56. See Peter Brooks, *The Melodramatic Imagination: Balzac, Henry James, Melodrama, and the Mode of Excess* (New Haven, CT: Yale University Press, 1976), 16, 10.

57. Agustin Zarzosa, "Melodrama and the Modes of the World," *Discourse* 32, no. 2 (Spring 2010): 236, 237, 238. For an analysis of melodrama as it both "exploit[s]" and "produces" "unsettled emotional states," see also Matthew S. Buckley, "Refugee Theatre: Melodrama and Modernity's Loss," *Theater Journal* 61, no. 2 (May 2009): 182.

58. Zarzosa, "Melodrama," 237.

59. Zarzosa, "Melodrama," 238.

60. Brooks, *Melodramatic Imagination*, 10; Zarzosa, "Melodrama," 238.

61. Zarzosa, "Melodrama," 237.

62. Brooks, *Melodramatic Imagination*, 10.

63. See François Delaporte, *Anatomy of the Passions*, trans. Susan Emanuel (Stanford, CA: Stanford University Press, 2008), 39.

64. Ginzburg, "Clues," 102.

65. See the register of physically observable facial characteristics Cesare Lombroso connected to the condition of moral imbecility, "born" criminality, and, following the influence of Darwin, the atavistic characteristics of monkeys and apes in *Criminal Man*, trans. Mary Gibson and Nicole Hahn (Durham, NC: Duke University Press, 2006), 53.

66. Brooks, *Melodramatic Imagination*, 47, 56.

67. Brooks, *Melodramatic Imagination*, 125.

68. Gunning, "Tracing the Individual Body," 35.

69. Brooks, *Melodramatic Imagination*, 75.

70. Brooks, *Melodramatic Imagination*, 76.

71. Brooks, *Melodramatic Imagination*, 76.

72. Brooks, *Melodramatic Imagination*, 78.

73. Garry Leonard, "He's Got Bette Davis Eyes: James Joyce and Melodrama," *Joyce Studies Annual*, 2008, 81. For insight into the leftist appropriation of the form by modernists such as Bertolt Brecht, W. H. Auden, and Christopher Isherwood, see also Benjamin Kolmann, "Awkward Moments: Melodrama, Modernism, and the Politics of Affect," *PMLA* 128, no. 2 (March 2013): 337-52.

74. Leonard, "He's Got Bette Davis Eyes," 80.

75. Leonard, "He's Got Bette Davis Eyes," 79.

76. Leonard, "He's Got Bette Davis Eyes," 79.

77. Leonard, "He's Got Bette Davis Eyes," 79.

78. See Emmanuel Levinas, *Totality and Infinity: An Essay on Exteriority*, trans. Alphonso Lingis (Pittsburgh: Duquesne University Press, 1969), 39.

79. Levinas, *Totality and Infinity*, 202.

80. I discuss Paul de Man's version of prosopopoeia, as it appears in *The Rhetoric of Romanticism*, more fully in chap. four.

81. Levinas, *Totality and Infinity*, 43, 46.

82. Levinas, *Totality and Infinity*, 46.

83. Levinas, *Totality and Infinity*, 202.

84. Levinas, *Totality and Infinity*, 202.

85. Levinas, *Totality and Infinity*, 202.

86. Levinas, *Totality and Infinity*, 202.

87. Levinas, *Totality and Infinity*, 202.

88. Zarzosa, "Melodrama," 238.

89. Levinas, *Totality and Infinity*, 202.

90. I quote here from Ford Madox Ford's 1913 essay "On Impressionism," where he writes that producing a proper impression requires an "altogether disproportionately enormous frame; a frame absolutely monstrous"; Ford Madox Ford, "On Impressionism," in *Critical Writings of Ford Madox Ford*, ed. Frank MacShane (Lincoln: University of Nebraska Press, 1964), 44.

91. Peter Brooks, *Reading for the Plot: Design and Intention in Narrative* (Cambridge, MA: Harvard University Press, 1984), 18.

92. Brooks, *Reading for the Plot*, 18.

93. Conrad, "Author's Note," 39.

94. Levinas, *Totality and Infinity*, 202.

95. I reference in this heading Ezra Pound's *ABC of Reading* (1934; repr., New York: New Directions, 1960) and his description of his ideogrammic method as directing what everyone already "KNOWS" (22).

96. Segal, "Deconstruction," 202.

97. Conrad, preface to *The Nigger of the "Narcissus,"* xlviii.

98. Arata, *Fictions of Loss*, 4.

99. Levinas, *Totality and Infinity*, 4.

100. See Sigmund Freud, *Beyond the Pleasure Principle*, ed. and trans. James Strachey (New York: Norton, 1959), 33-34, for Freud's idea that trauma results from a breach in the "protective shield," which, at its most efficient, is adept at "binding" and disposing of excess stimuli.

101. Freud, *Beyond the Pleasure Principle*, 30.

102. Christina Britzolakis, "Pathologies of the Imperial Metropolis: Impressionism as Traumatic Afterimage in Conrad and Ford," *Journal of Modern Literature* 29, no. 1 (January 2006): 6.

103. Britzolakis, "Pathologies of the Imperial Metropolis," 9.

104. Leonard, "He's Got Bette Davis Eyes," 80.

105. Leonard, "He's Got Bette Davis Eyes," 86.

106. For more on the concept of "display rules," or the cultural norms regard-

ing what affects are allowed to be displayed in various settings, see Wallace Friesen and Paul Ekman, "The Repertoire of Nonverbal Behavior: Categories, Origins, Usage, and Coding," *Semiotica* 1, no. 1 (1969): 75.

107. Levinas, *Totality and Infinity*, 46.
108. Brooks, *Melodramatic Imagination*, 10; Zarzosa, "Melodrama," 237.
109. See Joseph Valente, "The Accidental Autist: Neurosensory Disorder in *The Secret Agent*," *Journal of Modern Literature* 38, no. 1 (Fall 2014): 33, who contends that Stevie's "nominal idiocy . . . was never intended to designate an autistic mode of subjectivity," since pediatric medicine had not developed sufficiently enough in Conrad's time to make such a diagnosis (20).
110. Valente, "Accidental Autist," 22.
111. Valente, "Accidental Autist," 20, 27.
112. Pound, *ABC of Reading*, 22, 21.
113. Pound, *ABC of Reading*, 22.
114. Brooks, *Melodramatic Imagination*, 56.
115. Brooks, *Melodramatic Imagination*, 67.
116. Brooks, *Melodramatic Imagination*, 67.
117. Gunning, "Tracing the Individual Body," 32.
118. See, e.g., Ellen Harrington, "The Female Offender: The New Woman and Winnie Verloc in Conrad's *The Secret Agent*," *Conradian* 32, no. 1 (Spring 2007): 57-69.
119. Fried, "Almayer's Face," 213.
120. Ellenbogen, *Reasoned and Unreasoned Images*, 46.
121. Fried, "Almayer's Face," 213.
122. Fried, "Almayer's Face," 213.
123. Zarzosa, "Melodrama," 237.
124. Fried, "Almayer's Face," 230.
125. Fried, "Almayer's Face," 213.
126. Conrad, "Author's Note," 39.
127. The terms come from Stephen Best and Sharon Marcus, "Surface Reading: An Introduction," *Representations* 108, no. 1 (Fall 2009): 5.
128. Freud, *Dora*, 96.

Chapter 4. Modernist Prosopopoeia; or, Making Faces

1. T. S. Eliot, "The Love Song of J. Alfred Prufrock," in *The Complete Poems and Plays* (New York: Harcourt, 1930), 6, 4.
2. Eliot, "Love Song," 6.
3. T. S. Eliot, "Tradition and the Individual Talent," in *Selected Prose of T. S. Eliot*, ed. Frank Kermode (New York: Harvest, 1975), 40.
4. Eliot, "Tradition," 43.

5. For a description of the great portraitist's ability to "mobilize our projection," see E. H. Gombrich, "The Mask and the Face: The Perception of Physiognomic Likeness in Life and in Art," in *The Image and the Eye: Further Studies in the Psychology of Pictorial Representation* (New York: Phaidon, 1994), 117.

6. Jonathan Cole uses the term "facial loss" to characterize people suffering from both common and rarer conditions—such as Moebius syndrome—that impair their facial functioning and thus inhibit social relationships with others; Jonathan Cole, *About Face* (Cambridge, MA: MIT Press, 1999), 5.

7. See Suzannah Biernoff, *Portraits of Violence: War and the Aesthetics of Disfigurement* (Ann Arbor: University of Michigan Press, 2017), 167.

8. Biernoff, *Portraits of Violence*, 167.

9. Katherine Feo, "Invisibility: Memory, Masks and Masculinities in the Great War," *Journal of Design History* 20, no. 1 (Spring 2007): 17.

10. Julie M. Powell, "About-Face: Gender, Disfigurement and the Politics of French Reconstruction, 1918-24," *Gender and History* 28, no. 3 (November 2016): 605.

11. Powell, "About-Face," 610.

12. David Lubin, "Masks, Mutilation, and Modernity: Anna Coleman Ladd and the First World War," *Archives of American Art Journal* 47, no. 3/4 (2008): 13.

13. Feo notes the inconsistency of information regarding the actual number of masks Ladd's studio produced, which ranged from 97 to 220; Feo, "Invisibility," 17.

14. Suzannah Biernoff notes that more soldiers suffered from facial injuries than amputated limbs in "Flesh Poems: Henry Tonks and the Art of Surgery," *Visual Culture in Britain* 11, no. 1 (March 2010): 27.

15. Mina Loy, *Auto-Facial-Construction* (1919), in *The Lost Lunar Baedeker: Poems of Mina Loy*, ed. Roger L. Conover (New York: Farrar, Strauss & Giroux, 1997), 165 (hereafter cited in text as *AFC*).

16. Henri Gaudier-Brzeska introduces his concepts of "sculptural energy," "sculptural feeling," and "sculptural ability" in his "Vortex" manifesto, which appears in *Blast I*, ed. Wyndham Lewis (Santa Rosa, CA: Black Sparrow, 1997), 155. I take the word "organizational" from Ed Comentale's *Modernism, Cultural Production, and the British Avant-Garde* (Cambridge: Cambridge University Press, 2004), 184. For Harold Gillies's description of plastic surgery as a "strange new art," see the biography by Reginald Pound, *Gillies: Surgeon Extraordinary* (London: Michael Joseph, 1964), 30.

17. See Anna Coleman Ladd's "Address to the American Women's Association: Lecture about Being a Sculptor, circa 1930," May 5, 1925, box 2, folder 34, Anna Coleman Ladd Papers, ca. 1881-1950, Archives of American Art, Smithsonian Institution, Washington, DC. Quoted in Aaron Shaheen, "Spiritualizing Prostheses: Anna Coleman Ladd's Portrait Masks for Mutilated Soldiers of World War I," *Modernism/Modernity* 26, no. 3 (September 2019): 651.

18. See Hugh Kenner, *The Pound Era* (Berkeley: University of California Press, 1991), 234.

19. Carolyn Burke discusses the traditional nature of Loy's art education in *Becoming Modern: The Life of Mina Loy* (New York: Farrar, Strauss & Giroux, 1996), noting that Loy began in London with the copying of classical antiquities, heads in particular. While Gaudier-Brzeska received no formal training as an artist, more on his "prewar radical style" appears in Roberta Jeanne Marie Olson, "Graphic Gaudier-Brzeska," *Record of the Art Museum, Princeton University* 33, no. 1 (1974): 4; and Evelyn Silber, *Gaudier-Brzeska: Life and Art* (London: Thames & Hudson, 1996). I note here that despite Gaudier-Brzeska's associations with the vorticist movement, art historians and even contemporaries stressed that his work was not vorticist. See Horace Brodzky's letter in *American Magazine of Art* 8, no. 6 (April 1917), where he wrote that Gaudier-Brzeska "did not have anything in common with them" (252). As modernist literary critics, our understanding of Gaudier-Brzeska's work has more likely been filtered through Pound's assessment of it and through his contributions to *Blast*.

20. For Gombrich's definition of criticism and the idea that "likeness has to be caught rather than constructed," see Gombrich, "Mask and the Face," 124.

21. Catherine M. Soussloff, *The Subject in Art: Portraiture and the Birth of the Modern* (Durham, NC: Duke University Press, 2006), 8.

22. Soussloff, *Subject in Art*, 8.

23. Soussloff, *Subject in Art*, 10.

24. Sarah Blackwood, *The Portrait's Subject: Inventing Inner Life in the Nineteenth-Century United States* (Chapel Hill: University of North Carolina Press, 2019), 17.

25. For more on Silvan Tomkins's concept of "facial awareness" as it relates to our ability to understand what our expressions "feel like," see Silvan Tomkins, *Affect, Imagery, Consciousness* (New York: Springer, 2008), 119.

26. Tomkins, *Affect, Imagery, Consciousness*, 119.

27. Tomkins, *Affect, Imagery, Consciousness*, 119.

28. See also François Delaporte, *Anatomy of the Passions*, trans. Susan Emanuel (Stanford, CA: Stanford University Press, 2008), 126.

29. Lois Tyson, "Beyond Morality: Lily Bart, Lawrence Selden and the Aesthetic Commodity in 'The House of Mirth,'" *Edith Wharton Review* 9, no. 2 (1992): 3.

30. See Gaudier-Brzeska, "Vortex," 155.

31. Tim Armstrong, *Modernism, Technology, and the Body* (Cambridge: Cambridge University Press, 1998), 6.

32. See Denis Diderot, *On Art: The Salon of 1765 and Notes on Painting*, trans. John Goodman (New Haven, CT: Yale University Press, 1995), 214; and Georg Simmel, "The Aesthetic Significance of the Face," in *Georg Simmel 1858–1918: A Collection of Essays with Translations and a Bibliography*, ed. Kurt H. Wolf (Columbus: Ohio State University Press, 1959), 276.

33. According to Carolyn Burke, Loy began practicing the Mensendieck system of functional movement around 1914. Conceiving the body as a muscle-bound system of bones, the aim of the system is to develop an aesthetically pleasing musculature and beautify bodily protuberances. Armstrong (*Modernism, Technology, and the Body*, 107) also relates Loy's technique to her interest in Christian Science and the belief in "conscious human control of biological and psychological functioning," along with Matthias Alexander's Alexander Technique, which saw "*habit* as the point of entry for a bodily pragmatics."

34. For more on the performative aspects of Loy's "understanding of personality," see Christina Walter, "Feminist Manifesto and *Auto-Facial-Construction*" (July 25, 2010), in *Modernism Lab Essays*, ed. Pericles Lewis, https://campuspress.yale.edu/modernismlab/mina-loy/.

35. F. W. H. Myers, *Human Personality and Its Survival of Bodily Death* (Charlottesville, VA: Hampton Roads, 2001), 47.

36. Myers, *Human Personality*, 49.

37. James Paxson, "Personification's Gender," *Rhetorica: A Journal of the History of Rhetoric* 16, no. 2 (Spring 1998): 176.

38. Paxson, "Personification's Gender," 176.

39. Eliot, "Love Song," 6.

40. Paxson, "Personification's Gender," 156.

41. Paxson, "Personification's Gender," 156.

42. Paul de Man, *The Rhetoric of Romanticism* (Cambridge, MA: Harvard University Press, 1984), 76.

43. De Man, *Rhetoric of Romanticism*, 92.

44. De Man, *Rhetoric of Romanticism*, 92.

45. De Man, *Rhetoric of Romanticism*, 92, 89.

46. De Man, *Rhetoric of Romanticism*, 90.

47. De Man, *Rhetoric of Romanticism*, 90.

48. Eliot, "Love Song," 5.

49. Eliot, "Love Song," 4, 6.

50. Eliot, "Love Song," 5.

51. De Man, *Rhetoric of Romanticism*, 78. Michael Rifaterre analyzes these shifts as "chiasmus" in "Prosopopoeia," *Yale French Studies* 69 (1985): 112, and Barbara Johnson, in *Persons and Things* (Cambridge, MA: Harvard University Press, 2008), theorizes prosopopoeia as exhibiting a similar dynamic of call and reply.

52. J. Hillis Miller, *Versions of Pygmalion* (Cambridge, MA: Harvard University Press, 1990), 55.

53. Miller, *Versions of Pygmalion*, 222.

54. Miller, *Versions of Pygmalion*, 222.

55. Ezra Pound, *A Memoir of Gaudier-Brzeska* (New York: New Directions, 1970), 49.

56. Pound quotes Gaudier-Brzeska in *Memoir*, 50.

57. Unable to afford stone, Gaudier-Brzeska generally sculpted in plaster. Kenner (*Pound Era*) writes that Pound spent two months' income on the four-foot piece of marble that would become his head.

58. Quoted in Jon Wood, "Heads and Tales: Gaudier-Brzeska's *Hieratic Head of Ezra Pound* and the Making of an Avant-Garde Homage," in *Sculpture and the Pursuit of the Modern Ideal in Britain, c. 1880–1930*, ed. David J. Getsy (Hants, UK: Ashgate, 2004), 198.

59. Lisa Tickner, "Now and Then: The Hieratic Head of Ezra Pound," *Oxford Art Journal* 16, no. 2 (1993): 58, 57.

60. Tickner, "Now and Then," 58.

61. Pound, *Memoir*, 49.

62. In general, the relationship between the two men has been read and understood from Pound's point of view, particularly as presented in *A Memoir of Gaudier-Brzeska*. For example, Horace Brodzky claimed that the bust was done "by way of disapproval and in contempt of Pound"; quoted in Timothy Materer, "Ezra Pound and Gaudier-Brzeska: Sophie's Diary," *Journal of Modern Literature* 6, no. 2 (April 1977): 315. Aside from Pound's memoir, H. S. Ede's *Savage Messiah* (New York: Outerbridge & Lazard, 1972), originally published in 1931, offers the most complete account of the author's life and work.

63. Wood, "Heads and Tales," 199.

64. Wood, "Heads and Tales," 199.

65. Wood, "Heads and Tales," 200.

66. Materer ("Ezra Pound and Gaudier-Brzeska," 319) notes Gaudier-Brzeska's weariness of Pound as quoted in Sophie's diary: "I've just about had enough of him. He comes and stays for hours without speaking. After all, I think that he is superficial, and this idea prevents me from working well on his portrait—it's not coming along."

67. E. H. Gombrich, "On Physiognomic Perception," in *Meditations on a Hobby Horse and Other Essays on the Theory of Art* (London: Phaidon, 1985), 45.

68. Pound quotes Gaudier-Brzeska in *Memoir*, 50.

69. Eliot, "Love Song," 15.

70. Kenner, *Pound Era*, 258.

71. Kenner, *Pound Era*, 259.

72. Scholars have suggested that Gaudier-Brzeska had in mind the Easter Island statue Hoa-Haka-Nana-La, which he had seen in the British Museum, as he was carving the head. See Jonathan Blackwood, "Gaudier-Brzeska, Henri (1891–1915) and *Gaudier-Brzeska: A Memoir*," in *The Ezra Pound Encyclopedia*, ed. Demetres Tryphonopoulos and Stephen J. Adams (Santa Barbara, CA: Greenwood), 129–32.

73. De Man, *Rhetoric of Romanticism*, 89; Kenner, *Pound Era*, 258.

74. See Ezra Pound, "A Retrospect," in *Literary Essays* (New York: New

Directions, 1918), 3, for Pound's three "principles" of poetic composition. Pound comments most fully on his "ideogrammic method" in *ABC of Reading* (1934; repr., New York: New Directions, 1960), 27, 25.

75. See Gombrich, "On Physiognomic Perception," 45, for his idea of "physiognomic perception." For the description of Kris and Gombrich's anti-fascist collaboration and their analysis of propaganda for the BBC in the 30s, see Louis Rose, "Interpreting Propaganda: Successors to Warburg and Freud in Wartime," *American Imago* 60, no. 1 (2003): 124.

76. Eliot, "Love Song," 15.

77. Charles Darwin, *The Expression of the Emotions in Man and Animals* (1872; repr., Minneapolis: Filiquarian, 2007), 5.

78. See Pound, *Memoir*, 50.

79. "Letter Written from the Trenches" appears in Pound, *Memoir*, 28.

80. Eliot, "Tradition," 43.

81. Paxson, "Personification's Gender," 176.

82. Delaporte, *Anatomy of the Passions*, 154.

83. Pound, *Memoir*, 49.

84. Quoted in Ede, *Savage Messiah*, 47.

85. Soussloff, *Subject in Art*, 10.

86. Gaudier-Brzeska, "Vortex," 156.

87. *The Graduate*, directed by Mike Nichols (Los Angeles: Embassy Pictures, 1967).

88. For Gillies's quotation, see Pound, *Gillies*, 30.

89. In "Masks for Facial Wounds," Wood explains his intention to use his skill to "make a man's face as near as possible to what it looked like before he was wounded"; Francis Derwent Wood, "Masks for Facial Wounds," *Lancet* 189, no. 4895 (June 1917): 949.

90. Feo, "Invisibility," 21.

91. Feo, "Invisibility," 22.

92. For the original, see Anna Coleman Ladd Papers, 1881-1950, Archives of American Art, Smithsonian Institution; quoted in Feo, "Invisibility," 23.

93. Harold Gillies, *Plastic Surgery of the Face Based on Selected Cases of War Injuries of the Face Including Burns, with Original Illustrations* (London: Frowde, Hodder, & Stoughton, 1920), 5.

94. Harold Gillies and A. H. McIndoe, "The Late Surgical Complications of the Fracture of the Mandible," *British Medical Journal* 2, no. 3805 (December 9, 1933): 1063. I take the term "sub-structure" from an unpublished paper that was likely authored by Gillies's partner, Thomas Pomfret Kilner, in the late 1930s; papers from Thomas Pomfret Kilner, box 9, British Association of Plastic and Reproductive Surgeons Archive, London, England.

95. See Harold Gillies, "Facial Injuries due to Road Accidents and Their Repair,"

Medical Press and Circular (1934), published papers by Sir Harold Gillies 2, 1927-60, box G, folder 24, British Association of Plastic and Reconstructive Surgeons Archives, London, England.

96. Gillies, "Facial Injuries."
97. Gillies, "Facial Injuries."
98. See Andrew Bamji, *Faces from the Front: Harold Gillies, The Queen's Hospital Sidcup and the Origins of Modern Plastic Surgery* (West Midlands, UK: Helion, 2017), 30.
99. For the quotation, see Andrew Bamji, "Facial Surgery: The Patient's Experience," in *Facing Armageddon*, ed. Hugh Cecil and Peter H. Liddle (London: Leo Cooper, 1996), 495.
100. Horace Sewell, Letters to Reginald Pound, 1955-72, MS 0336, Royal College of Surgeons, London, England.
101. See Harold Gillies and D. Ralph Millard, *The Principles and Art of Plastic Surgery* (London: Butterworth, 1957), 50.
102. Harold Gillies, "The Development and Scope of Plastic Surgery, The Charles H. Mayo Lecture for 1934" (lecture, Northwestern University, Chicago, IL, 1935), 1.
103. Gillies, "Development and Scope," 1.
104. Gillies, "Development and Scope," 1.
105. Gillies, *Plastic Surgery*, 6.
106. Gillies, *Plastic Surgery*, 5.
107. Gillies, *Plastic Surgery*, 139, 55.
108. Tomkins, *Affect, Imagery, Consciousness*, 119.
109. The remark appears in Sir Archibald McIndoe's unpublished lecture from 1958, "Total Reconstruction of the Burned Face," MS 0368, Royal College of Surgeons, London, England.
110. McIndoe writes in "Total Reconstruction of the Burned Face" that "finally we have now arrived at the time when form, colour, harmony and contour are of immense importance, when we can within a reasonable time create order out of chaos and make a face which does not excite pity or horror. By doing so we can restore a lost soul to the normal living."
111. For this reference to structure, see Gillies and McIndoe, "Late Surgical Complications," 1063.
112. Tomkins, *Affect, Imagery, Consciousness*, 119.
113. François Delaporte, *Figures of Medicine: Blood, Face Transplants, Parasites* (New York: Fordham University Press, 2013), 82, 65.
114. Delaporte, *Figures of Medicine*, 77.
115. Delaporte, *Figures of Medicine*, 82.
116. The idea that facial disfigurement results in isolation, social death, and the cessation of social viability is part of what Heather Lane Talley terms the "disfigure-

ment imaginary" in *Saving Face: Disfigurement and the Politics of Appearance* (New York: New York University Press, 2014), 28, 39.

117. Delaporte, *Figures of Medicine*, 82.

118. I quote here from a particularly depressing example from the patient case file of F. H. Adams, who was patient number 1292 on the register and suffered a "total loss of vision"; British Patient Files, 1915-25, MS0513, Royal College of Surgeons, London, England.

119. For Tonks's drawing of Lumley and the accompanying case file, including a "before" picture, see Samuel JMM Alberti, ed., *War, Art and Surgery: The Work of Henry Tonks and Julia Midgley* (London: Royal College of Surgeons of England, 2014), 148-49.

120. Biernoff, *Portraits of Violence*, 167.

121. Quoted in Biernoff, "Flesh Poems," 56.

122. Biernoff, "Flesh Poems," 31.

123. Biernoff, *Portraits of Violence*, 4.

124. Biernoff, *Portraits of Violence*, 132.

125. Biernoff, *Portraits of Violence*, 131.

126. See Emma Chambers, "Fragmented Identities: Reading Subjectivity in Henry Tonks' Surgical Portraits," *Art History* 32, no. 3 (June 2009): 579.

127. Chambers, "Fragmented Identities," 579.

128. Chambers, "Fragmented Identities," 587.

129. Chambers, "Fragmented Identities," 587.

130. Chambers, "Fragmented Identities," 593.

131. Soussloff, *Subject in Art*, 8.

132. This analysis appears in Emma Chambers, "Wounded Soldiers and the Memory of War," in Alberti, *War, Art, and Surgery*, 56.

133. Chambers, "Wounded Soldiers," 56.

134. Biernoff, *Portraits of Violence*, 131.

135. De Man, *Rhetoric of Romanticism*, 92.

136. De Man, *Rhetoric of Romanticism*, 92; Gillies, "Facial Injuries."

137. De Man, *Rhetoric of Romanticism*, 92.

138. Biernoff, *Portraits of Violence*, 131.

139. Chambers, "Fragmented Identities," 591.

140. The quote, originally from Henry Tonks to Dugald Sutherland McColl, June 1916, MacColl Papers, Glasgow University Library, appears in Chambers, "Fragmented Identities," 588.

141. Eliot, "Tradition," 64.

142. Chambers, "Wounded Soldiers," 55.

143. Bamji, *Faces from the Front*, 50.

144. Biernoff, *Portraits of Violence*, 116.

145. Biernoff, *Portraits of Violence*, 117.

146. Biernoff, *Portraits of Violence*, 117.

147. Allen Grossman, "The Passion of Laocoön: Warfare of the Religious against the Poetic Institution," in *True-Love: Essays on Poetry and Valuing* (Chicago: University of Chicago Press, 2009), 77.

148. Grossman, "Passion of Laocoön," 77.

149. Grossman, "Passion of Laocoön," 73.

150. Grossman, "Passion of Laocoön," 75.

151. Grossman, "Passion of Laocoön," 76.

152. Grossman, "Passion of Laocoön," 77.

153. Grossman, "Passion of Laocoön," 77.

154. Grossman, "Passion of Laocoön," 88; italics in the original.

155. Grossman, "Passion of Laocoön," 77.

156. Grossman, "Passion of Laocoön," 87.

157. Grossman, "Passion of Laocoön," 87; italics in the original.

158. Pat Barker, *Toby's Room* (New York: Penguin, 2012), 273.

159. Barker, *Toby's Room*, 273.

160. Grossman, "Passion of Laocoön," 77.

161. Grossman, "Passion of Laocoön," 115.

162. Soussloff, *Subject in Art*, 8.

163. Soussloff, *Subject in Art*, 8; Tomkins, *Affect, Imagery, Consciousness*, 119.

164. Tomkins, *Affect, Imagery, Consciousness*, 119.

165. De Man, *Rhetoric of Romanticism*, 81.

166. Biernoff, *Portraits of Violence*, 167.

Chapter 5. Unreadable Persons: The "Face-Scape" of Old Age

1. Humphrey Carpenter recounts this commentary in *W. H. Auden* (New York: Houghton Mifflin, 1981), 423.

2. Auden's remark to a reporter about his face also appears in Carpenter, *W. H. Auden*, 423.

3. See Hannah Arendt's deeply felt piece, "Remembering Wystan H. Auden, Who Died in the Night of the Twenty-Eighth of September, 1973," *New Yorker*, January 20, 1975, 39.

4. Hockney's reputed question appears in various places on the internet and has been memorialized in Alan Bennett's 2009 play *Habit of Art*, without a clear attribution of its source. One online commentator traces this anecdote to Paul Johnson's *Brief Lives* (London: Hutchinson, 2010), but I could not actually locate it in the book. Recent respondents claim that Hockney never inquired about the condition of Auden's nether regions, but rather that the question was addressed to Hockney by either Jim Dine or Noel Coward.

5. For more on this disease and Auden's face, see Jeffrey K. Aronson and Manoj

Ramachandran, "The Diagnosis of Art: W. H. Auden's Face," *Journal of the Royal Society of Medicine* 104, no. 1 (January 1, 2011): 38-40.

6. Arendt, "Remembering Wystan H. Auden," 45.

7. Georg Simmel, "The Aesthetic Significance of the Face," in *Georg Simmel 1858-1918: A Collection of Essays with Translations and a Bibliography*, ed. Kurt H. Wolf (Columbus: Ohio State University Press, 1959), 277.

8. Simmel, "Aesthetic Significance of the Face," 277.

9. Simmel, "Aesthetic Significance of the Face," 277.

10. Pound's letter is quoted in Jon Wood, "Heads and Tales: Gaudier-Brzeska's *Hieratic Head of Ezra Pound* and the Making of an Avant-Garde Homage," in *Sculpture and the Pursuit of the Modern Ideal in Britain, c. 1880-1930*, ed. David J. Getsy (Hants, UK: Ashgate, 2004), 198.

11. Mina Loy, *Auto-Facial-Construction* (1919), in *The Lost Lunar Baedeker: Poems of Mina Loy*, ed. Roger L. Conover (New York: Farrar, Strauss & Giroux, 1997), 165 (hereafter cited in text as *AFC*). See also Ezra Pound, *A Memoir of Gaudier-Brzeska* (New York: New Directions, 1970), 30, for Gaudier-Brzeska's definition of sculpture as a "virile" art. For Pound's notion of "hygiene," see Ezra Pound, "The Serious Artist" (1913), in *Literary Essays of Ezra Pound* (New York: New Directions, 1935), 45.

12. W. H. Auden, "Old People's Home" (1970), in *Collected Poems*, ed. Edward Mendelson (New York: Modern Library, 1976), 852-53 (hereafter cited in text as *CP*).

13. See W. B. Yeats, "Before the World Was Made," in *The Collected Poems of W. B. Yeats* (New York: Scribner, 1996), 270.

14. I take the phrase from Theodore Martin, "The Dialectics of Damage: Art, Form, and Formlessness, A Reply to Jennifer Ashton," *nonsite* 18 (October 19, 2015); and Jennifer Ashton, "Totalizing the Damage: Revolutionary Ambition in Recent American Poetry," *nonsite* 18 (October 9, 2015), https://nonsite.org/9500/.

15. I elaborate more fully on Michael Taussig's *Defacement: Public Secrecy and the Labor of the Negative* (Stanford, CA: Stanford University Press, 1999) later in the chapter.

16. Edith Wharton, *The House of Mirth*, ed. Janet Beer and Elizabeth Nolan (Peterborough, ON: Broadview, 2005), 62.

17. See Melanie Dawson's *Edith Wharton and the Modern Privileges of Age* (Gainesville: University Press of Florida, 2020) for more on the relationship between Wharton and American literature's more general preoccupation "with aging's significance" in the early decades of the twentieth century (2).

18. George Orwell, *The Collected Essays, Journalism and Letters of George Orwell: In Front of Your Nose 1945-1950*, ed. Sonia Orwell and Ian Angus (New York: Harcourt, 1968), 515.

19. Orwell, *Collected Essays*, 515.

20. Margaret Morganroth Gullette, *Aged by Culture* (Chicago: University of

Chicago Press, 2004), 38. See also Margaret Morganroth Gullete, *Agewise: Fighting the New Ageism in America* (Chicago: University of Chicago Press, 2010).

21. Tim Armstrong, *Modernism, Technology, and the Body* (Cambridge: Cambridge University Press, 1998), 6.

22. See Armstrong, *Modernism, Technology, and the Body*, 147. For more on Yeats's interest in rejuvenation, see Richard Ellman, "Yeats' Second Puberty," *New York Review*, May 9, 1985, https://www.nybooks.com/articles/1985/05/09/yeatss-second-puberty/; and Richard Ellman, *Yeats: The Man and the Masks* (New York: Norton, 2000).

23. Armstrong, *Modernism, Technology, and the Body*, 147.

24. Michael Pettit, "Becoming Glandular: Endocrinology, Mass Culture, and Experimental Lives in the Interwar Age," *American Historical Review* 118, no. 4 (October 2013): 1052. On the relationship between rejuvenation and reproductive technology, see Susan Squier, "Incubabies and Rejuvenates: The Traffic between Technologies of Reproduction and Age-Extension," in *Figuring Age: Women, Bodies, Generations*, ed. Kathleen Woodward (Bloomington: Indiana University Press, 1999), 88–111.

25. Herring argues that the "astonishing creative output" of figures such as Djuna Barnes, Charles Henri Ford, Mabel Hampton, and Samuel Steward "extend[s] modernism's temporal expansion"; Scott Herring, *Aging Moderns: Art, Literature, and the Experiment of Later Life* (New York: Columbia University Press, 2022), 1, 5. For works on literature and aging, see also Kathleen Woodward, *Aging and Its Discontents: Freud and Other Fictions* (Bloomington: Indiana University Press, 1991); and Amelia DeFalco, *Uncanny Subjects: Aging in Contemporary Narrative* (Columbus: Ohio State University Press, 2007). For other studies that stress the continuity between "modernism" and its later iterations, see Alys Moody, *The Art of Hunger: Aesthetic Autonomy and the Afterlives of Modernism* (Oxford: Oxford University Press, 2018); Madelyn Detloff, *The Persistence of Modernism: Loss and Mourning in the Twentieth Century* (Cambridge: Cambridge University Press, 2009); David James, ed., *The Legacies of Modernism: Historicising Postwar and Contemporary Fiction* (New York: Cambridge University Press, 2009); and Susan Stanford Friedman, "Alternatives to Periodization: Literary History, Modernism, and the 'New' Temporalities," *Modern Language Quarterly* 80, no. 4 (2019): 379–402.

26. Herring, *Aging Moderns*, 11.

27. Heather Lane Talley, *Saving Face: Disfigurement and the Politics of Appearance* (New York: New York University Press, 2014), 28, 39. For studies that specifically address the intersection of disability and age studies, see Jane Gallop, *Sexuality, Disability and Aging: Queer Temporalities of the Phallus* (Durham, NC: Duke University Press, 2019); and Margaret Morganroth Gullette, *Declining to Decline: Cultural Combat and the Politics of the Midlife* (Charlottesville: University of Virginia Press, 1997).

28. Talley, *Saving Face*, 38.

29. In *Thinking about Dementia: Culture, Loss, and the Anthropology of Senility* (New Brunswick, NJ: Rutgers University Press, 2006), Annette Leibing and Lawrence Cohen link this instability and illegibility to a cultural idea of "senile form" (5). Read more positively, "senile form" might also be approximated to Eve Sedgwick's notion of the "senile sublime," which, as she argues in *Touching Feeling: Affect, Pedagogy, Performativity* (Durham, NC: Duke University Press, 2003), refers to a "more or less intelligible performance by old, brilliant people," which makes evident the "bare outlines of a creative idiom" (24).

30. Armstrong, *Modernism, Technology, and the Body*, 151.

31. Armstrong, *Modernism, Technology, and the Body*, 149, 151.

32. Armstrong, *Modernism, Technology, and the Body*, 149.

33. See Armstrong, *Modernism, Technology, and the Body*, 151, for his discussion of a number of letters Yeats wrote in his later years to younger women, in particular Dorothy Wellesley, who was a lesbian, where he "reiterated . . . the embarrassments of an aged sexuality and what can be made of it in terms of the poet's ability to 'enter' the consciousness of others."

34. Peter Schmidt, *The Conquest of Old Age: Methods to Effect Rejuvenation and Increase Functional Activity* (London: George Routledge & Sons, 1931), 25.

35. Schmidt, *Conquest of Old Age*, 25–26.

36. Schmidt, *Conquest of Old Age*, 25.

37. Schmidt, *Conquest of Old Age*, 26.

38. Schmidt, *Conquest of Old Age*, 24–25.

39. Jay Prosser, *Second Skins: The Body Narratives of Transsexuality* (New York: Columbia University Press, 1998), 142–43.

40. Prosser, *Second Skins*, 142; Prosser cites Hubert Kennedy, *The Life and Works of Karl Heinrich Ulrichs, Pioneer of the Modern Gay Movement* (Boston: Alyson, 1988); and Richard von Krafft-Ebing, *Psychopathia Sexualis: With Especial Reference to the Antipathic Sexual Instinct*, trans. F. J. Rebman (London: Rebman, 1901).

41. Emma Heaney, *The New Woman: Literary Modernism, Queer Theory, and the Trans Feminine Allegory* (Evanston, IL: Northwestern University Press, 2017), 5.

42. Heaney, *New Woman*, 5.

43. See Chandak Sengoopta, "Secrets of Eternal Youth," *History Today*, August 2006, 54.

44. See Roisin Kiberd, "Early Body-Hacking: When Men Got Goat Testicle Grafts to Boost Their Sex Drive," *Vice*, April 16, 2015, https://motherboard.vice.com/en_us/article/early-body-hacking-when-men-got-goat-testicle-grafts-to-boost-their-sex-drive.

45. For more on Lili Elbe, see Jessica Berman, "Is the Trans in Transnational the Trans in Transgender?," *Modernism/Modernity* 24, no. 2 (April 2017): 217–44, which examines how gender status supports or compromises civic and national identity.

46. Armstrong, *Modernism, Technology, and the Body*, 166.

47. Stephen Katz, *Disciplining Old Age: The Formation of Gerontological Knowledge* (Charlottesville: University of Virginia Press, 1996), 41.

48. J.-M. Charcot, *Clinical Lectures on the Diseases of Old Age*, trans. L. H. Hunt (New York: William Wood, 1881), 13; quoted in Katz, *Disciplining Old Age*, 81.

49. Arendt, "Remembering Wystan H. Auden," 45.

50. Katz, *Disciplining Old Age*, 82.

51. See I. L. Nascher, *Geriatrics: The Diseases of Old Age and Their Treatments Including Physiological Old Age, Home and Institutional Care, and Medico-legal Relations* (Philadelphia: P. Blakiston's Son, 1914), 2.

52. Nascher, *Geriatrics*, 3.

53. Nascher, *Geriatrics*, 3.

54. Nascher, *Geriatrics*, 12.

55. Nascher, *Geriatrics*, 13.

56. Nascher, *Geriatrics*, 12.

57. Nascher, *Geriatrics*, 14-15.

58. Nascher, *Geriatrics*, 14-15.

59. Nascher, *Geriatrics*, 19.

60. Nascher, *Geriatrics*, 19.

61. Schmidt, *Conquest of Old Age*, 61.

62. Schmidt, *Conquest of Old Age*, 81. I note here the number of very recent studies on the effects of older fathers on their children, including the recent Swedish study claiming that children of middle-aged fathers were 25% more likely to be mentally ill. See Brian M. D'Onofrio and Paul Lichtenstein, "The Age Gauge: Older Fathers Having Children," *Cerebrum*, July-August 2014, https://www.ncbi.nlm.nih.gov/pmc/articles/PMC4445596/, which reviews the Danish and Swedish studies of advanced paternal age in more detail.

63. Lee Edelman, "Occupy Wall Street: 'Bartleby' against the Humanities," *History of the Present* 3, no. 1 (Spring 2013): 115.

64. Herman Melville, "Bartleby, the Scrivener: A Story of Wallstreet," in *Billy Budd, Bartleby, and Other Stories* (New York: Penguin, 2017), 24 (hereafter cited in text as "BS").

65. Nascher, *Geriatrics*, 13.

66. Osler's retirement speech appears online in the National Institute of Health's US National Library of Medicine, https://profiles.nlm.nih.gov/ps/access/GFBBYH.pdf#xml=https://profiles.nlm.nih.gov:443/pdfhighlight?uid=GFBBYH&query=%28fixed%20period%29.

67. Laura Davidow Hirshbein, "William Osler and *The Fixed Period*: Conflicting Medical and Popular Ideas about Old Age," *Archives of Internal Medicine* 161 (September 24, 2001): 2076.

68. George F. Corners and A. S. Blumgarten, *Rejuvenation: How Steinach Makes People Young* (New York: Thomas Seltzer, 1923), xi.

69. Corners and Blumgarten, *Rejuvenation*, 50.
70. Katz, *Disciplining Old Age*, 91.
71. Katz, *Disciplining Old Age*, 91.
72. Aldous Huxley, *After Many a Summer Dies the Swan* (Chicago: Elephant, 1993), 10, 12, 14.
73. Huxley, *After Many a Summer*, 69.
74. David Sterritt, "*Seconds*: Reborn Again," *Criterion Collection*, August 13, 2013, https://www.criterion.com/current/posts/2867-seconds-reborn-again.
75. Quoted in Sterritt, *Seconds*.
76. See Richard Settersten Jr. and Jacqueline Angel, eds., *Handbook of the Sociology of Aging* (New York: Springer, 2011), particularly their introductory essay, "Trends in the Sociology of Aging: Thirty Year Observations," 3–16.
77. Stephen Farber, "Review of *Seconds* by John Frankenheimer," *Film Quarterly* 20, no. 2 (Winter 1966-67): 27.
78. Farber, "Review of *Seconds*," 28.
79. Sean Easton, "The Old Vines Are Buried Deep: Classical Motifs in John Frankenheimer's *Seconds*," *Illinois Classical Studies* 37 (2012): 209.
80. For more on the stylistic and technical distortion in the film, see Peter Wilshire, "A Key Unturned: *Seconds*," *Senses of Cinema*, no. 18 (December 2001), http://sensesofcinema.com/2001/underrated-and-overlooked/seconds/.
81. David Ely, *Seconds* (New York: Harper Voyager, 2013), 76.
82. Taussig, *Defacement*, 2.
83. Taussig, *Defacement*, 2.
84. Taussig, *Defacement*, 3.
85. Taussig, *Defacement*, 6, 208; see also Kenneth Surin's excellent review essay on Taussig's *Defacement*, "The Sovereign Individual and Michael Taussig's Politics of Defacement," *Nepantla: Views from the South* 2, no. 1 (2001): 205–20.
86. Nascher, *Geriatrics*, 19.
87. Taussig, *Defacement*, 37.
88. Taussig, *Defacement*, 43.
89. See Martin, "Dialectics of Damage"; and Ashton, "Totalizing the Damage."
90. See Ben Lerner, *10:04: A Novel* (New York: Picador, 2015); quoted in Ashton, "Totalizing the Damage."
91. Herring, *Aging Moderns*, 5.
92. See Blake Gopnik, "Cindy Sherman Takes on Aging (Her Own)," *New York Times*, August 21, 2016.
93. Quoted in Gopnik, "Cindy Sherman Takes on Aging."
94. Quoted in Gopnik, "Cindy Sherman Takes on Aging."
95. See Sarah Blackwood's analysis of Lily Bart's "performed portrait" in *The Portrait's Subject: Inventing Inner Life in the Nineteenth-Century United States* (Chapel Hill: University of North Carolina Press, 2019), 1.

96. See Parul Sehgal, "Ugly Beauty: Cindy Sherman's New Self-Portraits Are Her First Pure Protagonists: Gloriously, Catastrophically Themselves," *New York Times Magazine*, October 5, 2018, https://www.nytimes.com/interactive/2018/10/05/magazine/instagram-cindy-sherman-ugly-beauty.html.

97. Simmel, "Aesthetic Significance of the Face," 277.

98. Taussig, *Defacement*, 252.

99. Taussig, *Defacement*, 252, 249.

100. Taussig, *Defacement*, 251.

101. Taussig, *Defacement*, 252, 253.

102. I refer again to one of the outlined practices in Stephen Best and Sharon Marcus, "Surface Reading: An Introduction," *Representations* 108, no. 1 (Fall 2009): 18.

103. Frankenheimer, *Seconds*.

104. Taussig, *Defacement*, 3.

105. Simmel, "Aesthetic Significance of the Face," 271.

Epilogue. "Getting Out" of the Face

1. While "*carnet*" officially refers to an identification card, the word is used more colloquially in Spain to refer to the photo itself.

2. Jenny Edkins, *Face Politics* (New York: Routledge, 2015), 3.

3. See Edkins, *Face Politics*, 7.

4. See Edkins, *Face Politics*, 7. See Walter Benjamin, "Little History of Photography," in *Selected Writings: Volume 2, Part 2, 1931-1934*, ed. Michael W. Jennings, Howard Eiland, and Gary Smith, trans. Rodney Livingstone (Cambridge, MA: Harvard University Press, 1999), 507, 510, for his analysis of a picture's "spark of contingency" and the agency of a subject that "will never consent to be wholly absorbed in art." For more recent work on facial agency as it relates to "biopolitical normalizations . . . within a culture" and the idea of "face-habits," see Cristina Voto, "Artificial Skin and Biopolitical Masks, or How to Deal with Face-Habits," *Signs and Society* 10, no. 1 (Winter 2022): 127.

5. See E. H. Gombrich, "On Physiognomic Perception," in *Meditations on a Hobby Horse and Other Essays on the Theory of Art* (London: Phaidon, 1985), 55. For his account of the effect of an artist's rendering of a face, see E. H. Gombrich, "The Mask and the Face: The Perception of Physiognomic Likeness in Life and in Art," in *The Image and the Eye: Further Studies in the Psychology of Pictorial Representation* (New York: Phaidon, 1994), 135.

6. Roland Barthes, *Mythologies*, trans. Richard Howard and Annette Lavers (New York: Hill & Wang, 2013), 74.

7. Barthes, *Mythologies*, 74.

8. Edkins reflects on the selfie as an example of portrait photography in *Face*

Politics, as does Sarah Blackwood in the conclusion to her recent book *The Portrait's Subject: Inventing Inner Life in the Nineteenth-Century United States* (Chapel Hill: University of North Carolina Press, 2019).

    9. Hans Belting, *Face and Mask: A Double History* (Princeton, NJ: Princeton University Press, 2017), 142.

    10. Josh Cohen, *How to Read Freud* (New York: Norton, 2005), 112.

    11. Cohen, *How to Read Freud*, 112.

    12. Mina Loy, *Auto-Facial-Construction* (1919), in *The Lost Lunar Baedeker: Poems of Mina Loy*, ed. Roger L. Conover (New York: Farrar, Straus & Giroux, 1997), 165.

    13. On Madonna's face, see Jennifer Weiner, "Madonna's New Face Is a Brilliant Provocation," *New York Times*, February 8, 2023, https://www.nytimes.com/2023/02/08/opinion/madonna-grammys-2023.html.

    14. Belting, *Face and Mask*, 153.

    15. For this terminology, see Scott Herring, *Aging Moderns: Art, Literature, and the Experiment of Later Life* (New York: Columbia University Press, 2022), 5.

    16. Robyn Citizen neatly taxonomizes *Get Out* and *Seconds* as part of a genealogy of speculative "body swapping" films in "The Body Horror of White Second Chances in John Frankenheimer's *Seconds* and Jordan Peele's *Get Out*," in *Jordan Peele's "Get Out": Political Horror*, ed. Dawn Keetley (Columbus: Ohio State University Press, 2020), 87.

    17. For a review of *Get Out* and the Whitney Museum of American Art's exhibition of Dana Schutz's *Open Casket*, See Zadie Smith, "Getting In and Out: Who Owns Black Pain," *Harpers*, July 2017, https://harpers.org/archive/2017/07/getting-in-and-out/.

    18. *Seconds*, directed by John Frankenheimer (New York: Criterion, 2013), DVD.

    19. Smith, "Getting In and Out."

    20. Gombrich, "Mask and the Face," 124.

    21. *The Skin I Live In*, directed by Pedro Almodóvar (Spain: Warner's España, 2011).

    22. See David Edelstein, "Exteriors," *New York Magazine*, October 6, 2011, https://nymag.com/movies/reviews/the-skin-i-live-in-edelstein-2011-10/.

    23. Belting, *Face and Mask*, 153.

    24. Loy, *Auto-Facial-Construction*, 165. For an explanation of how we may visualize another's experience while respecting it as other, see Allen Grossman, "The Passion of Laocoön: Warfare of the Religious against the Poetic Institution," in *True-Love: Essays on Poetry and Valuing* (Chicago: University of Chicago Press, 2009), 87.

    25. Cohen, *How to Read Freud*, 112.

    26. Erving Goffman, "On Face-Work," in *Interaction Ritual: Essays on Face-to-Face Behavior* (New York: Pantheon, 1967), 5.

    27. François Delaporte, *Figures of Medicine: Blood, Face Transplants, Parasites*

(New York: Fordham University Press, 2013), 65. For more on the "disfigurement imaginary," which sees facial disfigurement as occasioning "social death" or the "cessation of social viability," see Heather Laine Talley, *Saving Face: Disfigurement and the Politics of Appearance* (New York: New York University Press, 2014), 39.

28. Delaporte, *Figures of Medicine*, 77.
29. Delaporte, *Figures of Medicine*, 82.
30. See Edkins, *Face Politics*, 5, for her analysis of these ideas in Deleuze and Guattari's *A Thousand Plateaus*. For the reference, see Gilles Deleuze and Félix Guattari, "Year Zero: Faciality," in *A Thousand Plateaus*, trans. Brian Massumi (Minneapolis: University of Minnesota Press, 1987), 171.
31. Deleuze and Guattari, "Year Zero," 171; quoted in Edkins, *Face Politics*, 5.
32. Working from Deleuze and Guattari, Edkins also notes Giorgio Agamben's *Nudities*, trans. David Kishik and Stefan Pedatella (Stanford, CA: Stanford University Press, 2011), arguing that, for Agamben, the "mask" acquires the same meaning as a "face," which is linked to "social identity" (quoted in Edkins, *Face Politics*, 5). While I do not address his work on the face in detail here, Giorgio Agamben, in "The Face," in *Means without Ends: Notes on Politics*, trans. Cesare Casarino and Vincenzo Binetti (Minneapolis: University of Minnesota Press, 2000), 92, writes that the face expresses nothing because it is only appearance—and therefore essential to human attempts to "image" or "name" things, or to make them like themselves.
33. Grossman, "Passion of Laocoön," 75.
34. Grossman, "Passion of Laocoön," 75, 77.
35. Grossman, "Passion of Laocoön," 77.
36. Grossman, "Passion of Laocoön," 77.
37. Silvan Tomkins, *Affect, Imagery, Consciousness* (New York: Springer, 2008), 113.
38. Tomkins, *Affect, Imagery, Consciousness*, 113.
39. Tomkins, *Affect, Imagery, Consciousness*, 119.
40. E. H. Gombrich, "Action and Expression in Western Art," in *The Image and the Eye: Further Studies in the Psychology of Pictorial Representation* (London: Phaidon, 1982), 100.
41. Gombrich, "Mask and the Face," 126.
42. Gombrich, "On Physiognomic Perception," 55.
43. I refer again to Stephen Best and Sharon Marcus's "Surface Reading: An Introduction," *Representations* 108, no. 1 (Fall 2009): 5, and its critique of the symptomatic reading practices the authors attribute to Fredric Jameson.
44. Tomkins, *Affect, Imagery, Consciousness*, 113. For the reference to "immediate reading," see Ellen Rooney's critique of "surface reading" in "Live Free or Describe: The Reading Effect and the Persistence of Form," *Differences* 21, no. 3 (2010): 116.
45. Jonathan Cole, *About Face* (Cambridge, MA: MIT Press, 1999), 3.

46. Cole, *About Face*, 3.
47. Cole, *About Face*, 77.
48. See Jonathan Cole's more specific account of Moebius syndrome in "Relations between the Face and Self as Revealed by Neurological Loss: The Subjective Experience of Facial Difference," *Social Research* 67, no. 1 (Spring 2000): 215.
49. See Deleuze and Guattari, "Year Zero," 171; Djuna Barnes, *Nightwood*, 92.
50. For her discussion of facial injury and World War I, see Suzannah Biernoff, *Portraits of Violence: War and the Aesthetics of Disfigurement* (Ann Arbor: University of Michigan Press, 2017), 167. For his account of prosopopoeia, see Paul de Man, *The Rhetoric of Romanticism* (Cambridge, MA: Harvard University Press, 1984), 81.

Index

Page numbers in italics indicate illustrations.

Adorno, Theodor, 14
aestheticism, 39-44, *40, 43*, 122
affect, 25, 32-35, 39-44; Allport on, 29; anti-intellectual view of, 47, 51; Wyndham Lewis on, 36; Simmel on, 69-70
Agamben, Giorgio, 24, 234n32
ageism, 154, 175, 185. *See also* old age
Alexander, Matthias, 221n33
allegory, 18, 19; Conrad and, 87, 97, 99, 101, 107
Allport, Gordon, 29, 32-33
Almodóvar, Pedro, 24, 186-90
American Civil Liberties Union (ACLU), 13
Arata, Stephen, 87-88
Arendt, Hannah, 23, 150, 151
Armstrong, Tim, 123, 155, 157, 159
artificial intelligence (AI), 13
Ashcan School, 76-77
Ashton, Jennifer, 174
Auden, W. H., 23, 150-57, *151*, 162, 173, 188
Auden, W. H., works of: "Doggerel by a Senior Citizen," 153, 176; "Old People's Home," 150, 153-54

Bacon, Francis, 9
Balzac, Honoré de, 58
Bamji, Andrew, 135, 145
Barker, Pat, 116, 119, 145, 148
Barnes, Djuna, 1, 8-9, 188, 192
Barthes, Roland, 15, 106, 182

Baudelaire, Charles, 28, 79, 177, 190; on "artificial" form, 69-72; on *flâneurs*, 72
Baudelaire, Charles, works of: "On the Essence of Laughter," 18-19, 45-49, 53; "The Painter of Modern Life," 71; "Some French Caricaturists," 82
Beall, Edgar C., 38
Beckett, Samuel, 103
Beerbohm, Max, 18, 28, 44-46
Beeston, Alix, 56
behaviorism, 29
Bellows, George, 20, 57, 76-78, *78*
Bell's palsy, 191
Belting, Hans, 7, 184, 185
Benjamin, Walter, 54, 179, 182; on photography, 10, 15
Bennett, Alan, 226n4
Bergson, Henri, 120
Berman, Louis, 6, 18, 25; on "normality," 36, 38; on personality, 31-33, 35, 37; on Wilde, 28-29, 31-32, 36
Bernard, Claude, 38
Bernardin de Saint-Pierre, Jacques-Henri, 45-46, 206n98
Bertillon, Alphonse, 10, 20-21, 111, 113; de Man and, 22; identification sciences and, 21, 91-100, *94, 98*
Best, Stephen, 16-17
Biernoff, Suzannah, 14, 117, 141, 149, 192, 219n14
"biocertification," 92
biometrics, 38-39

blackface, 41-42, 186, 196
Blackwood, Sarah, 60, 121, 233n8
Blanchard, Mary, 41
Blumgarten, A. S., 165
Botox (drug), 184-86
Boucicoult, Dion, 102
Brecht, Bertolt, 216n73
Bristow, Joseph, 26
Britzolakis, Christina, 108
Brodzky, Horace, 222n62
Bronstein, Michaela, 215n44
Brooks, Peter, 81, 82, 87; Barthes and, 106; on melodrama, 100, 104, 110; on novels, 102
Burgess, Ernest W., 69
Burke, Carolyn, 124, 220n19
Burrows, Stuart, 56

Campers, Petrus, 196n47
Canguilhem, Georges, 12, 38, 144
Caravaggio (Michelangelo Merisi), 9
caricature, 44-50; Baudelaire on, 45-49; Beerbohm on, 44-46; of Currier & Ives, 39-42, 40; of Duval, 42-44, 43; Gombrich on, 48-50
Carus, Gustav, 196n47
Chambers, Emma, 141-42, 144-45
Charcot, Jean-Martin, 10, 23, 160-62, 162
Citizen, Robyn, 233n16
Clearview AI app, 13
Cleveland Street Scandal (1889), 39
Cohen, Ed, 32
Cohen, Josh, 184
Cohn, Elisha, 50
Cole, Jonathan, 181, 191-92, 219n6, 235n48
Cole, Sarah, 99
commedia dell'arte, 8
Conrad, Joseph: Dreiser and, 87; Fried on, 68, 99, 113; Lombroso and, 90, 91, 101, 112, 114; Valente on, 109-10, 218n109; Wilde and, 90
Conrad, Joseph, works of: *Almayer's Folly*, 113; *Heart of Darkness*, 99; *Lord Jim*, 99; *The Nigger of the "Narcissus,"* 68, 211n73; *The Secret Agent*, 8, 17, 20-21, 85-115, 187
Corners, George F., 165
COVID pandemic, 13
Coward, Noel, 226n4

Crafts, Hannah, 197n59
Crane, Stephen, 57, 68; "When Man Falls, a Crowd Gathers," 20, 75-76
Crary, Jonathan, 4-5, 54
critical race studies, 11-12
cubism, 137
Currier, Nathaniel, 39-42, 40

Daly, Augustine, 65, 210n61
Damasio, Antonio, 33-34, 50
dandy, 37
Danish Girl, The (film), 159
Darwin, Charles, 5, 10; Berman on, 28-29; on Duchenne, 14; *The Expression of the Emotions in Man and Animals*, 29, 85, 131, 213n8
Dean, Tim, 201n119
defacement, 177-78; definition of, 154; Taussig on, 172, 173, 178-80
Delaporte, François, 10, 29-31, 121-22; on expression, 35, 39, 143, 211n94; on face transplants, 188-89; on identity, 140; on physiognomic ideal, 132
Deleuze, Gilles, 4, 9, 24, 47, 189
de Man, Paul, 21-22, 142, 190; New Historicism and, 201n119; on prosopopoeia, 22, 126, 127, 192, 235n50; *The Rhetoric of Romanticism*, 125-26
Den Tandt, Christophe, 58, 62
Descartes, René, 9
Diderot, Denis, 82, 124
Dinoire, Isabelle, 188
disability studies, 11-12, 197n57
Doane, Mary Ann, 5, 11
Dreiser, Theodore: Ashcan School artists and, 76; Conrad and, 87; *The "Genius,"* 76, 212n101; realism of, 57-58; Trilling on, 58. See also *Sister Carrie*
Duchenne de Boulogne, Guillaume-Benjamin-Amand, 5, 10, 25, 29-31, 30; Darwin and, 14; Tomkins and, 35
Duval, E. G., 42-44, 43

Easter Island (Rapa Nui), 222n72
Easton, Sean, 170
Ebershoff, David, 159
Ede, H. S., 222n62
Edkins, Jenny, 182, 197n64, 233n8, 234n32
eidos, 147-48

Index

Ekman, Paul, 13, 85-86, 196n43, 213n8; on physiognomic ideology, 10, 88; on signs of criminality, 90-91
Elbe, Lili, 159-60
Eliot, T. S., 116-17, 145; on impersonality, 7, 117, 209n39; modernism of, 118; on prosopopoeia, 116
Eliot, T. S., works of: *The Cocktail Party*, 60; "The Hollow Men," 60; "The Love Song of Alfred Prufrock," 116-17, 125, 126-27, 154; "Tradition and the Individual Talent," 117, 132
Ellenbogen, Josh, 93-94
Ely, David, 166, 171
empiricism, 59
Empson, William, 4-5
endocrinology, 2, 6; Berman and, 18, 28-29, 31, 38; Leys and, 33; Schmidt on, 155-59, *158*; xenotransplantation and, 157, 159
Engels, Friedrich, 73
eugenics, 92, 157, 163. See also racism
expression: Brooks on, 87; Delaporte on, 35, 39, 143, 211n94; Gaudier-Brzeska on, 132-33; "neutral," *183*, 183-84; "plastic," 45

face blindness. *See* prosopagnosia
"faceicity" (*visagéité*), 4, 13
"face-scape," 150-57, *151*, 162
face transplant, 188-89
face-work, 11, 13, 63-69, 79; Goffman on, 5-6, 188, 210n53; Gombrich on, 7
"facial awareness," 121, 140, 181, 190-91, 212n106, 220n25; Tonks on, 148
facial behavior, 25-26
facial exercises, 6, 22, 119, 124, 154
"facial integrity," 119, 120, 184, 188
facial recognition technology (FRT), 13, 24, 88
facial repair surgery, 2, 22, 117-20, 133-49; aging and, 155; Biernoff on, 235n50; Delaporte on, 188; illustrations of, *138-40*, *144*, *146*, *189*; Talley on, 156
facial types, 156; Berman on, 28; Gillies on, 136-37, 143-44
Farber, Stephen, 170
Faulkner, William, 60
Feo, Katherine, 117, 219n13
fingerprints, 21, 91-92

Fisher, Philip, 66
Foldy, Michael, 39
Ford, Ford Madox, 215n44, 217n90
formalism, 17-18
Foucault, Michel, 54, 145
Franju, Georges, 185
Frankenheimer, John, works of: *The Manchurian Candidate*, 169; *Seconds*, 2, 23, 155, 166-74, *167*, 178, 185-87; *Seven Days in May*, 169; Wilde's *Dorian Gray* and, 171
Freud, Sigmund, 48, 85, 86, 184
Fried, Michael, 17, 68, 200n99; on Conrad, 68, 99, 113, 114; on "will-to-see," 75
Friesen, Wallace, 85-86

Galton, Francis, 5, 10, 20-21, 91-92
Garbo, Greta, 15, 182
Gaudier-Brzeska, Henri, 110, 149, 222n62; on expression, 132-33; *The Hieratic Head of Ezra Pound*, 22, 118, 120, 128-33, *129*, 151-53, 188, 222n57; Loy and, 131, *132*; Pound's memoir of, 128, 222n62; vorticism and, 122, 219n16, 220n19
gaze, 69-70; clinical, 145; male, 63
generation gap, 153
geriatrics, 23, 155-63; Charcot on, 160-61; as medical specialty, 167-68; sexology and, 160, 228n27, 230n62. *See also* old age
gerontology, 161
Get Out (film), 24, 185-87, 190, 233n16
Gillies, Harold, 22; facial surgeries of, 119, 120, 133-40, *136-38*, 148, 189; *Plastic Surgery of the Face*, 134, *137*, *138*, 143; *The Principles and Art of Plastic Surgery*, 135-36; Tonks and, 135, 139, 143-46
Gilman, Charlotte Perkins, 63
Gilman, Sander, 11
Ginzburg, Carlo, 91-92, 101
Giovanni di Paolo, 117
Goffman, Erving, 5-6, 188, 210n53
Gombrich, E. H., 4, 12-18, 28, 97, 186, 190; on aesthetic remoteness, 182; on caricature, 48-50; on "face-work," 7; on fascist propaganda, 131; "The Mask and Face," 14-15; on masks, 1, 14-15; on personality, 61; "On Physiognomic Perception," 15-16; on "physiognomic perception," 35, 61-62; on reading, 191

Gordon, Rae Beth, 81
Gould, Stephen Jay, 196n47
Gross, Daniel M., 14, 33-34
Grossman, Allen, 3, 12, 22-23, 147-48, 189-90
Guattari, Félix, 24, 47, 189
Guillory, John, 199n95
Gullette, Margaret Morganroth, 155
Gunning, Tom, 91, 102

Haire, Norman, 155, 159-60
Harris, Frank, 26
Hartley, Lucy, 10
Heaney, Emma, 159
Hepburn, Audrey, 15, 182
Herring, Scott, 156, 228n25
Herzog, Werner, 197n59
Highmore, Ben, 72-73
Hirschfeld, Magnus, 159-60
Hockney, David, 150-52, 173
Homer, 3, 190
homophobia, 28, 36. *See also* queerness
Horkheimer, Max, 14
House of Mirth, The (Wharton), 5, 20, 63-69, 79, 154
Hoyers, Niels, 159
Hudson, Rock, 166-74, *167*, 188
Huxley, Aldous, 166, 169
hysteria, 81, 85

identification sciences, 90-100, *94*, *98*
identity, 140, 174, 188-89
impersonality, 82; Eliot on, 7, 117, 209n39; Lukács on, 60; Sherman on, 176; Wilde on, 52
impressionism, 96-99, 108, 113-15; Ford on, 215n44, 217n90; Gillies and, 136-37
Instagram, 1-2, 176, 177, 179
Institute for the Study of Sexual Sciences (Berlin), 160
"inverts," 159
Iraq War veterans, 182
Isherwood, Christopher, 150, 216n73
Ives, James Merritt, 39-42, *40*

James, Henry, 58, 60, 195n31
Jameson, Fredric, 199n95
Jens, Salome, 169
John, Augustus, 119

John the Baptist, 116-17
Joyce, James, 103, 108

Kafka, Franz, 103
Kaplan, Amy, 57
Katz, Stephen, 160, 161, 166-67
Kenner, Hugh, 120, 130-31
Kern, Stephen, 89
Kiberd, Roisin, 159
Kilner, Thomas Pomfret, 223n93
Kornbluh, Anna, 17
Krafft-Ebing, Richard von, 159
Kramnick, Jonathan, 199n98
Kris, Ernst, 14, 18, 28; on caricature, 48-50; on fascist propaganda, 131
Kurnick, David, 16, 19

Ladd, Anna Coleman, 118, 119, 120, 134, 219n13
Laforgue, Jules, 7-8
Laocoön (Trojan priest), 3, 147, 190
laughter, 45-49, 53
Lavater, Johann, 10, 29, 31, 38
Le Brun, Charles, 9
Le Doux, Joseph, 34
Leonard, Garry, 103, 108
Lerner, Ben, 174
Levinas, Emmanuel, 12, 87; on "ethical relation," 21, 104-9, 113-15
Lewis, Wyndham, 36-37, 44, 152-53; Tonks and, 119; vorticism and, 120, 122
Leys, Ruth, 10, 13, 33-34; Baudelaire and, 47; on Ekman, 88; Sedgwick and, 34, 51; "The Turn to Affect," 18
LGBTQ+. *See* queerness
Lombroso, Cesare, 10, 20-21; Conrad and, 90, 91, 101, 112, 114; Nordau and, 95
Loy, Mina, 15, 149, 179; on ageing, 165, 176; *Auto-Facial-Construction*, 118-24, 132, *133*, 152, 176; facial exercises of, 6, 22, 119, 124; on "facial integrity," 119, 120, 184, 188; Gaudier-Brzeska and, 131, *132*; Mensendieck system and, 221n33; training of, 220n19
Lubin, David, 118
Lukács, Georg, 19-20; on impersonality, 60; on modernism, 83; on naturalism, 58-60; on personality, 60; on reading, 68
lying, 85-86, 88, 104, 107

Index

Lyon, Janet, 67
Lyon, Robert, 182

Macho, Thomas, 193n2
Madonna (pop star), 184-85
mannequins, 6-7
Man Ray (Emmanuel Radnitzky), 7
Mao, Douglas, 57
Marcus, Sharon, 16-17
Martin, Theodore, 174
masks, 7-8, 118; Barthes on, 15; Gillies and, *137, 138*; Gombrich on, 1, 14-15. *See also* Ladd, Anna Coleman
Massumi, Brian, 47
"material physiognomy," 36-37
Matz, Jesse, 21, 97, 101
M'charek, Amade, 11, 42
McIndoe, Archibald, 139, 224nn109-10
melodrama, 21, 81-82, 100-107; Arata on, 87-88; Brooks on, 100, 104, 110; Cole on, 99-100
Melville, Herman, 163-65
Mensendieck system, 221n33
Merrick, Joseph, 197n59
Metchnikoff, Élie, 166
Michaels, Walter Benn, 62-63, 68, 69, 83
Millard, D. Ralph, 133
Miller, J. Hillis, 12, 127, 145, 190
mime. *See* pantomime
modernism, 7-8, 28, 60-61, 79; aesthetic, 154; aftereffects of, 174-80; ageism and, 154; avant-garde, 119; formalist, 17-18; Herring on, 156; Lukács on, 83; naturalism and, 58-59
Moebius syndrome, 24, 191-92, 219n6, 235n48
Myers, F. W. H., 124
Myers-Briggs personality test, 7

Nascher, I. L., 161-63, 165
Nash, Paul, 119
Nersessian, Anahid, 199n98
neurodiversity, 109
neuroscience: Leys on, 33; Wilde and, 50
"neutral" expression, *183*, 183-84
New Historicism, 201n119
Ngai, Sianne, 12
Nichols, Mike, 133
Nietzsche, Friedrich, 28-29

Nightingale, Florence, 28-29
Nordau, Max, 95, 97

Occupy Wall Street movement, 163-65
old age, 150-63; Botox and, 184-86; Charcot on, 160-61; "face-scape" of, 150-52; Frankenheimer on, 166-74, *167*; generation gap and, 153; Loy on, 165, 176; Melville on, 163-65; prejudice against, 154, 175, 185; Sedgwick, 229n29; Sherman on, 175-80. *See also* geriatrics
Opton, Suzanne, 182
Orwell, George, 10-11, 150, 154
Osler, William, 165, 167

pantomime, 7-8, 81, 82
Park, Robert E., 69
Parkinson's disease, 191
Parrington, V. L., 58
Paxson, James, 125, 132
Peele, Jordan, 24, 185-87, 190, 233n16
personality, 52, 94, 182; Berman on, 31-33, 35, 37; definition of, 7; disintegration of, 90; flexibility of, 162; Gombrich on, 61; ideology of, 26-27; Loy on, 122, 125; Lukács on, 60; Myers on, 124; Simmel on, 75; Soussloff on, 121, 141; Susman on, 6, 66; Wilde on, 71. *See also* impersonality
"petropus," 8, 195n33
Pettit, Michael, *151*, 152-57, 216n73
photography, 102; Benjamin on, 10, 15; Crary on, 54; of facial repair surgery, 136-39, *137, 138*. *See also* selfies
physiognomic ideology, 10, 88, 95
physiognomic perception, 35, 61-62
Picasso, Pablo, 82, 118
Picture of Dorian Gray, The (Wilde), 26, 49-53, 80, 121, 123, 171
Pierrot figure, 82-83
plastic surgery. *See* facial repair surgery
Poe, Edgar Allan, 57, 72-75, 79
Pound, Ezra, 7, 118, 151; *ABC of Reading*, 14, 110, 131; Gaudier-Brzeska's sculpture of, 22, 118, 120, 128-33, *129*, 151-53, 188; *A Memoir of Gaudier-Brzeska*, 128, 222n62; on vorticism, 128
Pound, Reginald, 135
Powell, Julie, 117-18

prosopagnosia, 20, 78, 79, 80, 83, 187
prosopopoeia, 24, 78, 104, 139, 149; as defacing, 124-27; definitions of, 116, 126, 154, 192; de Man on, 22, 126, 127, 192, 235n50; female, 125; Tonks and, 142-43, 146-48; Yeats and, 153
Prosser, Jay, 159
"pseudo-totalizing" strategies, 62
puritanism, 36

queerness, 19, 32, 200n110; Cleveland Street Scandal and, 39; endocrinological experiments and, 157-59; homophobia and, 28, 36; trans people and, 156-60, 173

racism, 11-12, 39-44, 40, 43, 47; blackface and, 41-42, 186, 196; eugenics and, 92, 157, 163
Randolph, John, 166
Rapa Nui (Easter Island), 222n72
reading, 2, 107-11; close, 87-88, 200n98; Gombrich on, 191; Lukács on, 68; "paranoid," 200n104; surface, 16-17, 115, 199n95, 199n98, 211n70; symptomatic, 115
"revisaging," 23-24, 153-54, 155
"rhetoricity," 14
Rhys, Jean, 57; *Voyage in the Dark*, 20, 79-80, 83; Zola and, 212n105
Rifaterre, Michael, 221n51
Rooney, Ellen, 17, 211n70
Rose, Louis, 14, 131
Rose, Sam, 17
Rousseau, Jean-Jacques, 100, 111
Rwandan genocide, 182

Sachs, Oliver, 78
Sade, Marquis de, 111
Samuels, Ellen, 11, 92, 101
Sarony, Napoleon, 38, 41, 54, 55
Sarpell, Namwali, 12
Schmidt, Peter, 155-59, *158*, 163
Schmitt, Cannon, 59, 209n32
Schneider, Sara K., 7
Schweik, Susan, 11
Seconds (film), 2, 23, 155, 166-74, *167*, 178, 185-87
Sedgwick, Eve Kosofsky, 12, 190, 200n104,

200n110; Leys and, 34, 51; on "senile sublime," 229n29
Segal, Alex, 107
selfies, 1-2, *2*, 176-79, 182-83, *183*, 233n8. *See also* photography
Sengoopta, Chandak, 159
Serpell, Namwali, 197n59
sexology, 155, 157-60; geriatrics and, 160, 228n27, 230n62
Shakespear, Dorothy, 128
Sheehan, Aaron, 120
Shelley, Mary, 105, 166-67
Shelley, Percy, 21-22
Sherard, Robert, 26
Sherman, Cindy, 23; on Impersonality, 176; self-portraits of, 1-4, *3*, 155-56, 174-80, *175*
Sherry, Vincent, 8, 195n33
Simmel, Georg, 69-70, 77-78, 177, 190
Simmel, Georg, works of: "The Aesthetic Significance of the Face," 2, 4, 124, 152; "The Sociology of Sociability," 67, 75; "Sociology of the Senses," 69-70
Sister Carrie (Dreiser), 5, 8, 19-20, 54-84, 121, 187; Conrad's *Secret Agent* and, 21; Fisher on, 66; Sherman and, 177; Wharton and, 63-69
Skin I Live In, The (film), 24, 186-90
Sloan, John French, 57, *58*, 76
Smith, Zadie, 185-86
social death, 156, 179
Somme offensive (1916), 135
"soul's emotions," 122
Soussloff, Catherine, 121, 141
Steinach operation, 23, 155, 157-59, 165
Sterritt, David, 166-67, 169
Stevenson, Randall, 90
Stewart, Martha, 184-85
Storey, Robert F., 7-8, 82
surveillance, 11, 12, 20, 88-90, 94
Susman, Warren, 6, 66
Symons, Arthur, 26, 49, 53

Talley, Heather Lane, 156, 224n116
Taussig, Michael, 12, 23-24, 172, *173*, 178-80, 190
Teshigahara, Horoshi, 185
Tickner, Lisa, 128-29

Index

Tomkins, Silvan, 25, 35, 49; on "facial awareness," 121, 140, 181, 190-91, 212n106; 220n25; Sedgwick and, 34
Tonks, Henry, 15, 22, 119, 140-49, 188; drawings of, *144*, *146*, 189, 192; on "facial awareness," 148; Gillies and, 135, 139, 143-46
Toulouse-Lautrec, Henri de, 26-28, *27*, 37-38
Touraine-Solente-Golé syndrome, 150, 162
trans people, 156-60, 173. *See also* queerness
Trilling, Lionel, 58, 209n22
Trollope, Anthony, 165
Tyson, Lois, 20, 64, 122

Ulrichs, Karl Heinrich, 159
Under the Gaslight (Daly), 65, 210n61

Valente, Joseph, 109-10, 218n109
vasectomy. *See* Steinach operation
Verloc, Winnie, 88-89
visagéité ("faceicity"), 4, 13
Voltaire, 46
Voronoff, Serge, 159, 166
vorticism: Gaudier-Brezska on, 122, 219n16, 220n19; Kenner on, 120; Wyndham Lewis on, 120, 122; Pound on, 128

Walter, Christina, 124
Waugh, Evelyn, 166

Wechsler, Judith, 82
Wegener, Einar, 159-60
Wharton, Edith, 57, 122; *The House of Mirth*, 5, 20, 63-69, 79, 154
White, Richard Grant, 54, 55
Wilde, Oscar, 2, 18, 25-54, 183; Auden and, 150; Berman on, 6, 28-29, 31-32, 36; caricatures of, 39-44, *40*, *43*, 121, 187; Conrad and, 90; on impersonality, 52; Wyndham Lewis on, 36-37; Loy and, 123; on personality, 71; *The Picture of Dorian Gray*, 26, 49-53, 80, 121, 123, 171; Toulouse-Lautrec's portrat of, 26-28, *27*, 37-38; trials of, 32, 37-39; Wharton and, 154
Wood, F. Derwent, 134
Wood, Jon, 130
Wordsworth, William, 126, 127

xenotransplantation, 157, 159

Yeats, William Butler, 7, 150, 179; prosopopoeia and, 153; Steinach operation of, 23, 155, 157, 159

Zapatistas, 172
Zarzosa, Agustin, 100, 105
Zola, Emile, 79, 212n105
Zurier, Rebecca, 76